Korean War and
Twin Sisters

Yong N. Chung

PRESS

Korean War and Twin Sisters
by Yong N. Chung

Printed in the United States of America

ISBN 978-1-60791-630-7

Unless otherwise indicated, Bible quotations are taken from The NIV Korean-English Study Bible. Copyright © 2004 by Word of Life Press Songwol-dong, Jongno-gu, Seoul, Korea.

www.xulonpress.com

Preface

In 1945 Korea was liberated from the thirty-six year stranglehold of Japanese dominion. However, Korea was immediately occupied by Russia in the north and the United States in the southern half of the peninsula. Three years later in 1948, the first governments were established for both the north and south regions. Two years thereafter, on 25 June 1950, the Korean War had broken out. The fratricidal war continued for three years and one month ending in 27 July 1953.

The aftermath of the war cost the lives of nearly two million people, in addition to two hundred thousand women having been widowed, and one hundred thousand children orphaned, along with ten million others left torn from their families according to official war statistics.

The first ten years following the 1945 liberation were the most turbulent times in Korean history. Coming through the historic turmoil and witnessing unprecedented human tragedies throughout the war, the author happened to know twin sisters who had been separated through a catastrophic midnight air-raid. Thence, the twin sisters were cast into two different worlds; one into the light and the other into the darkness. One became a world famous physician and the other was ruined to a hopeless street prostitute.

As fish are caught in a cruel net, pitiful are the men who are trapped by evil times that fall unexpectedly upon them. For the trapped the Merciful Hand has been waiting all along with fingers crossed. Truly the war devastates our body but even worse is the corporeal arrogance of today that may easily insinuate us into a pit of total corruption. Though it may not be enjoyable reading history, I strongly recommend the rising generation of today to leaf through it.

Yong N. Chung
Stockton, California

Content

1.

The Gust Wind Ripping through a Mountain Village

Climbing up along the mountainside from a village which was nestled at the foot of steep mountains on the northern tip of Cholwon, there stood a solitary cottage. Huddled in front of a thick pine-forest, the cottage looked down over the village through a copious opening on the ridge cloistered within woods. It was quite reminiscent to an enshrouded scholar sitting on folded legs. Though the cottage looked secluded and lonely, it surely was a sweet home for twin sisters, sweeter than a honey comb.

The cottage was part of the estate given to the twins' great grandfather by the Kwons' Clan years ago in compensation for watching the clan's cemetery. The twins' great grandfather and grandfather grubbed, toiled, and cultivated the land, expanding it patch by patch down to the glen throughout their lives.

Thanks to his forefathers, the father of the twin sisters reaped the field in abundance every year all the while holding the position as a clerk at the county office. For firewood, he scraped piles of pine needles under the pines, and stored them in the open shed next to the main shelter. In winter, he would climb up the back forest in the snow and cut frozen pine branches to heat up the hot floor. The frozen branches burnt fierce due to being coated in sap. Having been content they had all that they wanted in abundance and lived in peace.

It was almost a mile walk from the cottage to the heights of the northern highway. The highway ran through the village on the level in which the county office, school and sheriff's office were seated and thence the highway elevated abruptly to the heights.

Coming down the heights, on the right hand side in the alcove were army guards, through which army trucks rolled in and out and infantry men were seen marching in and out, shouting commands. From this point up to the heights, the highway exposed its bare year-round isolation.

Beyond the heights was the 38th Parallel Line, the demarcation line of North and South Korea.

Along the highway down past the Army guards, on the left hand side were the county office, school and sheriff's office. On the right laid a rice mill, an oil extract house, a general store and a tavern. Coming along further down the highway for another spell to the ravine was a stream flowing into the Han-tan River, which the locals called the lamentation river, over which a lengthy concrete bridge was built connecting both hillsides.

On both sides of the highway, some eighty thatched and brick roofed buildings snuggled together to shape up a county subdivision. It was also widely known that not a single soul had ever crossed over to the northern heights the past several years.

∙∙

Dismissed from school, passing by the county office across a big tree in front of the village church, the younger twin, Jean had always led the way ahead of the elder, Suk, frolicking and romping along the road to the foot of an abrupt cliff. It was there that marked the end of the road as the cliff stood aloft like a mammoth wall.

At the foot of the cliff was a stream in which the younger Jean loved to soak her feet, waiting for the elder Suk to wade across together. The elder always walked at her foot's pace behind the younger Jean, snickering or frowning sometimes in silence.

Wading across the stream, they trod on a trail hidden in bushes to the southern edge of the cliff, and thence the trail swung up on a steep ridge to which even the spunky Jean had to scramble up on rainy days. Both sisters would climb up the trail pushing their bodies

10

forward. Their mother toiling in the field would hail them cracking a big smile, as they made it safely up the ridge.

Jean who came into the world minutes late on the heels of the elder Suk appeared to be brighter in babbling baby talk. As they entered their teens, Jean went right ahead of her elder sister Suk, in regards to sociability possessing a snap talk with humorous gestures among friends.

The twins looked much alike; the lengthy slim shape, an attractive charming figure with smooth complexion and round shiny eyes, the straight forehead along with a poppy nose. They were so much alike that it was quite a chore for a stranger to tell one from the other at a moment's glance.

If one was to insist, the younger Jean had a little darker complexion taking after her father and her eyes were slightly larger and brighter than her elder sister's. Above all, Jean was much more active and expressive than her sister Suk. That might be why the younger Jean was always given an upper hand within the confines of school and church.

Two years ago the twins' Sunday school teacher Sun, the pastor's only daughter, was admitted to a seminary through a government qualification test, bypassing the high school diploma. Upon hearing the news that Sun had to leave for seminary, Jean had burst into a cry on the spot, while the elder Suk had a sore heart for weeks.

To them, their teacher Sun was not only a wonderful Sunday school teacher, but a dear friend as well. Sun taught them about our God the Creator, since their childhood until they fully grasped the meaning and purpose of our being His creations. Sun explained to them that we are created to do good works which God prepared in advance for us to do.

Sometime ago, teacher Sun had a serious talk on living a blessed or cursed lifestyle. "God created us for Him to do good works through us. Therefore if we think, speak and do good things to please Him, He is delighted to award us accordingly. As God is Love, He wants you to be happy, healthy and smart just like your mother does. But evil things come from the Devil who watches to steal you and destroy the world. If you were caught in the Devil's temptations to turn from God's word and if you were bent on thinking, talking and committing evil things to please the Devil, what do you think would happen to you? As I told you, all evil things come from the Devil. Therefore we should not even think of such evil things not to mention touching them. We should not even come close to them to see what they look like. What do you think? Jean, speak up."

The teacher pointed at Jean and Jean stood up, asking,

"Teacher Sun, how can we tell good things from evil things?"

"That's a good question." Nodding her head, teacher Sun paused a minute and then responded,

"To be honest with you, it is beyond our strength and wisdom. If we could, there wouldn't be sinners on earth. But our God is almighty, as you know. If you are with Jesus, He will give you the strength and wisdom. He is our shepherd and we are His flock. Do you understand?"

To this, the elder Suk took the words by heart and said,

"Yes, I do."

However, the younger Jean was not quite satisfied and questioned,

"Why do you always talk about Jesus? Why can't we? My father is a very respectful strong man. Why can't he?"

At such inappropriate remarks, the elder Suk would snap in, silencing her younger sister with a nudge to her side. Teacher Sun liked Jean's straightforwardness but in heart she was fonder of Suk's prudent thoughtful attitude.

■■■

The twins' mother, a slim lady whose belly was so thin that one could not imagine her giving birth to twins, did all the domestic and field chores at home. For the last thirteen years until the twins reached the fifth grade, she served the village church as a kindergarten caretaker.

An episode in her life that left her heart broken was in regards to her father in law, who had a severe pain in his left groin three years ago. They could not seek professional medical help as hospitalization was a luxury expense that they could ill afford. They first tried herbs and sapwood until they came to hear of a well known acupuncturist in the highlands.

They took him to the acupuncturist who administered a giant needle to pry out the pain, which knocked him into a sudden fit of violent seizures that left him collapsed on the floor and stopped his breathing on the spot. She wailed,

"Money, money is the killer!" Since then, she often wailed in memory of her father in law who could have been saved if they had money.

Other than that, she was pretty content, blessed with a wonderful husband and two beautiful daughters in good health. She had a plenty of food to cook for her family such as the beans sprout budding over the rim on the upper floor, braided strings of dried radish, mushroom, ferns, and leaves hanging down on the ceiling racks.

She was always rich in heart and shared their food surplus with the poor. Besides, she could get her hands off the spinning and knitting sericulture that was shared among common housewives on account of her husband's extra income.

On her husband's payday, whatever clothes or shoes her family needed, she could just as easily pick them up at a fortnight market, and on those days they also dined out in excitement on special foods such as noodle and steamed buns.

On their way back home from such a day, the family collectively sang aloud

"I Know not why God's Wondrous Grace," and quickened their steps to climb up the ridge before the fall of dusk. When they returned home hand in hand, what was a lonely cottage turned into paradise.

···

On Saturdays, the twins' father upon returning home from work would pull up his sleeves to pump water to fill the furrows in the field in front of the cottage, and then went up to the pine forest in the back to scrape pine needles or to pick out tree stumps to chop into fire wood for the winter.

His open shed was filled with firewood year round and he stored enough kimchee in the under ground pots to last the winter. The shed and latrine were detached from the main shelter.

13

On this particular Saturday, June 24, 1950, he filled the field's vegetable, corn and potato furrows, and then mended the pigpen and chicken cages until twilight. As night fell, the family of four sat around the dinner table under a petroleum lamp.

"Whose turn is it tonight?" Father had asked. Jean without hesitation immediately started saying grace,

"God Father. Thank you for watching over us today. We also thank you for this wonderful dinner. With this food, make us healthy and make us good children of yours. I pray this in the name of Jesus Christ."

They all responded in concert, "Amen."

After dinner, they shoved off the dinner table to the upper floor for daily family worship and shared the daily bread of words. Following worship, every one returned to finish up their assigned chore of the day before finally crawling into bed; mother clearing the table, father scheduling for tomorrow, and the sisters touching up the last page of home work. Truly, there was no other place like home, the home that was fully blessed.

•••

That following day, Sunday June 25, 1950, the family did not have predawn service at church, which was the only day of the week for them to relax and sleep in. Around dawning, someone knocked on their door whispering in a pressing tone,

"Are you not up yet, twin's dad? It's me..."

"Who's this at this early hour of the day?" Twin's father pushed the door open and stuck out his head. There stood in an early morning dense fog, Mr. Ahn, the owner of the general store on the highway, visibly shaken.

The general store owner, Ahn, was a close friend to Twin's father. Sometime ago, Ahn was arrested and taken to the District Police Bureau on suspicion of being a communist agent, where he was about to be mistakenly executed.

Twin's father, a county clerk, ventured himself to visit the police chief and the city council to attest Ahn's innocence and stood adamantly for his release home. Since then, they became intimate friends in the village.

The majority of suspected communist agents that had been taken to the police bureau along with Ahn were either imprisoned or executed following summary judgments.

"What's up, Ahn? Come on in," Twin's father beckoned.

"I can't! Wake up, my friend. The red army is pouring tanks and armed corps over the northern heights. Hurry Up! Move on!" Ahn's voice was pitching in tremor.

"What?! Did you say the red army?!" Frightened, Twins' father sprang out of bed.

"Yeah, the red army! Our pastor is running with other community leaders and asked me to wake you up and let you know. The northern army is swarming over the northern heights. Come on!" So alarmed was Ahn that he quickly vanished into the dismal fog before Twin's father had time to put on his pants.

Twin's father hurried after him but Ahn was nowhere to be seen within the dense fog. When he hit the arbor tree at the bottom of the ridge, the day was breaking in the eastern sky.

Lo and behold! A great multitude of armed forces were flooding the highway. In the distance, it looked more like a lengthy funeral process rather than an assaulting force. Intermittent shouting of commands with shrieking whistles here and there in the ranks chilled the liver sending a freezing spasm to the spinal nerves like a gale wind ripping through the mountainous terrain.

Perched behind a tree, Twins' father surveyed the invading forces and wondered,

"Why is the army marching and shouting? Can the world be changing hands overnight? Shall I run away? To where and for what? What did I do wrong? ... But you have to. You have to what? You have to pack up and run away or you'll be killed.... Who's going to kill me and why? This is total nonsense...Yes, I will pack up. No, you don't have to. You just stay where you are..."

Loping his way back up the ridge home like a frightened stallion, two different ideas tussled in his mind.

As he rushed back to the cottage, his wife approached and queried,

"What's the matter?"

15

"The red army is pouring over the northern heights, I just saw them," he sighed.

"Did you say the red army and they are crossing over the heights?" She blanched in fear, trembling.

"No need to get frightened, my dear. We haven't done anything wrong in the first place. God knows us. Suppose we have to run away, but it is too late now."

"Oh, My Goodness!" She fell to her knees in despair.

The couple held each other tight in silence when Jean was heard rustling up in the upper room.

"Our God is fair. He is good you know..." he muttered, releasing his wife.

"You are right. You are very right." No sooner had she uttered the words, a sudden explosion of cannon balls from the south thundered the mountain village, followed by successive popping of machinegun bullets.

The twin sisters were jolted upright off the bed and scurried down to the master room to cling to their parents, screaming aloud, "Mom! Mom!"

Soon enough the uproar of machine gun violence was silenced like a receding squall. Instantly the peaceful sweet home transformed into a freezing igloo of fright and terror.

In the middle of breakfast, Twin's father dropped his spoon and flurried out of his home, fretting in anxiety. He regretted not having held his friend Ahn long enough to discuss what to do next in this emergency. He was haphazardly making his way down the ridge trying to find an answer.

In contrast with his frantic motions, the late June morning sun was nonchalantly spreading its warm wing of benevolent beam as the mist lifted over the exposed opening on the ridge, tenderly embracing each and every green leaf. Green vines and tendrils of cucumber and pumpkin crawled all over in vigor and verdure. The fat cones stuck to the corn-cane were shooting up their tender tassels bashfully, the bottom of summer potatoes were bulging out and fresh green peppers hanging in strings were ready to be chewed crunchily.

Harvest on the ridge was plump and rich, but today he was apathetic and hustled by them in haste.

He ran down to the arbor tree and narrowed his eyes to see if there was any change, only to be stunned at the scene he witnessed. Still, more military personnel were flooding the highway with tanks and armored vehicles ahead as if they were in a parade, all the way from the northern heights down to the county sheriff office and further down to the bridge at the entrance of the village. At the sight, he turned aghast and dared not to stick his neck out. He felt dizzy and blinded momentarily.

Slouching back home, his heart was weighed upon by some insurmountable force and he felt as if he was trapped in a cave with no loophole, especially with the expeditious nature of the chaos. He had good reasons for that as history would later reveal.

••

By the time U.S. forces withdrew from South Korea in June 1949, the infantile South Korean military totaled only 65,000 strong in addition to 4,000 coast guards. The Air Force, not even equipped with a single anti-aircraft gun, was made up of some L-4 and L-5 reconnaissance planes along with ten antiquated aircrafts purchased from Canada with the funds raised among citizens. The Army had not a single tank or armored vehicle. They did possess a few 105mm cannons and 4.2 inch mortars with cannon balls that had been exhausted on the first day of combat.

On the other hand, the North Korean army had 135,000 well-trained ground forces with 242 Soviet T-34/85 tanks, 200 Soviet fighters and IL bombers plus a great number of giant cannons and mortars. It wasn't even a match to begin with.

••

Twins' mother was in prayer when her husband came into the room,

"Have you seen anything new?" She asked suspensively.

"No, nothing new. The northern army is still pouring over the pass…"

"Is that right? Let me go out and take a close look at them. They wouldn't do any harm to an old lady like me, would they?"

"Don't be so sure. It's not the proper time, anyway." Twins' father held his wife and continued,

"Look, we are secluded on the mountain. No one will come all the way up here to catch us. Besides, are we criminals?" His tone was very convincing.

"You are right," She agreed and continued,

"All we have to do is look out and watch. Should anyone climb up the ridge, you could jump right onto the attic to hide in it, couldn't you?"

"That's not a bad idea. In that case, you should be ready to tell a white lie that I took refuge with our pastor and other community leaders. Can you do that?"

"I'll try and I think I can do so. I will also train the girls to do the same. It is really a matter of life or death."

She paused for a moment, wearing a serious face, and then exclaimed,

"If we had foreseen this day, we should have purchased extra batteries for the transistor radio last week when we dined out to the fortnight market. How forgetful we are!"

"Yes, we are," he regretted.

They noticed that the radio batteries were running low some time ago and they had forgotten about it when they were at the market last week.

•••

The following morning, Twin's mother came down to the general store to see Mrs. Ahn. They were close friends to the point that Mrs. Ahn called Twins mother 'elder sister,' as she was three years her junior.

"Hello, elder sis. Come on in. Thanks for coming." Mrs. Ahn pulled her in.

"How is everything here? How is Mr. Ahn? Is he home?" Twin's mother asked.

"Yes, sister. He has been cooped up in the room all morning, complaining why he should run away when he hasn't done anything wrong. He just stepped out, saying that he would find a place to dig a hide-out in the storage room just in case," Mrs. Ahn whispered to her elder's ear.

"It's nice to hear that he is around. I was afraid if he had gone on refuge. By the way, the northern army coming down in flocks wouldn't do any harm to our people, I wonder."

"Not at all. They just kept marching down with machineguns on their shoulders. No one has ever snooped in the store so far. I was amazed at so many tanks and armored vehicles ahead of them."

"That's what Twin's father said too. He was shocked at the number of armed vehicles. This is not like the wars we see in movies. We heard just one bout of brief gunfire and that was it!"

"You are right, but my husband kept saying that the situation doesn't look good according to the radio he plugged in his ear ever since."

At this, Twin's mother interrupted and asked,

"In fact, I am here for that matter. Do you have any extra batteries to share with us? We should have bought some at the fort-night market last week."

"Oh, please don't mention it. My husband whined over it too. He said he had the last battery in his radio."

Twins mother was quite at loss, deeply disappointed she replied,

"I fully understand. I just checked if you had any remaining. By the way, what makes your husband think the situations aren't too good? Can you tell me?"

"Why of course. He is afraid that a major war may break out if the North Korean armies keep coming down. As you can see they keep pouring down, don't they? My husband said that the United States and U.N. Forces may end up using atomic bombs to check the aggression just like they did against Japan. In that case, we will all be killed."

"Let's pray that it wouldn't come to that. In the mean time, see if there is a way to get batteries and please let me know."

She realized her attempts of finding a battery were futile, but she desperately needed it to keep her husband informed of what's going on. She prayed,

"Lord, help me to find a way to get a battery, please."

Crossing the stream at the foot of the cliff, she arrived at the idea of making daily visits to the general store to receive news and deliver it to her husband. A dangerous endeavor yet worth taking, as she would risk anything for her husband.

She hurried home with renewed strength and hope, thanking the Lord for giving her another test. She believed that life is a series of tests we shouldn't fail. She also believed that in all things God works for the good of those who love Him and who have been called according to His plan. She thought it was just a matter of faith in Him and she confessed she had been fretting in anxiety due to her weakness in faith.

When she got back home, she picked a hand hoe and worked in the front field all day, as if nothing had happened, to show a good example of how to face a crisis to her family. The twin sisters who were mature for their age of thirteen years wanted to help, if not to protect their parents, sensing that danger was approaching, and they grasped readily what to do as the situation dictated.

The following morning the 27th June, the younger Jean came to her mother's side and announced without a seconds thought,

"Mom, I am going to the radio shop in the city today and I will bring some batteries home for you, okay?" She pressed her mother for money to purchase the batteries.

"Wait a minute. Are you saying that you are going down to the radio shop in the city? That is more than twenty miles away! In the middle of this war and through the marching red army on the highway? You must be joking!" Mother queried in surprise.

"Of course I am not joking. I mean business." Jean retorted.

To the elder Suk and her mother, this was a really wild idea.

"Are you telling me that you are going to the city to buy batteries?" Twins' father next to Suk asked with upturned eyes.

"Yes, father. I am. If sister Suk doesn't want to come let me go with mom."

She demanded persistently.

Presently, Twins' mother ventured herself to set out with a firm determination to accept death in the worst case, while Jean was descending the ridge sprightly, kicking morning dews.

It just so happened that the battery was the most crucial thing in their world. Therefore the night before, the entire family missed a good night's sleep, tossing about in their beds. That was the case except for Jean who slept soundly on a comforter with a mindset to get batteries from the city at daybreak.

On the way to the city, Twin's mother noticed that the number of the red army marching in formation was tellingly thinning down.

Approaching a soldier shouldering a machinegun, Jean warmed up to him,

"Hi, uncle soldier."

"Hello, cutie," greeted the soldier, and asked with a big smile,

"Where are you going?"

"We are going to catch up with our father. He took refuge leaving us behind." She had created a story.

"Are you with your mom? Wish you good luck, cutie." They exchanged pleasantries.

Jean thought the northern soldier looked much younger and nicer than the southern soldiers she often met before. She wanted to keep conversing with him, but her mother stopped her with menacing eye signals.

The sky was intensifying its heat, and fat stumps of rice with shredding tassels on the paddy seemed bathing in the sun, a wide variety of grains and flowers in the field looked wiggling and wallowing in the sweet of the early autumn heat. At last, Jean, escorting her mother by hand, was coming down a highway pass looking down over the city.

The city was desolate and the streets empty. They knocked on the door of the radio shop which was tightly closed. They kept banging until someone came out. It was the radio shop owner. They swooped up all the batteries in the shop paying twice the regular price. When they returned home safely on that day, the sun was almost sinking in the scarlet western sky.

21

At home, the elder sister Suk stood guard waiting on her father. She set out to be like teacher Sun who passed the National Qualification Test, leafing through a fifth-grade drill book all day long.

That night, Twin's father suggested at the dinner table his hiding place. He suggested that the open shed detached from the main house was ideal and better than the attic under the sweltering summer heat. They all agreed.

The following morning, the third day of the war, Twin's mother and Jean came down to the general store and handed a couple of batteries to Mrs. Ahn.

That night, well past midnight, Mrs. Ahn frantically knocked on the door of the twins' house,

"Sister! Twin's mother! Please wake up and help me!"

Twins' mother bounced out of the bed, asking,

"Is that you sister Ahn? What's wrong? What happened at this time of night?" Twin's mother tugged her inside.

"Resentful. Bitterly lamented," Ahn cried out, breathing violently and vented out,

"That rascal Choi and his bandits stormed into my house to seize upon my husband and brutally battered him. As my husband was knocked unconscious, they bundled him away. I followed them but they vanished in the dark. What shall I do?"

"Who is this rascal Choi? Calm down and speak slowly," Twin's mother tried to appease her. She was enquiring to figure out who this rascal Choi was, when Twin's father suddenly sat up from bed and stroked a match to light the lamp. At this, Ahn got further frenzied and sternly interrupted him, alarming in terror,

"Dangerous! Blow the light out! These bandits are ransacking the entire village to round up reactionaries. They may swoop upon you any minute!" She screamed in whisper.

Then the father instantly blew the light out recognizing the time had come and rose up in the dark to grope for a sleeping bag out of the attic and hurried out.

He trotted toward the open shed, made sure that no one was on his heels watching his furtive action, pitched his sleeping bag down into the bulk of pine needles and buried himself.

●●●

As a matter of fact, Choi was a man widely known within the county. It was just that Twins' mother couldn't figure it out offhand due to the panic of her frantic friend.

Five years ago upon liberation in 1945, the muddy torrent of so-called 'Liberation and Freedom' rushed the shores of this land on the heels of withdrawing Japanese. The liberation and freedom itself was clean like the living water, however the dirt of ignorance encrusted on the receptacle had turned the clear water into a murky mess.

One day, Choi's father had gotten dead drunk and howled into the rice mill he had worked as an employee for the last thirty years. There he picked up a mallet in the mill and jumped onto the jar stand to smash every single sauce jar, shouting,

"I have been a slave to this mill owner long enough to raise hell! I'm no longer his slave!"

When he was taken to the sheriff's office, he howled even louder drunkenly, "Didn't you know that the time has changed? Isn't it freedom to do whatever you feel like doing? Isn't it the liberation to be liberated from the bondage of owners? I'm free now and I am liberated! We human beings are all equal. I won't be fooled anymore!" Since the incident, villagers kept a wide berth to his foolhardiness.

On another occasion, Choi's father, dead drunk yet again, played the village messenger on his way home from a fortnight market. He got on the back-bed of a moving truck and howled about 'liberation and freedom' again when the truck, coming down the hill, jolted him off the bed. He was killed on the spot.

The village was quiet for awhile. Then Choi and his brother were arrested and taken to the police bureau on suspicion of conspiracy within the Southern Labor Party against the government. According to hearsay, Choi's brother was beaten to death during torturous interrogations while Choi was imprisoned following his summary judgment. It was rumored that Choi's brother was executed as the mastermind behind the conspiracy.

This Choi, at the news of the northern army pouring south, broke out of prison and joined the County Communist Party. As a revolutionary, he could not wait to mop up the reactionaries before they found time to escape.

Along with like minded red-banded comrades, he rushed the village searching for reactionaries hounding them to their deaths with bloodshot eyes, shouting hysterically day to night.

He also hailed his deceased father and brother as great patriotic revolutionary heroes whose lives had been martyred for the cause of the communist revolution led by Chief Comrade, Kim Il-Sung, the head of Northern Government.

On the list of reactionaries Choi carried, the general store owner Mr. Ahn was one of the top suspects. The reason being that Ahn at the beginning was involved in the conspiracy, only then to backtrack, flatly denying his involvement, thus betraying Choi. There were eleven other such reactionaries in the village according to Choi's list.

Since the liberation in 1945, Korea was at arms having been divided north and south, separated by the 38th parallel line. During this transitional period, no one on this tiny peninsula could be excused from the ties of mutual entanglement in terms of blood, birth place, school and religion. Almost everyone was either a communist sympathizer or reactionary some way or another. During the seesaw game throughout the war, the reactionaries were slaughtered by communist revolutionaries, and the communist sympathizers were drag netted and executed by the retreating southern police.

••

In the wake of southern forces on the run like receding ebb, the communist occupied zones turned into an infernal ground for slaughtering innocent people.

Choi declared that now was the turn for the communist revolutionaries to annihilate reactionaries.

"Who is this rascal Choi?" Twins' mother barely finished her question when the bloodthirsty figure of Choi entered her mind.

Stunned and frightened, she stammered,

"Oh, my, that brutal guy! I thought he was imprisoned."

Shuddering in terror, she embraced Mrs. Ahn tight. Both had been in lost for words.

Thus, Twins' father ended up digging into the pile of pine needles in the open shed, with his panic-stricken wife standing vigil over him against slaughterers with the help of twin sisters.

At predawn the following day, Twins' father pulled himself out of the piles of pine, tiptoed like a stray cat around the sauce jar-stand, sneaking himself into the master bedroom through the back door of the house.

"Are you alright?" His wife's voice was trembling. The twins were asleep sound in the upper room.

"I am alright, how about you my poor lady? But we have no choice, my dear. If Mr. Ahn was the first one to be picked up, I would surely be targeted next," he muttered in her ears.

Frightened, she pleaded,

"P l e a s e, hide deep into the pile towards the hind wall of the shed. It is a great relief that you just had the pine needles piled up to the front edge of the shed."

"You are right. God prepared it for me. I will dig further towards the back wall.

We can always turn to Jesus for help. He is always with us, isn't He?" He responded.

Last Saturday, Twins' father came across piles of pine needles stacked in the forest. He scraped them and hauled them to the shed. He made three roundtrips to fill up to the ceiling with pine needles.

Twins' father continued, "I will come out of the shed at 12 o'clock sharp at midnight to get the news you collected from the village during the day, especially on Choi's movements. I will get national news as long as I have the receiver plugged in my ears, you know."

At daybreak, he picked up rice balls his wife prepared and a bottle of water that would last him for the day, and then dug into the piles toward the hind wall to hide deep within.

There he listened to the radio. Through the radio he learned for the first time that Seoul had been occupied by the northern army, and that the southern government withdrew to Suwon, twenty miles south of Seoul. He also learned that the retreating army exploded the only Han River Bridge to impede the assaulting northern forces.

United Nations Security Council adopted military aid to South Korea, and United States President Harry S. Truman issued the presidential order to General MacArthur to commence the army, navy and air operational supports to the South Korean Government.

Digesting the news, Twins' father realized that he had to be confined in the hideout for some time. He then realized that the immediate threat to his life was not so much the war, as that of Choi and his comrades. He also knew that in order for him to survive, his name had to be taken off and completely erased off Choi's list of wanted reactionaries. That could only be done when Choi was fully convinced that he ran away with the pastor on refuge.

His wife was also aware of the situation. She trained her daughters thoroughly how to pretend that their father took refuge with their pastor and other village leaders that night, until the act became watertight. For this, the elder Suk was scared to death, while the younger Jean found it a little amusing biting her lower lip, rolling her big eyes at her mother's directions. At any rate, both girls appeared firmly determined to safeguard their father.

••

One day when the sun reached its apex, pouring down heat, the older Suk was reviewing her 5th grade drill book, while the younger Jean was trimming fresh spinach and green peppers with her mother on the front floor, when three men with bamboo spears stormed in, causing the dog from under the wooden floor to bark fiercely against them. Behind the three spearmen was the rascal Choi, flashing his white teeth.

At the dog's barking, Suk sprang out of the room. Twins' mother turned pale in terror at the sight of Choi, trembling all over.

However, the younger Jean unfazed bounced off the floor and ran to greet Choi.

"What brings you here, uncle comrade? If you have seen our father, please..."

"Shut up, girl! We are here to arrest him. Now are you asking me if I have seen him?"

This exploded her into a desperate cry, she babbled,

"My father took refuge with our pastor and other elders of the village. I was afraid that you caught him and brought him back today!" She whimpered louder.

Then Choi shouted, turning to the other three,

"Comrades, what are you waiting for? Search! Ransack every nook and corner and catch him!"

The three spearmen jumped onto the floor and flung the doors open to the rooms, swaying their bamboo spears. One went up the attic, while the other thrust through the master and storage rooms. They thoroughly searched under the rear and front floors.

The third dashed into the kitchen and kitchen storage jumping onto the sauce jar-stand opening every lid. As they were poking and thrusting all over, Jean clung to her mother, and with Suk all three cried aloud. In fact, Twins' mother cried out in tongues,

"Lord, you saved us from disaster and disease. You picked us out from the valley of death. You saved us from the fire and the flood!" It was not an ordinary prayer. It was a heart breaking supplication in tongue to the Almighty.

This unusual scene sparked uncertainty in Choi's mind, momentarily arousing a doubt if the suspect truly had run away, but soon enough he shook it off. Then the three bamboo spearmen collectively attacked the detached latrine and the open shed.

One of them violently poked into the piles of pine needles trying to gain footing on top of the pile, when the piles turned loose, he slipped to the ground.

In dangerous proximity to Twins' father, Choi who had been watching with arms akimbo shouted in the nick of time,

"That's good enough! The damn reactionary must have truly run away. Beat it! Let's get going, Comrades."

Just one more thrust of the bamboo spear could have exposed him and ended his life. Thus Twins' father escaped death by a hair, another live testament of our living God. Twins' parents took it as a trial strengthening their trust in God.

••

When both needles on his G.I.watch pointed at 12:00 AM, Twins' father shoved through and pulled himself out of the piles of pine needles. Feeling his way through the pitch darkness, he passed by the jar-stand and breezed into the master bedroom through the back door.

The first thing he would do was to fumble for his twin daughters in the dark to make sure they were safe and sound, and then approached his wife,

"Brace up, my dear. It's not going to be that much longer. According to the radio news, the U.N. forces of sixteen countries such as America, England, France, Canada, Columbia and Turkey are being dispatched to the scene to fight and push back the red army. Also the U.S. Army 21st Regiment of the 24th Division in Japan landed on Busan shore to counterattack the invading forces. With such direct U.S. intervention, the odds are easily predictable, isn't it?" He whispered into her ears. Then his wife would draw closer and passed along to him all the news she gathered in the village on that day.

At the first crow of the rooster, he would pick up rice balls and a bottle of water that his wife had prepared the night before, and sneaked out of the room to return stealthily back to the piles of pine needles before daybreak.

Once he sunk deep into the pile, he was confined to his own little world. To pass time he would hark back to the old days, as he laid buried deep in the pine needles.

As he recalled the old days, the time flew swiftly like flitting birds.

His days had been scheduled with activities every day with the exception of Wednesdays and Sundays, on which the entire family went to church to praise and worship the Lord together. Now his once busy lifestyle had halted as he lay buried in the piles.

At the thought of his being a live corpse, a cold shiver ran down his spine, and the only thing defying his death seemed to be the radio constantly straining his ears. He wanted to stay alive, not only to stay alive but also to stay awake.

All he could do to stay awake was to replay sweet memories, mincing and regurgitating every bit of it; such as the moment he was cheerfully descending the ridge with his twin girls ahead bouncing and leaping through the morning dew embracing the rising morning sun, while his lovely wife was watching them off at the gate every morning. The color, the taste and the depth of such sensational moments varied depending on seasons and ambiance. Sometimes he was so deeply absorbed in such moments that the time seemed affixed in oblivion for good.

As a matter of fact, he was gratified for his wife's being such a beauty. He was well aware that her shape and figure, once stripped of the poverty, could be no less admirable and adorable than any beauty in the world. Furthermore her heart was so faithful that she submitted to her husband as to the Lord, and she was also a wonderful and thoughtful mother to his children.

Recalling his life with her, he had many blissful and exciting moments as well as many heart-aching and sore moments such as the time she was laboring with ripping pain to give birth to twins, in which he totally surrendered to God, supplicating,

"Oh Lord, I do confess that I did wrong to her. Please do not take her away. Just take her pains away, please." Such moments were so deeply and vividly engraved in his heart that as he recalled the scene, he was almost wailing the supplication unaware through the piles of pine needles.

Twins' father had never heard of Christianity until Twins' mother married him into the church. Though she was from a poverty stricken family, she was rich at heart with the priceless seed of Abraham's faith.

Later she became widely known and highly admired across the county as the prototypical dutiful daughter-in-law, and her dedicative care of her parents-in-law with pure love and respect was truly based on the words of God.

Can there be a husband who wouldn't appreciate and honor a wife who is truly loving and dutiful to his parents? Can there be any husband who would not thank to have such a wonderful and faithful wife? He started saying thanks to her for her genuine love and care toward his parents.

By then, he was ready to take God's words and she was ready to share all the good secrets hidden from the time of the creation of the world. Twins' father must have belonged to God from the beginning like all others as the Holy Bible revealed,

"He who belongs to God hears what God says."

As the words of God are living and active, he was daily transformed into a new being through hearing and receiving them. In this way, the cottage gradually turned to be a paradise and they were blessed with heavenly glory on earth.

But now what his life had turned upside down! Wasn't he breathlessly swaddled in a sleeping bag under the pile of pine needles? Yes, he thanked God for saving him from being skewered by Choi's bamboo spear, but then suddenly turned his back on God's will with a choking plea,

"You are fair and merciful, my Lord. Then why do you leave me abandoned in this suffocating ordeal and torture? You pour the summer heat upon grains and fruits to ripen them and for that we thank you, but your pouring heat upon me further aggravates my torturous pain and I can't keep my nose up in the stinking sweat and dirt.

You said,

'Consider it pure joy whenever you face trials of many kinds, because the testing of your faith develops perseverance, and perseverance renders you to be mature and complete not lacking anything.' Therefore I try to rejoice this suffering but my body resists, my Lord. I am limited and I cannot stand anymore. Please lift me out of this slimy pit, my Lord."

He often debated with Choi in his soliloquy,

"Comrade Choi. What have I done wrong?"

Twins' father and Choi were classmates of the same village county school.

"My friend, was it that wrong for my great grandfather to take over those 600 pyungs of open fields on the ridge and cultivated it into corn and vegetable fields, grubbing day and night? Was it that grave an offense for me to inherit that opening and other corn fields down to the glen? You call me 'bourgeoisie', the landowner, but you know well that that land was given to our great grandfather by the Kwon clan in compensation for overseeing their cemetery. That barren land was cultivated and further expanded down to the glen with my forefathers' blood and sweat.

For the last twenty years, I have been working for the county office as a clerk since we both graduated from school together. What's wrong with my being a clerk in the county office? Why did the county office manager and all other employees have to run away not to be tortured and slaughtered by you? Why?

My wife whispered in my ears last night that you publicly announced to mop up every single county worker and flog them to death. It seems I am inevitably branded as a reactionary because I served the county as a clerk, no matter what good works I have done for the people. Ask anyone what I did. God knows that I tried my best to help the poor and the needy. I don't mean to praise my actions as if I had done something great. I just want to let you know that I have tried my best to obey Heaven's will.

Then why is it that I should be buried in the piles of pine needles like a wriggling worm? I can't even wriggle. But for you, I might have boldly approached the soldiers coming down the northern pass and asked them what the purpose of carrying guns on their shoulders was about. Why on earth did you thrust the spear to kill me, comrade Choi?"

Many times a day, he suppressed impulsive fits to jump out and seize Choi by the neck to get an answer to the question of what his isms and ideologies represent. He continued his soliloquy,

"Besides, what's wrong with sharing the truth, the way and the life with others through Jesus Christ? Why is it so detestable to help others with God's words and lead them to rejoice in the heavenly glory on earth? Is it that felonious to help others out of the darkness into the wonderful light? How can it be a crime to teach others that God is so good that he comforts the persecuted and persecutes the persecutors? Those denying God's word will be thrown into an eternal darkness. Didn't you know that, Choi?"

....

On the third day of the war, the northern forces fully occupied Seoul, the capital city and were then stalled along the Han River as the Han River Bridge had been exploded by the withdrawing southern army. Since then, the southern government moved to neighboring Suwon then moved further south to Daejeon, ninety miles south of the capital Seoul, as the northern forces pressed on, crossing the river.

On July 5, the U.S. 21st Regiment had their first engagement with the northern army at Juk-mi-ryung, north of Osan. Seeing that the South Korean government hastily moved further down to Daegu from Daejeon following the battle, it is assumed that the U.S. 21st Regiment must have suffered a setback and lost the battle.

Twins' father was deeply disappointed at the news of the government's further southward mobility, the notion of returning back to Seoul logically seemed more distant. The South Korean President, Dr. Rhee Syngman, officially transferred the command of the Republic of Korea's Armed Forces to the U.N. Forces; placing the South Korean Army under the operational control of U.N. Command.

While on the southward flee, the withdrawing government dragnetted all the young men on the streets and marshaled them into the National Defense Corps with no logical plan whatsoever. A great number of recruits fell sick and starved to death, and finally turned into a shamble of confused throng to be disbanded on the road.

In a month or so, the withdrawing South Korean Government reached the southern tip port-city of Busan, and the U.S. 8th Army Command established the resistance line along the Nakdong River and issued the order to withdraw south of the line.

By this it was acknowledged that the entire peninsular north of the Nakdong River had completely fallen into the hands of the northern army. Busan port and its adjacent areas were overcrowded with refugees snooping around to fill their empty stomachs while looking for shelter to soothe their swollen feet.

The people under the control of the northern army swiftly changed their colors in order to survive by conforming, and started blabbing,

"The final battle is between the revolutionary army and U.S. imperialists."

"It is just a matter of time to expel the imperialists and drown them into the sea!"

"The end of the U.S. imperialists and the reactionaries is blinking around the corner."

The number of red-banded comrades and volunteer forces were increasing daily. Some of them got together to organize the People's Committee, and their immediate mission was to track down reactionaries for the people's summary court. The so called people's court was not a judicial court but a tragic scene of massacre against God and man, which was formed and executed by bandits such as Choi.

●●●

Yellow-trousered men of the northern army with shouldered machine guns were streaming in and out of the school, county and sheriff office buildings in the village.

Twins' mother, leaving her husband to her twins care, joined the women's volunteer movement in a gesture of being a patriot to convince others that her husband took refuge with the pastor and was not at home. She passed on the news she collected to her husband when he stealthily came in at midnight. In return, Twins' father passed on the news he heard on the radio to his wife and strengthened their belief that U.S. and U.N. forces would counterattack and repel the northern army in no time.

They believed that those against God will eventually perish, and they knew that their momentary troubles were achieving for them an eternal glory that far outweighed their earthly troubles. Therefore, when they got together, they thanked for the troubles they had and encouraged each other as one in Christ.

Besides, it became a unique pleasure for them to be able to whisper sweet talks into each other's ears at night and it was the very meaning of their being alive. They never forgot to thank and glorify God for His presence at this critical time of war.

As for the war situation, thousands of young lives spewed their blood along and over the Nakdong River in a tug of war of daily attacks and counter attacks.

Twin sisters pulled every string in their power to help their parents, adapting themselves to rapidly changing circumstances. They devised their own passwords and signal songs to be ready for unexpected situations.

While Jean posted herself at the front of the house acting as surveillance, the elder Suk roamed around the open shed conversing with her father. Rotating the role with their password and signal songs, they improved their technique and method in the matter of safeguarding their father.

Jean often visited her friend, Boksoon, a daughter to the owner of the rice mill in the village and collected news on new developments in town to keep her father informed. In the meantime, elder Suk pumped water to fill the furrows of the front field and did other house chores to help her mother.

As August approached, the unyielding summer heat was rampaging towards its zenith. The glowing sun kept burning, while trees and the greens seemed drooping mushily, dispirited in the sweltering heat.

To the shrill chirrup of a cicada, hens under the shade were croaking in slumber as if they were talking in their sleep. Then, all of sudden, a peal of thunder roared through the hillside villages, ripping through the tranquility as if bringing every roof down, with a succeeding explosion of bombs and machine gun fire.

A swarm of bombers emptied bombs in sheets, the fighter aircrafts diving and soaring up like hawks shook both heaven and earth violently, only to vanish into the blue carrying away its roar. Then smoky pillars spewed and jutted up instantly from the village and cumuli of fiery smoke rolled up like a giant wriggling caterpillar. The havoc had yet to conclude.

Another swarm of fighters swooped upon the village already on fire to bomb and destroy the northern highway pass and enflamed all the buildings and houses to ash. The havoc did not end there. Another round of air-raids poured its wrath upon the ruins and remains to the hilt and then vanished afar, concluding its fury.

Startled at the roaring thunder, Twins' mother dashed to the open shed and scanned both sides watchfully and then leaned against the earthen wall. She assured her husband in a flurry, faltering,

"Twins' Dad. Twins' Dad. It's me. Don't be frightened. There comes another round of raids. It is just an air-raid."

"I heard it, my dear. I know exactly what's going on there. Are you all right?

What about kids? Are they okay?" He questioned.

"Yes, everybody is just fine!" She shouted back yelling over the rolling thunder of explosions. This impelled Twins' father to stick his head out instinctively through the pile of pine needles. His eerie look with sunken eyes on the pale hairy face chilled her blood as if she had encountered a ghost. His features hidden away from the sun, in slightly a month or so period, were disfigured enough to raise her hair. Turning aghast, she waved her hand, shrieking in terror,

"Watch what you are doing! Downward! Beat it now!" To this, Twins' father sunk immediately into the pile. The twins, Suk and Jean, were also frightened and ran down to cling to their mother, and there they stuck together until the uproar receded and finally subsided.

As the sky was silenced, blatant whistling was heard from below the village. Jean ran down to the front and looked in the direction of whistle and reported back,

"Mom, soldiers are gathering at the bottom of the valley. I can see them."

Twins' mother rushed to Jean, and yes she saw soldiers boisterously gathering in the glen. Soldiers were climbing up the ridge in groups toward the pine forest. Alarmed pale in the face, she forced her daughters into the room, and then scurried to the open shed and warned her husband,

"Twins' father, soldiers are packed on the ridge and moving toward the pine forest behind our house. Keep your breath down, please."

She ran down to the front to push the thatched gate closed, then hurried back to the room to look out of the window.

Strangely enough, the soldiers climbing the mountain paid no attention to either their cottage or front field. It appeared that the soldiers gathered in the valley were moving along the Taebaek Mountain Ridge to another strategic point.

That night, Twins' mother's heart fluttered in fear at the thought of soldiers encamping in the pine forest within a stone's throw distance, all the while as her husband was breathing in the pile of pine needles. The crescent and twinkling stars were distinctively clear in the night sky, but it was pitch dark around the cottage shadowed in bamboo brush.

Slightly past midnight, Twins' father sneaked in through the back door,

"You were frightened, weren't you, my dear?" He asked.

"Yes I was, and I thought my liver melted away. I was really afraid that you had been knocked out by the pealing thunder."

"I was prepared for it, as I was warned by the radio. I anticipated it anyways. According to the radio news, the northern army launched all-out attacks to penetrate through the resistance line along the Nakdong River, but they were counter attacked. The bloody battles for the last two weeks must have turned the river into a sea of blood spewed by thousands of young soldiers."

Twins' mother interrupted, pleading,

"Please, that's enough. Why were there sudden air-raids to the village today? We are so far up north of the Nakdong River. Today's raids might have turned the village into an infernal shamble!"

"Why, that's a signal of a full scale counter attack by the U.S. They started with carpet bombing..."

"What is the carpet bombing?"

"Well, it is a strategic bombing over a certain designated area, pouring bombs in sheets like spreading a carpet. It seems the U.S. detected or located enemy logistics or operation commands somewhere in this village. That's why they poured bombs upon us, I guess."

"What a hair-raising scene! We were scared to death. Tomorrow I will go down to the general store to check how things are and I will let you know," confirmed Twins' mother.

2.

Complete Devastation

The following morning after the air-raids shook their village, Twins' mother went down to the village with Jean, leaving her husband to Suk's care. They were anxious to see what happened to the general store and rice mill. Jean asked,

"Mom, in case Boksoon got her house burnt, can she stay with us?"

"Of course, she will be more than welcome," Twins' mother answered open-heartedly.

When they came down to the arbor tree at the foot of the cliff, they came in sight of the bombed northern highway pass and the dilapidated concrete bridge at the entrance of the village.

The empty northern highway pass was badly caved-in like a camel's back, and upturned tanks and armored vehicles were scattered with a few having rolled onto their backs. The concrete bridge was gone, what stood instead were empty handed pillared columns.

Jean was at a lost for words. The once vibrant village turned into shambled ruins. The county office and the school had been smashed to pieces, having been gutted by bombs. Dead bodies were scattered all over, some overlapped in trenches. Roofs were gone; the ones that remained hung tilted on broken pillars or burnt walls. The village was completely devastated.

Astounded at the sight, they hurried toward the general store and to the rice mill. Where have they gone? There was a deep hollow where the store once stood, the same for the rice mill. All they could see were broken pieces of a generator, torn belts, burnt twisted empty drums, debris and scattered bodies.

"I am scared, mom!" Horrified, Jean screamed.

"I am too. Calm down, my baby. This is like hell, complete devastation!" Drawing Jean closer, her tongue dried up and stuck to her palate.

Mrs. Ahn and Boksoon, whom the mother and daughter came down to see, must have been lifted up in the fierce explosion, burst into pieces in the air and thrown over somewhere in the mutilated bodies that scattered all over.

Frightened and exhausted, their legs lost energy and languished, wobbling shakily. In the heat of August sun, the mother and daughter struggled to arrive back at the arbor tree; there they both sank under the shade to catch their breath.

In this inexorable stark reality, the mother and daughter tandem were pondering similar thoughts privately; Twin's mother had envied Mrs. Ahn who had a high school education, while Jean on countless occasions had envied Boksoon, the only daughter to the wealthy rice mill owner, who had so many things Jean had wanted.

Where were the envied now? The mother and daughter pairing desperately sought forgiveness from the deceased for their envious and jealous behavior, but could not atone to them for they were gone. They felt sorry for the dead, which reminded them of the fact that they were still alive. Instantly they perked up and became invigorated. Their steps hastened as they made their way back home.

••

That night, Twins' father, as usual sneaked inside from the back door. Twins' mother received him, still faltering in tremor,

"Twins' father, my husband. The village was completely destroyed. All the beautiful office buildings are gone, except broken pillars and tilted roofs. Mutilated bodies were everywhere!"

"How was the general store?" He asked.

"Inexpressible! It was totally blown away, same goes for the rice mill next door. The entire village turned into shambles, a complete devastation."

"At last, that was their end!" Sighing out his grief, Twins' father was recollecting the God's words that he had meditated today while buried in the pile of pine needles,

'My people committed two sins; they have forsaken me, the spring of living water, and have dug their own cisterns, broken cisterns that cannot hold water. If only they had paid attention to my commands, their peace would have been like a river, their righteousness like the waves of the sea.'

Then he asked again,

"If the general store was blown away, do you think the Ahn family is dead?"

"Yes, I saw it. They are dead, no longer alive like us," she answered.

"Well, man is destined to die once and after that to face judgment. However, let us not forget that the Lord disciplines those he loves, and he punishes everyone he accepts as a son. It's not too late for our people to repent."

"But I am worried about you," she sobbed.

"I am not afraid of death anymore," he confessed.

He realized that if these fleeting moments in life were for the eternal glory to come, he would gladly accept death with gratitude, far from being afraid. He was overcome with joy upon reaching his new stance regarding life and death. He wanted to testify and share his truth with others so that they too may prepare for their eternal life.

••

As predawn dew evaporated at the break of day, pressing for another sultry day, a carrion crow cawing in the early morning forebode an ill omen for the day. Thunderous air bombardment echoing through the hillside from afar further increased the wartime fear and horror. Another day of war was dawning.

The repair work for the broken concrete bridge and the caved-in northern highway pass continued throughout the nights. At night, soldiers and mobilized volunteers tied and knitted logs together and placed them on the broken pillars, as armored vehicles barely squeaked over them, followed by soldiers in rows. Then in broad daylight, bombers emerged from nowhere and knocked them down with a single blow. When night fell, soldiers and volunteer workers mustered up to repeat the same torturous mission only to have their efforts blown apart at another single blow the following day.

As the month of September set in, the number of soldiers in the back pine forest were noticeably increasing to a greater threat and fear to the twins' family.

Obviously, the northern army established a command post or a large number of combat units positioned in the safety of the forest. During daytime, it was dead silent in the forest when U.S. fighters swept over them to further freeze their activity, and the frequency of their flights seemed daily increasing.

In the meantime, Jean and Suck harvested corn and summer potatoes.

Often Choi and his comrades stormed the village without notice, menacing to kill any reactionary on the spot, having already killed many.

Twins' family was scared and were truly threatened when the red comrades clamored, bragging that they knew where every reactionary was hiding, and that it was just a matter of time for them to scoop them out. Indeed their hands were bloody, their feet were swift in bleeding the innocent and their vicious thoughts and so-called isms were in search for nothing but violence and massacre.

However, as time went by, twins family was getting used to them and knew how to cater to them wearing a serious face and calling them with the respectable title of 'uncle comrade,' all the while offering them steamed corn and potatoes unsparingly.

Twins' father unfailingly continued to sneak inside the back door at midnight. He whispered to his wife,

"We just need a little more patience. The northern army is exhausted following a month long full-scale attack to cross over the

Nakdong River, but it was all in vain. Did you notice the increasing number of aircrafts in the sky and they are all U.S. made? The war is almost at its end, I am positive."

Yet Twins' mother was not fully persuaded and in her trembling voice she cried, "You need to be on extreme care and caution especially in this moonlight. I would rather bring the things to your place, starting tomorrow."

"Nonsense, what makes you think that you can do a better job than I? Please be rest assured that I take extra caution even for breathing and sneezing. According to today's news, the U.S. command is about to launch an extensive counterattack at any moment."

....

The following morning, September 15th, a swarm of aircrafts floated in the southern sky. They were seen far off diving in head-first in turns and then swinging up in a flash, circling the space. This unusual maneuvering was prolonged almost all morning.

That night, Twins' father tiptoed in the back door and announced, panting,

"My dear, it is all finished! Only a couple more days of endurance! Early this morning the U.N. forces made a successful landing in Incheon and thrust right into the backbone of the enemy position. By now, they must have recaptured Seoul and the U.N. forces might be entering Seoul with flying colors right this minute."

"Still I am scared. I am always scared without you, my dear," she protested.

"No, you shouldn't be scared anymore. You should regain your peace of mind. Today's pain and sores are for tomorrows rest and comfort. Let us be hopeful and see the happiness that lies ahead, just like Stephan did while in the midst of being stoned to death. Stephan gazed steadily upward into heaven and saw the glory of God and Jesus standing at God's right hand. We should follow suit, that way we can get over death."

As U.N. forces landed in Incheon and launched toward Seoul, our friendly forces in the south broke through the resistance line, terminating almost forty days of bloody battles along the Nakdong River, and marched north at an incredible speed.

....

The red armies were crushed disastrously and routed frantically in scatters. As they fled northward or into nearby mountainous terrain, the red-banded comrades went on a rampage to mop up the reactionaries at large before they could join the red armies on the run.

It was Chuseok, a festival regarded as Korean Thanksgiving, the biggest holy day for people to pay respect to their ancestors and to Heaven for the bumper crop of the year. Yet, there was not a hint of festivity in the village.

Villagers sensed ominous signs in the air and they were seized with unutterable fear and apprehension. If they happened to meet their neighbors, they would have back-pedaled back in fear, for they knew it was in their best interest to distance themselves from each other. Indeed it was better for them not to know anything about the other party when questioned later by red-banded comrades.

The G.I. wristwatch pointed at twelve noon. With twelve more hours to go before he could meet his wife, Twins' father couldn't wait as he was extremely excited at the news he had just received on the radio.

More than one hundred days had passed since he slipped into the sleeping bag and buried himself deep in the pile of pine needles. He knew his torturous ordeal came to an end according to the radio and he couldn't wait to break the news to his wife. Yet he had to be extremely cautious since he was still right under the nose of the northern army positioned in the pine forest.

To further increase his heartbeat, shouting and whistling noise from the pine forest was being heightened and frequented increasingly, and he was even more on tenterhooks with crossed fingers.

The radio announced that U.N. forces recaptured Seoul and they were advancing northward towards the 38th parallel line. The number of prisoners was rapidly increasing, as those entrapped had no escape. He felt relieved and at the same time he was pleased to hear that the northern armies were being trampled. What a brutal guy he turned to be! Truly the war quickly changed man's inhumanness.

The movement of the needles on his watch was unbearably sluggish today. To repress his throbbing heart, he wanted to soak into every bit of sweet memories in the past and then, colliding with the cliff of stark reality, he had a freezing spasm running down all over, not necessarily because he was afraid of the death, but because he was in his flesh.

He believed that death is a route to the brighter eternal world. But for his wife and two daughters, he would rather have had the death. Therefore many a time, he prayed, asking God to take him. Truly he was ready to take death with thanks and honor if it was to be God's will.

In fact, he saw in his vision the wonderful eternal world beyond this wretched miserable reality, and he craved for it selfishly and more often proudly,

"Where, O death, is your victory? Where, O death, is your sting? Thanks are to our God! He gives us the victory through our Lord Jesus Christ." So swearing, he crushed the fear of death, and was already enjoying the eternal life.

••

It was Chuseok night. A strong wind was frantically swirling in the high nocturnal sky. In the open apex of the night sky, the illuminating full moon was skidding through shredded pieces of clouds. A shrill chirping of crickets filtered through the pine needles to ring his ears, while the smothering hustle-bustle of soldiers in the back forest reached its nocturnal pitch as usual. At last, the needles on the luminous watch overlapped to announce twelve midnight.

Twins' father pushed aside the pine needles and slipped through the piles. Dogs were heard barking fiercely from afar. His hair stood; inhaling deep he surveyed the land under the shadow of the bamboo shrubs. An electrifying chill ran down to his knees and he almost buckled as his knees were sapped of strength.

Coming out of the open shed, he glanced up at the sky and sensed uncanny winds swirling around. Inauspicious foreboding raised goose skin all over with fear. And he tolerated with it, swearing,

"I'll just break the news and come right back tonight."

He passed by the jar-stand as usual and groped his way around the back corner of the cottage in the pitch shadow of the thatched roof, when another stroke of electric chill ran down his spine from the scruff of his neck.

He felt like sinking into the depth as he stealthily groped on. He stressed at the abdomen and was about to turn the corner, holding his breath, when suddenly two dark figures swooped upon him. Instantly he collapsed. And he was hogtied in seconds.

After his capture, the two bullies turned their attention to the cottage. They pushed through the back door and bundled up Twins' mother who was trembling like an aspen leaf. Their capture was inevitable like a mouse sneaking in a snake's cage.

The couple was frozen pale; their demise left them with no words. Like an animal strangled by a brutal butcher, they were dragged on bare feet down the ridge, tumbling and rolling all over.

When they were splashing their way across the stream at the foot of the cliff, they heard the brutal slaughtering of the innocent from under the arbor tree. Their fates were sealed, regardless of the pleas of neighborhood dogs barking fiercely throughout the village

"You, cursed reactionaries. Sucking on people's blood without flipping a fingertip! What's so special about your son other than the dirty silver spoon in his mouth?"

The eerie thumping noise of flogging and the bewailing groans of the beaten innocent were curling the toes of the couple. Now it came to the turn of twins' parents.

"You, Jesus fanatics! You're a detestable reactionary. You have had a sweet easy life so far just rolling a pen around your dirty fat finger. Do you have anything to say for your pathetic existence?"

To this, Twins' father for the first time opened his mouth.

"Let me hold my wife in my arms. Receive Jesus Christ for your own sake."

"Here you go again. You silly reactionary! Where is Jesus? Is he not dead?"

A loud outcry reverberated through the night sky as Twin's father thanked,

"My Lord, we thank you for having us come to you hand in hand."

The shredded clouds were momentarily lifted and the moon revealed her full illumination as Twins' father held his wife tight in his arms.

Following the atrocious slaughtering rampage, the terrorists fled to faction themselves as partisans in remote mountain ridges. Solemn silence fell on the village as day was breaking to reveal nine slaughtered bloody bodies scattered under the arbor tree.

•••

That morning when Suk and Jean woke up, mom and dad were gone. Mom was neither in the master room nor in the kitchen. They rushed out to the front field. Mom was not there either. They cried out,

"Mom! Mom! Dad! Dad!" But there was no answer.

Frightened in fear and seized in sinister misgivings, they dashed out of the house and ran down the ridge, falling and rolling, crying out,

"Mom! Dad!"

As they descended down the ridge, they saw and heard villagers writhing and wailing under the arbor tree. They rushed to the scene and found their mom and dad among the cold bloody bodies.

Stunned at the sight, they dashed and scrambled over them, squealing frenziedly, shaking the bodies violently and rolling over them on all fours.

Until late in the evening, the air and artillery bombardments shook them, and this time U.S. army tanks and armored vehicles came rolling over the broken highway toward the northern pass.

•••

Two days had past. Suk and Jean were still crying themselves dry, shaking mom and clinging to dad, wheezing through swollen throats. On the heels of the U.N. forces, flocks of refugees were returning home. Among them were the pastor and his wife along with their only daughter, Sun, who left for seminary two years ago.

"Oh, Lord. That poor little one! Oh, no!" Sun's mother grieved as she recognized the twins huddled around their deceased parents. She gathered the elder Suk into her arms. Her daughter, Sun ran to Jean, shrieking,

"Jean, it's me, Sun. I am here! I am back!" She frantically tugged her in.

That evening, Pastor held the funeral service for those who were brutally massacred. Surprisingly the bell tower and Pastor's quarters remained intact except a few broken windows.

Teacher Sun helped Suk and Jean wash up with pumped water, while her mother prepared dinner in the kitchen. As they sat around the dinner table and Pastor was saying grace, a sudden dead sleep fell upon Jean, and she struggled to stay awake. That night, Suk and Jean slept like a log in their teacher Sun's bedroom.

After dinner, Pastor walked through the ruins in the village and returned to church with a serious face, and there in church he cried out on his knees throughout the night,

"Heavenly Father, I walked through the ruins. You promised, saying,

'if my people who are called by my name, will humble themselves and pray and seek my face and turn from their wicked ways, then I will hear from heaven and will forgive their sins and will heal their land.' As sins are rampant on this land, we deserve to be torn apart and devastated. However, Almighty God, send us your spirit to wake them up and have them shake off the devils. Have these people humble themselves before you and seek your mercy."

The following morning, Pastor held a meeting with village leaders to discuss on how to reconstruct the village.

Jean slept in until the sun was high above the window. In her dream, she was falling off a cliff with her mother, and in alarm she woke up with a throbbing heart.

Upon consciousness she shook her sister Suk violently,

"Suk, wake up!" Suk woke up and asked, looking around, "Jean, where are we?" Her horse voice was discordant.

Jean, pulling herself together stood up abruptly and shouted,

"We have to go! We have to go home!" hastening to find her way out.

Sun, who was helping her mother in the kitchen, ran after her, shouting,

"Jean, where are you going? Breakfast is ready, Jean!" Jean was already on the run toward her home.

"There is no way! They must be home. Mom and Dad must be home."

She climbed up the ridge as fast as she could, and then suddenly she halted and cried out,

"Mom! Mom! What happened to you, mom?" She shouted aloud for some time. Then, as if hallucinated, she stood up suddenly and made a dash through the opened thatched gate to jump onto the front floor, calling,

"Mom, mom..." and then, went through the kitchen door, crying out,

"Mom, mom, where are you?" and then, fell on the kitchen floor for another bout of crying.

After a short spell of silence, she sat up abruptly to make a run toward the open shed and madly searched through the pine piles, kicking and screaming,

"Papa, Papa! Where have you gone? Papa..." She gasped falling to the ground exhausted.

Another spell of dead silence, and then, as if something flashed upon her mind, she sat up again to run down to the front field and searched through the furrows helter-skelter, screaming,

"Mom! Mom! Why have you gone? Answer me, please." Now this time she collapsed, fully exhausted.

For the first several days, Sun stayed with the twin sisters over at the twins' house. The trauma and the hurt inflicted upon the sisters were beyond human remedy. Only God could heal them in his own time.

For the twins, it was very fortunate that their teacher Sun came in time to soothe their ripping pains and to bind their wounds. It was as if someone planned ahead of time the paths between the twins and their teacher.

However, Sun also had to help her mother at home and her father at church now as an Assistant Pastor. Not to mention she was needed in the village for the reconstruction project. Therefore, Sun arranged for the twin sisters to move in and stay with her at the pastor's quarters, the sisters obliged the move.

That night after evening service, Pastor said,

"Suk and Jean, you both have been our daughters in Christ. From now on, you two will become our real daughters. As I had only one daughter Sun, at times I wanted a few more. My prayers were answered. Now I have two more daughters from God. I am rich with my daughters. I am really thankful for these wonderful gifts."

Sun's mother, the madam lady, succeeded to his thanks, saying,

"You are right, Pastor. They have been beautiful daughters so far, but now, they are our real daughters and I don't know how to thank God for his gracious gift." She embraced the sisters in her arms, wetting her eyes. Suk and Jean were also shedding tears.

As days went by, Suk's sorrow was daily deepening and she sobbed silently throughout the night underneath her comforter, while Jean and Sun were sound asleep.

··

U.S. soldiers were not in need of A-Frame, not to mention of shovels and hoes. They overlooked the damaged concrete bridge and floated a pontoon bridge right next to it. In an hour or so, U.S. army trucks and other vehicles ran over it in full swing, while in the sky, fighters were rehearsing a fantastic air show.

The northern highway pass which was caved in from bombings, was refilled and straightened out as a couple of tank-like vehicles bulldozed over two to three rounds of tracking. It was amazing! At this pace, the village restoration process would be completed in no time. It would only take a half days worth of bulldozing to fill up the remaining hollows, push aside remains and debris of buildings and to level off the ground on which they could start the reconstruction work. For Pastor and other village leaders, what they witnessed was like a miracle, a miracle answered by God through prayers.

On the third day of their return from refuge, a U.S. Army jeep pulled up in front of the church. Two U.S. Army officers and a Korean Army officer got out of the jeep asking for the pastor.

Pastor was in a meeting with village leaders regarding plans for the reconstruction project. Sun was the only member of the village who was able to understand and speak English, as she studied the language hard at seminary to become a missionary.

She approached them and asked,

"Who are you looking for, sir?"

"We are here to see the pastor of this church," one of officers answered with glad eyes.

When she led them to the pastor's office, those at the meeting rose with wonder.

"Who are they?" The same officer asked. Sun explained who they were and what kind of meeting they were in the middle of.

Then the officer introduced himself. He was Captain Jonathan, U.S. Army Chaplain and the other was Captain Brown from U.S. Engineering Corps along with a Korean Army liaison officer.

"We came just in time. As a matter of fact, we are here to meet your pastor and other village leaders." Chaplain Jonathan introduced himself and then Captain Brown, the Engineering Officer and Lieutenant Kim, the interpreter.

Chaplain Jonathon continued,

"U.S. forces are advancing northward beyond the 38th parallel line, and we are looking for a site to establish a front line command post somewhere around here. Since we are in the mountainous zone, we can't find a better location than this village for the site. We don't know how long we will be stationed here, but I am sure we will be moving out pretty soon. We are here to get your approval on our plan."

The U.S. officers proposed they could level off the ground and establish the command within a day or two. They also guaranteed the safety and security of the village as long as they were stationed in the village.

When Chaplain Jonathan finished, the county manager intervened, saying,

"But as you see, we have to clear the ruins and debris for you. We cannot get it done that fast, sir."

"Oh, don't worry about that, sir. We'll take care of it. We'll also help you rebuild other buildings and houses as much as we can while we are here, if you'd like," Captain Brown offered.

In one day, the U.S. army established the command post with office buildings and quarters on the school ground.

"If you need a place for worship service, you may use our church," Pastor offered.

"Thank you very much Pastor, but we always carry our own church on our backs." Thanking, the Chaplain laughed aloud. Since then, Chaplain Jonathan and Pastor got together almost everyday, and they testified their oneness in Christ, budding a lasting friendship.

One evening at Pastor's office, Chaplain Jonathan absorbed in meditation and voiced,

"War is the most brutal weapon man can wield."

"Yes, it is an organized murderer and destroyer against God's will," Pastor agreed.

Chaplain Jonathan continued, quoting scriptures,

"In the wealthy home there are dishes made of gold and silver as well as some made from wood and clay," and then asked,

"Does the potter not have the right to make out of some lump of clay, pottery for noble purposes and some for common use?'

"You are right, Chaplain. We have all come from God: The rich, the poor, the noble and the base. The rich is to share with the poor. The noble are to help the base. We should all praise our Lord in chorus, showering his good will."

To this, Chaplain Jonathan, much enlivened, responded,

"That's why Paul warned, 'do not think of yourself more highly than you ought, but rather think of yourself with sober judgment, in accordance with the measure of faith God has given you.' Therefore, we should humble ourselves before God and obey his will. God wants unity not uniformity. We all can't be gold dishes, because it is against God's will."

"Of course it is against God's will if Christians of today seek uniformity. Even worse is that some of them advocate Christian community as Communistic community, harking back to the first century church. This is quite absurd, isn't it, Chaplain?"

"Yes, it is terribly misleading, but I have never heard of it."

"Well, that is only my view," Pastor answered.

••

Chaplain Jonathan was an Assistant Pastor to his father who was the Senior Pastor of the First United Spring Baptist Church in Denver, Colorado, before he joined the army as a Chaplain. First United had a large congregation of nearly 4,000 members and had four other assistant pastors. Chaplain Jonathan mentioned to Pastor that his church back home in Denver may be able to extend aid and help wartime orphans and widows in Korea. He gave the address and phone number of the Denver church to Pastor, and stated that he would write a personal letter to his father, explaining the situation here. At the time, ten U.S. dollars could provide one-month supply of food to an orphan in Korea. Pastor started praying.

Village seniors once invited Chaplain Jonathan and Captain Brown, offering them two oxen in appreciation for the reconstruction of their village. This sent them into a jovial laughter, Chaplain Jonathan replied,

"We highly appreciate your kind offer, but our soldiers carry their own chickens and cows on their backs. However, we'll definitely cherish your genuine love and friendship."

••

The village was secured as long as U.S. forces were stationed, and former red-banded volunteers came out one by one to register at the sheriff office, confessing their wrong doing of wearing the red bands. They humbled themselves divorcing their ties with the communist movement,

"Thank you for sparing our lives. I just followed them because I was forced to do so and I had no other choice. Therefore, please let us not talk about it anymore."

The village recovered its lost vigor, and people gathered to the village from neighboring towns, seeking safety and strength in numbers. However, the home of the rascal Choi was desolate as villagers kept their distance. The home sheltered Choi's old mother, who barely eked it out alone on skimpy foods supplied by anonymous hosts.

There were barbed wire entanglements on the ground between army units and school classrooms. The U.S. Army built four new classrooms with veneer boards and repaired four other classrooms. The school auditorium was partitioned into the needed number of classrooms. The church as well was used for classrooms during the day. The newly constructed classrooms were stuffy due to small windows, but they had sufficient power supply from the U.S. Army generators.

As school reopened, Jean was gradually animated both in school and church. An American soldier named Jack came to Sunday school with an armful of candies and chocolates, and he taught the village children how to speak English.

Jean was eager and quick to follow Jacks greetings such as: How are you? I am fine. I am glad. I am happy. I am tired. She had a knack in learning the foreign language, while Suk started with an English book, which Sun brought back from the Seminary. The elder Suk followed Jack's lips as well, but she couldn't pronounce as smoothly as the younger Jean.

Even in the middle of such exciting new endeavors, Jean had a fit of missing her parents. She would turn wild instantly, shedding tears whenever and wherever. Suk was different. She harbored her sorrow deep inside, crying in silence.

One of the church Deacons, Park moved into the twins' old cottage, since his earthen hut crumbled in the air-raid. Suk often visited her old house, spreading her comforter in her old room to cry her eyes out all night through. Teacher Sun would follow her and allowed her to cry out to her heart's content.

One day, sister Sun (the twins started calling her sister Sun) told the twins a story about Joseph,

"Joseph was the eleventh of Jacob's twelve sons. It was not recorded in the Bible when he lost his mother Rachel, but we assume he was about seven years old. His mother died laboring the birth of his only younger brother, Benjamin. Just imagine what Joseph was going through when his mother died." Sister Sun had used Joseph's loss to relate to the loss of the twins in order to give them hope of the future.

She continued, "Joseph was not crushed under the sorrow or yearning for his mother but he rose to overcome them. He was a man that dreamt on a large scale and a man of faith at the same time. Joseph had a dream in which his sheaf of grain rose and stood upright, while his eleven other brother's sheaves of grain gathered around Joseph's sheaf and bowed. Joseph's older brothers would later plot to kill him, as they felt ridiculed by Joseph's dream. However, the eldest Reuben suggested sparing his life, choosing rather throwing him into a cistern.

Can you imagine being thrown into a pit? Having been betrayed by his brothers, left for dead in the middle of hungry wild beasts, shivering in cold and hunger! Can you visualize his state?

"Scared to death, extremely exhausted too, I guess," Jean exclaimed.

"Not only scared of groaning lions but I would faint at the devil's thorny fingers reaching out to strangle my neck, if I were there," Suk added.

Sun continued,

"I would too, but Joseph was different. Of course he was frightened but he was with God who gave him a dream and a promise. Of course in this plight, he might have cried out for help to God, and God heard it, I think. The following morning they saw a caravan of Ishmaelite coming from Gilead. They were on their way to Egypt. When the Midianite merchants, I mean the Ishmaelite came by; his brothers pulled Joseph up out of the cistern and sold him for twenty shekels of silver.

Now these Midianite merchants must have traveled days and nights through the desert under the scorching heat and shivering cold at night. Do you think they gave Joseph a ride on the camel's back?

"No way. The camels were fully loaded with merchandise. Besides, Joseph was sold as a slave; his feet must have been blistered all over on the burning desert and his hand tied fast." Someone argued.

Sister Sun continued,

"I think so, too. Have you ever seen any cows or hogs on the carriage on the way to the market for sales? Joseph was on the way to the slave market for sale. He might have been brutally whipped and threshed, when he fell on the ground from exhaustion. How do you think Joseph responded to the cruelty? Do you think he cried out and begged to the merchant?"

"Well, he might." Suk answered.

"I don't think so. Joseph had to put up with it. He must have cried out to God for strength in silence." Someone opposed.

Sister Sun kept on,

"I think so, too. Joseph was a young man who had dreams. He was thoroughly taught by his father Jacob to endure present suffering for the glory to come, and I think he fully trusted in God and rather thanked him for the trials. In this way he strengthened his inner being and his faith in God. As I introduced Joseph many times before, at his age of thirty, thirteen years later, Pharaoh said to Joseph,

'I hereby put you in charge of the whole land of Egypt. Only with respect to the throne, will I be greater than you.' Pharaoh appointed Joseph the Prime Minister of then the strongest nation on the earth. Joseph held that position for eighty years until he reached the age of one hundred and ten years old.

Now let us look into how Joseph went through the pain of losing his mother at his young age, how he was maltreated and thrown into a pit by his brothers, and how he was sold as a slave and then went through all kinds of unbearable hardship, sufferings and mortification. And why?"

"That's because he was to be made a strong young man." Jean answered.

"You are right." Sister Sun agreed and continued,

"He saved a great number of people from starvation. He built Egypt to be the strongest nation in the world. He surely did many great things, as you know. Now, let me ask you a question. Can anyone do such a great thing?"

"There is no way! Not everyone can do it." Someone replied.

To this, Sister Sun stood up from her chair and said,

"I don't agree with you. If chosen by God for the same great job, anyone can make do. It is God, not we that do it. God chooses the one as He planned and trains him through sufferings and problems."

"If that's the case, can I do the same?" Jean asked, glaring her big eyes.

"Of course you can. First of all, you must be chosen by God as Joseph was. Otherwise you wouldn't be able to listen to and understand the story I told you. Do you follow me?"

"Yes, we do! We understand!" All responded.

"Then, we all must be chosen people."

"Yes, we are!"

"What we learned today is that God trains us through problems and sufferings, and strengthens us to be strong enough to take over whatever God planned for us. We should not be pressed under or defeated by the problems of today, but we should win over them, even the sorrow and pains! in order for us to grow stronger for tomorrow. When time comes, we should be used for His great purpose just like Joseph was. If you agree, let us not be saddened or dejected anymore but be hopeful and faithful in Christ!! Understood?"

"Understood! Amen!" All concerted.

The Southern Army and U.N. forces crossed the 38th parallel line and charged northward facing desperate oppositions, capturing Wonsan on October 10th 1950 and P'yongyang, the capital city of the northern half on October 19th the same year. Subsequently, the U.S. Frontline Command Post had to move their operations further north, extending beyond the 38th parallel line.

Chaplain Jonathan stopped by to report to Pastor before the U.S. Command Post moved out of the village,

"Pastor, I just received a reply to my previous inquiry from Denver Baptist Church. They said that they may be able to provide you with more extensive and larger scale aid through the Southern Christian Baptist Association. They are asking for the extent and scope of wartime needs, as well as the procedures to go by. This is the letter from Denver."

He handed the letter to Pastor, who was deeply impressed and thankful,

"Chaplain Jonathan, I don't know how to thank you. In regards to the aid, I only thought about the reconstruction of buildings and food aid to the farmers who could not harvest their crops due to war. It is quite amazing to hear that the Southern Christian Baptist Association would help us. I will go down to the city to meet the County Chief on this matter tomorrow and then I will reply to the Denver Church.

By the way, we are terribly sorry that you have to go. Please take a good care of yourself and let us know where you are stationed next. We do thank you again. And may God protect and bless upon you." They bid farewell and departed.

On October 26th 1950, the South Korean Army reached Chosan on the Apnok River, which prompted Chinese communist armies to launch their first attack without notice. In defiance of Chinese intervention, U.N. forces pressed on northward and on November 21st, the U.S. 10th Army Corps advanced to the northernmost city, Hae-san-jin, on the Tuman River. On November 24th, U.N. forces launched their final all-out offensive. There, Chinese communist forces poured out in whistling sleets, waves after waves, through mountainous terrain below the freezing point. An event later recalled as the 'Human Waves Strategy.' U.S. forces stood their frozen ground for a month and then on December 24th the same year evacuated a great number of refugees out of Heung-nam port and gave in, commencing to withdraw.

In the middle of December, a nipping cold hit the village. When the milky afternoon sun was hanging frozen on the bony branches of fruit trees, a peal of a cannon blast shook the earth and was approaching closer to the village. Villagers shrank again in fear and suspense with their mouths shut.

At sunset, in front of the county office, U.N. forces' armed vehicles were coming down in streams. A speeding jeep swerved off the highway and pulled up in front of the church. It was Chaplain Jonathan. He hurried into the church and met Sister Sun, who received him with a big smile,

"Hello, Chaplain Jonathan, It's so nice to see you again. You look like you are in a hurry."

"Yes, I am very much in a hurry, my dear. Is your father home?"

"No, he isn't. He is visiting a sick lady but I don't know who this sick lady is."

Chaplain Jonathan seemed indifferent to the sick lady. He cleared his throat with a serious look and said in grave tones,

"Chinese red armies are pouring down. We are ordered to retreat. I just came by to let you know this. It's best for all of you to come with us. Please pass this message to your dad. Again, it's best for all of you to come with us." He hurried back into the flow of vehicles. Sun and Jean came straight back home to deliver the urgent message to their mother.

In the meantime, Pastor was visiting the mother of the rascal Choi, who was abandoned. The lady was seventy-five years old and she had no means to survive but for Pastor's care and assistance.

Today Pastor and Brother Park, as usual, carried food and medication to the old lady. As they entered the place, the old lady, as if receiving angels, bowed and thanked,

"Gracious Pastor. This old one is still alive only to be a burden on you." Holding Pastor's hand and sobbed, choking in tears,

"I am a sinner not worth living!"

"Please calm down, ma'am and please listen. Our Jesus died on the cross to pay off our debt. He was crucified, shedding his precious blood to redeem us. He will not break a bruised reed and he will not snuff out a smoldering wick. He is saying now, 'Even to your old age and gray hairs, I will sustain you and I will rescue you.' He still loves you very much. He prays and comforts you as he always has." Pastor held her in his arms for awhile.

3.

Jean – Jean

As wintry dusk fell upon the frozen fields and mountains, hillside trails were engulfed in the sudden spread of darkness. The crescent moon and twinkling stars studded in the night sky zoomed its icy illumination upon to the mountain ridge.

Coming out of the trail from his visit with the old lady, Choi's mother, Pastor made his way out and hastened down the ridge toward home.

As he returned home, his wife approached,

"Where have you been all these critical hours, Pastor?" Breaking the news, she kept on,

"Chaplain Jonathan stopped by to give you this urgent message and then hurried back in retreat." Sun reinforced her mother's panic by adding,

"Yes, father, Chaplain Jonathan warned us to leave here right away."

To this, Pastor looked calm and nodded, saying,

"That's why the village sounded somewhat noisy this evening. What about other village leaders? Have you heard anything from them?"

"Of course we heard! They left already! We have no time! We should make haste!" Madam Lady, pressed on.

Pastor stuck his Bible and important papers into his traveling bag, which had been packed swiftly by his wife, and roped it across his back. Madam Lady put a large basket upon her head in which she carried immediate foods and provisions. Suk also put a big basket of aluminum kettle and other kitchen utensils in addition to her clothing and drill books, and set forth hand in hand with Sister Sun.

Jean had a package of clothing and some provisions upon her head and held tight onto Pastor's left sleeve. They wore as many clothes as they could from head down to heels, in doing so they found it difficult to walk briskly. They trudged and wobbled from the very first step, but they had no other way to carry extra clothing.

As the night deepened, the numbers of people were rapidly increasing to crowd the highway. The munching and crunching footsteps made on the frozen snow road could no longer be distinguished as the sheer number of refugees had trampled the snow into the earth

Pastor alerted Jean, who clung to his sleeve end,

"Jean, hold me tight and come close. Don't let it go," he warned.

"Yes, Pastor. I'll stick to you, though I can't see you clear," Jean assured.

It was not easy for her to tug at him with her right hand, her left hand clutching the package on her head, wobbling after him as she was bundled up with layers of clothes. Since it was pitch dark, it was a little more relaxing with her closed eyes to hear and count the munching foot steps on the frozen roadside, thus keeping herself awake.

Almost six months passed since the onset of war. The first three months were riddled with the red army parade and the rascal Choi's massacre, while the last three months witnessed the U.N. forces counter-attack capturing the northern capital P'yongyang, along with a series of bombings and air-raiding shows.

The Chinese 'human wave' swelled in numbers, inundating southward with a sinister march consisting of uniformed high kicks and whistles, resulting in a historic refuge exodus. This time almost every household was on the run southward, leaving everything behind.

Refugees jam-packed the highway and they trod all night through Uijung-bu at the heels of others ahead. Many of them followed the steps of those ahead with their eyes closed from fatigue. Walking throughout the night, their mouths dried up to the palate and their eye-lids drooped, weighed upon by the hefty load of slumber.

At dawning, the rising sun set the eastern sky aflame yet the refugees found no relief as the weather mocked them with a wintry chill. Suk, treading on the heels of Pastor with a firm clutch at the hem of sister Sun's skirt, awoke from a nodding state and,

"What is this? What am I gripping at?" To her alarm, she was clutching a strange woman' skirt, not sister Sun's skirt! She turned frantic, screaming to and fro,

"Sister Sun! Sister Sun!" She shouted in terror, "Jean! Jean!"

Through the hectic moment, she saw Sister Sun some distance ahead of her. Now scurrying towards her,

"You were here?! I felt my liver falling off. I was scared to death that I had lost you! By the way, have you seen Pastor and Jean? Where are they?" She came to think of her younger twin sister Jean. Sister Sun gathered herself, shaking her drowsiness and surveyed the highway, and then,

"Here we go. They are right there!" She exclaimed and ran to catch up with her parents. Suk scampered toward them and searched. But, alas! Jean was not seen there!

Jean was not there!

"Jean is not around!" She screamed. Everybody was alarmed and looked around to locate Jean, but Jean was not in their vicinity. Suk turned frantic and her heart was pounding relentlessly. Jean was nowhere to be seen! Suk almost went crazy, fretting over with goggling eyes. She shouted and screamed.

"Jean! Jean! Where are you?! That reckless one must be way behind! I'll definitely pinch her this time!" So irate, she looked back, only to find her stomach completely turned over at what she witnessed. What she saw were two to three armed vehicles tailing after the procession of refugees!

On both sides of the vehicles red flags were fluttering. As the vehicles approached, refugees opened the way reflectively for them, parting to the sides of highway. Suk urged with added fury, madly shrieking,

"Jean! Jean!"

Two armed vehicles were seen coming within her eyesight. Then all of sudden a thunderous explosion followed by machinegun-fire, burst the flow of refugees into a frenzied chaos. The swarm of aircraft was already afar, sweeping the thunder away, bursting the flocks of refugees into agonizing cries and appalling confusion.

Out of the armed vehicles, black pillars of fiery smoke shot up, and in no time the departed aircrafts came back for another round of diving and soaring raids, pouring bombs in sheets again to powder the shambles. Thus the sky crumbled down and the earth upturned in a rampage and then the air attackers disappeared afar. Bodies torn apart from the havoc fell onto the hollows. Pieces of ripped body fell on the edge and instantly congealed with a faint trace of steam.

Mercy was not yet given as air-raiders came back again to bomb and riddle the broken road and fallen people. Another round of air-raids could have caved the edge of roadside where Sister Sun and Suk lay flat on their stomachs.

As silence fell, Suk rose quickly and perked up to look around for Jean. She ran down back down the highway through chaotic shambles but the road sank having been caved in. Her legs enfeebled and shaken could not support her body upright through the uneven terrain, she fell down to the ground.

She felt the world crumbling upon her and was choking in fear and suspense. Overwhelmed by unutterable pain and sore anguish of despair, she was frenziedly stamping on the ground, screaming,

"Jean! Jean!" But Jean did not reply her call. Sister Sun followed at her heels and embraced Suk tight, but let her writhe in the agony to her heart's content.

Scattered refugees gathered back on the highway to resume their aimless migration. Sister Sun led Suk in the direction of Pastor and their mother. In the frozen sky, the wintry sun was smearing her opaque gleam, while untiring Suk kept on screaming and whimpering,

"Jean! Jean!" Sister Sun, holding Suk in her arms, finally cried out together.

Madam Lady came and embraced Suk, and with Sister Sun, all three cried together. The horror and sorrow stricken procession of migrating refugees kept their southward march, now at a swifter pace. They had no room to look back. They had to quicken their steps.

Pastor, holding Suk in his arms, tried to console her grief,

"I believe that our good Father keeps Jean safe somewhere in his own way. We are separated for a while due to unknown reasons, but I am sure that the time will come when we get together again with joy. Let's keep our good faith for it and let's pray together for that day." However, her aching heart was not soothed.

The somber sky was groaning all day with the thunder of air-raids, and dusk fell when they arrived in Seoul. Different from the Pastor's first flight, this time every household seemed packed for an escape.

Pastor originally planned to stop overnight in Seoul but had a change of heart. He decided to keep on proceeding with the accompanying flocks through the sleet and blizzard. He thought it best to get out and away from a city as large as Seoul, and find a place much smaller and less susceptible from the northern marauders.

Now, Suk was so deadly exhausted that she could not walk anymore. A fully loaded oxcart was passing by. Sister Sun brightened at the sight of the oxcart, ran after the cart driver, and begged for his favor,

"Mister, please do me a favor in the name of Jesus." So pressed was she that she asked in the name of Jesus.

"In the name of Jesus?" To this unusual plea, the cart driver flinched a moment.

He must be a good Christian, Sun thought in her mind. She became so convinced that she gloatingly broached the subject,

"Sir, my younger sister is in trouble. She is awfully sick. I have to carry her on my back, but as you see, I have been on my feet all night. Could you please help her just for awhile? If I could sit her on the back of the cart and I hold her. I know it is too much asking for you and your ox."

The cart driver mutely examined Sun and Suk, and then, arranged a space in the back for Suk. He returned to his front post to goad the ox as if nothing had happened.

"Thank you, sir. Thank you, sir." Thanking repeatedly, she hurriedly sat Suk on the back of the oxcart. Unequivocally, she experienced the Lord's touching hand of lifting us out of a slimy pit. At last, they arrived at the Han River.

In the night sky, flickering sleets were turning into flakes of snow. The refugee procession dragged in a long line as they were crossing over the frozen Han River.

Among them was a couple from the Mapo region. They were babbling a hair-raising story without a hitch.

"Early this morning, a heavily laden oxcart sunk at the Mapo pier as the ice cracked." Husband announced.

"What happened to the cart driver?" His wife shrieked.

"Do you ask what happened? Why of course, the frozen river swallowed them all, the driver, the ox and the cart!"

"Alas, that's sad!"

"That's not all. Those who followed the cart sank to be frozen and became water ghosts. In a war, people are to die either this way or that way. But be convinced that there is always a way to stay alive. That's why I didn't take that route and came this way. Do you understand now?" Husband played a hero.

When they reached the other side of the river, Pastor let out a sigh of relief,

"Now, we may slow down a little." However Suk was indifferent. She added to her agony. As she stepped on the Noryangjin bank, she shouted again, facing toward Seoul,

"Jean! Jean!"

Pastor took off his back bag and held her in his arms. He sobbed,

"Suk, my dear daughter. Jean is your younger sister and she is my precious daughter. She was gifted to me by the grace of God. If you

lost your sister, I lost my daughter. Therefore, let us cry out together."
As he mourned loudly, Suk's grief seemed a little soothed.

Pastor continued,

"At the sight of the ornamented robe stained in animal blood, and at the news that his beloved son, Joseph had been torn to pieces by a wild beast, Jacob's heart must have been crushed and shattered into pieces." Facing Suk, Pastor kept on,

"You know what a dear son Joseph was to Jacob, don't you?"

"Yes, I do. He was his first son to his beloved wife, Rachel," Suk whined.

"You are right. Rachel died while laboring to give birth to Benjamin, Joseph's only younger brother. Joseph was the apple of Jacob's eye. I mean that Joseph was more attached to Jacob than any other son, and he was strikingly smart and also very obedient to his father.

One day he was sent on his father's errand. Later Jacob was told that Joseph was killed by a wild beast. Can you imagine how much in grief Jacob was at the news?"

"Yes, I can." Suk answered curtly.

"Now let us look into what really was going on. Did God leave Joseph at the mouth of a wild animal or was God working something special through Joseph?" To this, Suk turned serious and answered,

"Yes, God was working something special through Joseph."

"You are right. God trained him in those troubles to use him as a bigger tool in his later days." Suk nodded. Pastor kept on,

"Very well. As you know, God trained Joseph to make him into a bigger vessel. Now I am convinced that our God plans to use you as a similar instrument, seeing that you are in similar predicament as Joseph was. Besides, if we further look into this matter, what do you think God is working with your sister, Jean? If you ask me, I am convinced that our God is working something special unknown to us through Jean. I would like to trust in God. Do you like to trust in God?"

"I like to, but…"

— —-

Pastor once talked about Abraham,

"The Lord had said to Abraham,

-Leave your country, your people and your father's household and go to the land I will show you-" Abraham obeyed and did as God commanded. In this way Abraham became our forefather of faith."

Explaining that God might be asking the same for us, Pastor continued,

"Suk, this story teaches us that God's words come before anything; birth, blood and all other worldly ties. In other words, God has a special plan for you. His plan comes before your own plan. His will comes before yours. It may not be easy for you to follow, but was it easy for Abraham to follow? No, it wasn't." Suk was nodding again and said,

"I understand, but I can't be that big, Pastor."

"Well, no one can tell so sure. It remains to be seen whether or not what you two sisters are going through will be greater than what Abraham or Joseph went through. We all are equally important to God.

One thing we should remember is that our good Lord came to the world for the poor, the sick and the wounded to give them strength, healing and peace." He said,

"In this world you will have troubles but take heart! I have overcome the world. And I will not leave you as an orphan and I will always be with you to the very end of the age."

The first thing the refugees would look for when they realized that they were in a safety zone was shelter in which they could stretch their aching legs. The railway station, church, school and other public buildings were primarily targeted for such shelter as the aforementioned facilities had water, restrooms and windbreaks, though most of the water taps were frozen hard. Some refugees took rural routes, as people there tended to warm them with greater hospitality.

Pastor chose a highway to head his family to Suwon. They sheltered for some time in an empty roadside stable. When they passed by Anyang, he heard for the first time that Chinese communist forces had captured Seoul yesterday, January 3rd 1951. The capital had now been turned over to the invading forces for the second time since the outbreak of war, June 25th 1950.

The southern government now in Suwon further moved southward to Taejon. U.N. Command pulled the final resistance line further southwards- across Pyungtaek to Samchuk. This time pastor decided to head his family to his in-law's in Jinjoo near by Busan, the southernmost port of peninsula.

Recalling the last ten days of refugee procession in which Pastor led his family, every minute, every hour and every day of these torturous days was ironically the most blessed and precious time in his and in his family's history. Our good Lord had prepared their way in every trial and tribulations they inevitably had to face.

Pastor tended to Suk's wounds of missing her sister Jean. To treat her mental anguish, Pastor taught Suk about God's plan, which was deeply engraved in her heart. Through their ongoing saga, the entire family was bound in unity to cry out on the roads they traveled. God was more responsive to unanimous appeal than to a single plea. They didn't have the confines to worship in a warm comfortable church. They cried out in hunger, in thirst, out in the cold and on rugged roads and frozen fields.

In their state of emergency with communist forces trailing on their heels and fighters constantly snarling in the sky, they stepped up their pace hand in hand and embraced together to cry out. God's comfort and love flowed in precious words through Pastor's lips and they were comforted as if they had been bathed in his precious blood. They then heard God saying,

'If you know the plans I have for you, plans to prosper and not to harm you, plans to give you hope and a future, consider it to be pure joy whenever you face these trials.'

God also promised through his words that they would be restored and made strong, firm and steadfast, after they have suffered.

To those in that tiring refugee procession, God's words were their strength and hope. Those suffering thanked God for the hardships they went through. As Sister Sun recited Gods words to Suk, Suk held Sun's hand tight, giving her legs the strength to walk another mile. Many other refugees joined the family of four to praise and worship the Lord on the road as the situation allowed.

There were also refugees, smacking tongue, passed by, ridiculing,

"These Jesus fanatics are totally out of their mind in this time of war. How can anyone dare to open their mouth to sing a song and thank God while on the run from being killed? Thanks to whom and for what?"

Yet those who thirsted for God's words like a deer pants for the stream of water, gathered to offer an altar and had their sorrow and anguish turned into exaltation and gratitude. Though the group was small in number, they were powerful in their prayer for heavenly joy in this bleak procession.

Truly speaking, they learned and experienced the absolute truth that our Jesus comes in our life to bring us out of darkness into his wonderful light; to save us from death, to give us joy instead of sorrow, and to lift us from despair and into the ray of hope. Jesus performs all these miracles through the trials and tribulations in our life, and He is not afar. He is always with us.

At last they were coming down a hill pass, looking down on the city of Jinjoo. Hills and fields were snow covered from late blizzards, and the icy wintry sun hung frozen half way to the western sky. Freezing winds shook pine branches to sprinkle the heaped snow upon them.

Madam Lady quickened her steps as they were closing into her hometown. She figured that they would be able to get home before sundown if they hastened. As they hastened, they forgot that they were in the middle of the coldest month of the year, January.

Approximately ten miles east of the highway from the city of Jinjoo, there was a high mountain pass, and if you make a right turn along the country road at the half way point of the pass, you would go through an orchard, at the bottom of which was the Madam Lady's home village.

Coming down the hill pass, they made an east turn at the crossroad and there across the highway they saw an old country school in which Madam Lady graduated from, a stationery store and a bakery she often visited.

On the corner of the crossroad was an old stable and deserted cottage. Seeing that the door of the cottage had been ajar due to a break, the cottage must have been abandoned for some time.

Wait! In the stable, two children were seen shuddering in the cold under the straws. Pastor stood at the sight and turning to madam lady, he suggested,

"Go ahead, keep going. I'll just take a look at the kids."

"Yes, Pastor. Don't take too long, please." Madam Lady pleaded. Turning to Sun and Suk who rather waited for their father, she pressed on,

"Come on. Let's keep going." She quickened her steps ahead.

In the stable, two boys were shivering within the straws. They must have been abandoned children. Pastor shook the larger one awake and asked,

"What's your name?"

Looking up, the boy answered,

"My name? My name is Yong the Second."

"What's his name?" Pastor pointed at the younger.

"He is Yong the Third." Obviously they were brothers.

"How old are you?" Pastor asked.

"I am eleven years old."

"How old is your brother, Yong third?"

"He is eight." The younger one raised his unkempt head from the straws, shuddering with cold and looked up at Pastor.

Pastor addressed him,

"Where is your home?"

"I don't know." The big one dropped his head, as he tugged in his younger brother.

Pastor was saddened at the sight. Tears welled up in the corner of his eyes, prompting him to look up in an effort to contain his tears. He took off his overcoat and gloves, handing them to the boys, saying,

"Cover yourselves with these. It's very cold. I will be back in a few days. Don't go anywhere." Then emptied his pocket to give them what money he had.

Leaving the children behind in the cold, Pastor couldn't help but cry out,

"Father, what am I supposed to do with them? They need shelter. They need food. They shouldn't be deserted in the cold and hunger like that. They are innocent and helpless!"
In the distance, he saw his wife and daughters making a right towards the orchard.
He trotted along to catch up with them.
Looking back at him in a hasty gait, Madam Lady caught a glimpse of him stripped of his overcoat, and inquired,

"Pastor, what happened to your overcoat?" After a pause, she continued her inquiry only to confirm,

"Again? Did you do it again, Pastor?" She was resigned. It surely was not the first time for Pastor to take off his overcoat for the needy this winter.

Barren fruit trees with haggard branches and twigs stood on the snow-covered slope, and the sun blushing scarlet was about to sink in the western hill. As they were coming down the slope, a reservoir was seen in the valley, the surface of which was glaring on the reflection of the setting sun. Underneath the reservoir were frozen rice fields in a gradual downgrade. Alongside the slope was a naked village of snow-covered thatched roofs completely devoid of foliage, it was here where Madam Lady was raised.

The following morning, Pastor excused himself out of the in-laws and hastened toward the deserted stable at the crossroad. This time another boy, much larger was shivering in the cold.

"What is your name?" Pastor asked the boy.

"My name is Yong the First, sir." His eyes were sparkling.

"Yong the First? Then you must be an elder brother to Yong the Second and Third."

"That's right, sir." He stood up and bowed his head, and continued,

"I don't know how to thank you for your benevolence of giving up your overcoat and gloves plus the money for our food, sir." His wording was unusually articulate for a child his age and his thanks were heartfelt.

"How old are you?" Pastor asked.

"I am fifteen years old, sir."

"Fifteen years old? Where were you yesterday, son?" When Pastor called him 'son,' the boy became enlivened at it.

"I worked at the wine shop to get some food for my brothers." Yong was not an ordinary boy. He was very smart and matured for his age.

"Where is your home?"

"We don't have a home now, but we used to live in Sunchon up until two years ago, sir."

"Did you say Sunchon? It's in the Jeulra Province."

"Yes, we are from that province, sir."

"Then how did you happen to be here in Jinjoo. It's a long way, isn't it?"

"Well, I don't know myself. We just moved from one place to another, looking for nice people." His answers were straight and candid.

"Did you say that you lived in Sunchon until two years ago?" Pastor continued, " "Then, where are your parents?" To this question, the boy turned his head and suddenly sealed his mouth. Seeing the boy's frigid reaction to his question, Pastor conciliated in a gentle voice,

"Don't worry, my son. I am not a bad man. I just want to help you. Can you tell me what happened?"

"You are not going to kill us, are you?" The boy's question was very serious.

Stunned at his words, Pastor retorted.

"What do you mean by that? Kill you and why?" Silence fell for awhile. Then Pastor patted the boy on the shoulder, appeasing him, and the boy hesitatingly but very cautiously whined out,

"My dad was a communist. He was a Captain in the army. People said my father instigated a rebellion against the government and took other soldiers with him to the mountain."

Pastor paused a minute to figure out the year and the place of the military uprising in Sunchon area. Pastor piecing together the timeline came back asking,

"So, your father was one of the leaders in that Yo-Sun military uprising. Then what happened to him?"

"He ran into the Chiri Mountain to become a partisan."

"What happened to your mother?" Pastor pursued.

"My mother? As my father ran into the mountain with other soldiers, my mother followed him to cook for them and was killed by punitive forces, sir" The boy raised his head as if beseeching for condolence. Pastor continued,

"I am terribly sorry to hear that. Then, what happened to your house?"

"Our house was set on fire by the punitive forces. Not only our house but also all our relatives' homes were destroyed as well. Most of our relatives, uncles, aunts and cousins were arrested and shot to death. But we escaped death by a hairbreadth, because they searched to annihilate to the last seed of red communist."

Pastor nodded his head and asked,

"What grade were you in?"

"I was in the fifth grade of our elementary school, sir." Changing the subject, the boy seemed a little relaxed.

"What about your brother, Yong the Second?"

"He was in the second grade." Answering, the boy wanted to be reassured,

"Sir, you must be a good man. You are not going to maul us to death, are you?" His question was as serious as his first inquisition.

"On the contrary. No one can dare to maul you little ones to death, and why?" His pitching tone and gesture convinced the boy, and he answered,

"The punitive soldiers and police forces said so. Some villagers did too. That's why we were scared and ran away. Now the war broke out, things got worse I guess."

According to what this boy stated, their father was one of leaders of the October 19th 1948 Yo-Sun Military uprising against the government. Last two years, this boy had been on the run with his two younger brothers, begging door to door for food. He had to find shelter and food for them in a hostile land. Surprisingly this boy appeared straight and honest in such difficult times. It was amazing and adorable to see a boy of such integrity and responsibility for his age through the turmoil of war. Pastor felt ashamed of himself and somehow a sense of guilt gripped him. Now, Pastor in a soothing tone,

"Yong, have you been to church?"

"No, sir. We don't know about church. I have never heard of it."

Pastor searched around and found a small country church nearby the village. However, the church was not financially strong enough to support these boys. Pastor took the boys to the small church with a word that he would come back in a few days, and returned to the in-laws late that night.

When pastor came home, he immediately went on a fast, and cried out walking through the orchard at the dark sky and asked what to do next. There was a small storage shack in the orchard. In the shack, he prayed for days. On his third night, he was crying out towards the cumulus of dark clouds, asking what he can do to glorify the Lord. Then he saw a streak of light. He struggled to stand and rather crawled out of the shack. He struggled again to catch the light and to stand in it. Finally he made it. He was in the middle of the light. Then, he heard a voice resounding in his heart,

'You are my servant. Be strong and courageous as I am with you. My heart is broken with the wartime orphans and widows forsaken on the street. Arise and Go! Animals can not help the weak. You can do it."

Pastor stood up, soaked in sweat. He had no fear whatsoever.

He left the in-laws with Suk and his family, and picked up the three Yongs on the way to Busan. He secured a shanty nearby the 5th pier of Busan harbor and dedicated himself to be the hand and foot of God in serving the orphans on the street. Thus was the origin of the House of Immanuel, Pastor's elaborate plan to house and educate orphans.

That night after dinner, Madam Lady said,

"In this time of war, people struggle to find food and shelter for their own family. You, on the other hand, are asking God's favor to help those orphans on the street. Truly you are a good servant to our God, but are you really sure about it?"

Pastor cleared his voice and said,

"Madam Lady, as you know I am not strong enough to get food and shelter even for my own family, but He will give me strength when I am weak. This is his business. I am only his servant. He will take care of everything. Therefore, let us not worry. Let us just obey and follow Him."

Sister Sun responded to her father,

"Father, tell me what to do. I will do my best to build the house God asked you to build, and I know Suk will do the same. Won't you, Suk?"

"I am more than happy to do so but I wonder if I could be of any help. If I could, I will do my very best," Suk responded enthusiastically. At this, Madam Lady intervened,

"My dear Suk, all you have to do is to be a good daughter of ours. The old has gone and the new has come. If we three get together I think we can become a good strong team. Don't you think so?" Everyone in the room seemed excited and enthused, when the eldest Yong stood up and exclaimed, interrupting everyone's oath of allegiance,

"Pastor and Madam Lady, I do not know anything about what you are discussing, but I do know that my two younger brothers and I are no longer forsaken as beggars. I would like to swear that we will listen to you and do whatever you expect us to do to be a good sons of yours. For the work Pastor plans to do, I will not only take off my shoes to run but I will also stick my neck out!" He yelled boldly, straightening his shoulder with clenched fists. Pastor, much impressed, nodded with smile and said,

"Yong, I am very much encouraged at your confession. I feel as if I had a thousand soldiers and horses replenished. But we can't do much about this. All we can do is to listen humbly and obey His words. By the way, let me confess one thing to all of you: I have been very much gratified with my second daughter Suk, when I watched her getting over the hardship and pains as Joseph did in the Bible, cherishing her dream in her heart. Now with my first son Yong, who has just sworn his will, we will make a good team to serve our Lord.

I know all these blessings were planned long before we met, and we all direct our thanks to God for this."

As spring comes even in time of war, so was the adolescence approaching Suk onto her flimsy heart. Ever since her only sister Jean went missing on the heels of the sudden death of both parents, Suk had been an easy target for the devil to entrap her into the net of despair and sorrow. On top of that, an adolescent stimulus began shaking her swollen heart in an eerie way, especially in the midst of confusion and disorder of the times. She was an easy prey. However, she had words deep in her heart as she made an oath,

"I will be a good girl like Sister Sun." Her oath was unshakable.

Last two weeks, Sister Sun taught Yong and Suk on the subject of 'the meaning and purpose of life.' Sun's lesson could be summed up as followed: we are not accidental. We were set apart before we were born and our days were numbered and written in His book. We were born to be loved and to love others through the precious blood of Jesus Christ. The purpose of life is to please and glorify God. For this, we should obey God's word and then we will be fully blessed. It is God who works in us to will and to act according to his good purpose. God gives us dreams. To realize our dreams, we should be led and guided by his holy guidance.

Sun also had Suk and Yong recite the following verses at predawn service.

'How can a young man keep his way pure? It is only by living according to His word. It is good for a man to bear the yoke while he is young.'

In this way, Suk and Yong were guided and led to the light in this bleak world of darkness, and were duly trained to do good everyday.

Pastor enrolled nine more orphans from the streets, placing before them two teachers and role models, Suk as their sister and Yong as their elder brother. Suk and Yong were ready to fill the shoes of a role model for them. In each service, Pastor emphasized that they should thank God for the grace and love of keeping them in the light, saying,

"We should walk in the light and have fellowship with one another, and the blood of Jesus purifies us from all sin. God is the light. Jesus came into this world as a true light. Through him all things were made but the world did not receive him. The light shines in the darkness, but the darkness has not understood it. But we are in his light as we were chosen by his grace. What a wonderful blessing we have!"

Sometime ago, they had one last bag of flour left for their provisions. What they normally did with flour was to knead it and then hand-cut it into noodles, or clump the flour to make steamed buns.

Kitchen personnel opened the final bag only to discover that it was full of weevils. Turning pale, they reported to Madam Lady,

"Madam Lady, the flour is full of weevils! What shall we do?" One of the kitchen workers raised her voice in vexation.

Madam Lady knew that bag was the last of the provisions they had and they had to eke out one more day on that flour until they receive new supply of food.

She turned serious at the report and warned with a gesture,

"Hush!" After a pause, "Mix it up with the wormwood we picked in the field yesterday and hand-cut into noodles for dinner."

While kneading the flour with wormwood, Sun and Suk felt temporarily a little nauseated. That evening at dinner, Suk said grace for all the members of the House of Immanuel,

"Heavenly Father, in this time of war, many people out there are starving with no food. We should have been discarded among them to starve to death or to conduct inhumane acts to survive. But our good Father brought us here and now we are going to have a delicious noodle dinner together. We thank you indeed for this meal. Please give your blessing to this food and water and take away sickness from among us so that we could be healthy and strong to please you. We thank you again for your presence in our dinner. I pray this in the name of Jesus."

"Amen!" All responded and ate without a doubt very deliciously. Suk and Sun also ate the meal delightfully.

The war situation still consisted of daily blood battles along the new resistance line. Busan area was jam-packed with daily increasing refugees. Among them was one man whose prayer God never overlooked and God lifted him high up to use him as His essential tool.

This man was neither rich nor strong. All he did was cry out to the Lord asking what to do to rise to the occasion. Then God gave him the strength and courage to embark on God's project on earth, hence the House of Immanuel.

4.

The House of Immanuel

Korean forefathers called themselves the 'White-Robed Race,' as they preferred to wear white robes around the year. As the color white is the symbol of purity and peace, they sought for and placed purity and fidelity before anything in life.

Korea was first founded approximately 4,435 years ago on the principle of 'Hong-Ik-Ingan which is translated 'Humanitarianism'. Hong-Ik-Ingan means in a broad sense to be beneficial to all human races on earth and in a practical context, it means a national spirit of dedication to the cause of White-Robed People. In a word, Korean ancestors advocated for the Law of Love thousands of years ago and adopted it as national policy.

Since the foundation, Korean forefathers had built altars and worshipped the Heavenly Father until shamanism and other religions infiltrated the land.

As mentioned in the preface of this book, Koreans were liberated from the thirty-six year Japanese domination in 1945 and were immediately occupied by Russia in the north and by America in the southern half of the peninsular. Three years later in 1948, the first governments were established both in north and south. And a year later in 1949, all stationed U.S. armed forces withdrew from Korea.

And again a year later, on June 25th 1950, Korean War broke out. The war continued for three years and one month, and ended in

1953. During the brutal fratricidal war, almost two million people were killed, two hundred thousand women were widowed, and one hundred thousand children were orphaned along with ten million others torn apart from their families according to an official statistics. Most of government and industrial facilities across the nation were destroyed and cities were practically leveled off. However, in the midst of this war, our God built the House of Immanuel for his chosen children.

Less than a month, twenty more orphans were added to the house. Also a large amount of relief fund in the amount of twenty thousand dollars was delivered to the house through the Denver church. When the fund came, Pastor realized that God had been working on an enormous plan, on a much larger scope than an ordinary orphanage.

Pastor went on fasting and prayed. In his prayer, he heard a voice.

Immediately he started working on a five-year development plan for the House of Immanuel. He secured the ground on which he would place facilities to accommodate as many orphans as possible.

The House of Immanuel was now planned to be an orphan town just like the one in Nebraska, the Father Flanagan's Boys Town, which consisted of school, church, office and different houses such as House of Faith, House of Hope, House of Love, House of Barnabas, House of Cornelius, House of Paul and House of Peter to accommodate orphans by age, sex and academic level. Pastor forwarded the five-year development plan to the financial supporters through the Denver church.

On March 15th 1951, the U.N. forces recaptured Seoul.

Chinese and northern armies withdrew back to the 38th parallel line. General Macarthur's plan to pursue further north to Manchuria was denied, and General Ridgeway took over command. The war became a stalemate along the parallel line.

Since the armistice negotiation commenced in July 1951, the war was phased into an unprecedented limited war (the demarcation line to be established along the occupied line at the time of signing the truce), which further intensified the battle.

For instance, the Baek-ma-gochi (White Horse Height) Battle which was launched by the Chinese red army on October 6th 1952 changed hands twenty-four times within a ten day period of fierce battles, exploding 300,000 cannon balls. The height lost its original grandeur to be disfigured like a wounded white horse. Hence it was named 'White Horse Height.'

With the help of the U.S. Engineering Corps, Pastor initiated putting houses on the secured property, and God sent him helping hands from all over the world in such an accurate and timely manner that Pastor often found himself unbelieving his own eyes.

As the number of orphans increased, so too were the facilities needed to accommodate them, and the aid and relief arrived in time as if planned and scheduled ahead. Pastor kept records and took pictures of ongoing projects to show how God worked his miracles phase by phase and forwarded them to the Denver church.

In every matter, Pastor looked upon God and prayed for His holy guidance. He placed first priority to feed his family on God's words and to implant them in every little one's heart. Madam Lady and Sister Sun were teachers, and Suk and Yong were role models as an obedient daughter and son, and also as exemplary students.

Pastor embraced teachers with love, teachers embraced students with love, seniors embraced juniors with love, brothers and sisters embraced themselves with love, thus the entire house made every effort to keep the unity in Christ through the bond of love and peace.

Those young orphans who were once abandoned and deserted out in the world were well fed in Christ, and some of them learned from infantile years how to praise and love our Lord and love their neighbors. As they grew, their shiny eyes were filled with light and hope. As they grew taller, they were fully convinced,

"Yes, we can. We can do better, since we are chosen like those in the Bible." Thus, their morale and spirit were highly elated in emulation with their predecessors in the Bible.

Suk was no longer alone. One day in the middle of service at church, Jesus came to her in person. Instantly her aching heart for missing her mother, father and Jean were soothed, and her lonely empty heart was filled with peace and joy. It was an esoteric experience. It was not an illusion. It was real.

Since then, she frequented the sanctuary to sit in her accustomed seat, the first seat in the middle, and then He comes without fail to embrace her in His arms. Her irresistible longing for her family and her insurmountable pains from her stark reality were lifted like the morning fog, and again her heart was filled with thanks and joy. It was incredible and it was truly real.

Lately something exciting happened to her. She didn't even have to go to the sanctuary, as He came to her place whenever she called,

"Father, My Lord or Master."

She was truly no longer alone. Whenever and whatever she was doing, He was always with her.

In the House of Immanuel, Suk was a ready-made symbolic criterion for all other orphans. Madam Lady quoted Suk quite often in encouraging as well as disciplining them,

"Look at sister Suk, didn't she make the first honor student in junior high school this time again?

Look at sister Suk, wasn't she the first one to attend the pre-dawn service to praise and worship our Lord this morning?

Look at sister Suk, wasn't she the one who always kept her room neat and clean?

Look at sister Suk, isn't she the one that washes the last dish in the kitchen before she goes back to her room to finish up her assignment in the study?"

Madam Lady took full charge of feeding the orphans with nutritious food so that they could have healthy bright eyes to navigate through the dark world. She also exerted no less effort in bringing them up intellectually to equip them with intellectual eyes through habituating to studying and doing daily scholastic assignments according to schedule. As years went by, word spread that those from the House of Immanuel were healthy, smart and diligent.

New comers must spend the first three months with Pastor or sister Sun until they became accustomed to the new environment. It was not easy to have new comers fit in the house without the help of Holy Spirit. Therefore, they started with prayer.

For new comers, the first three months were not easy, especially for those ten years or older. They had come from the streets and the streets were calling, as ninety percent of the orphans sought ways to run away. It surely is much harder to build a person straight than to build a skyscraper.

Their days started with prayer. They made confessions before each service. They confessed, looking back on not only immediate yesterdays but also on all those tragic years of war the nation suffered through.

Pastor used to start the service with a prayer,

"Heavenly Father, have mercy on this land and people and forgive us. Please heal this land. Have these people turn from the wicked way and seek your face. The night before the war broke out, on June 25th **1950**; most high-ranking military leaders of this country were merrymaking in a party throughout the night. We repent this. Please forgive us.

Even in this time of war, many people are engrossed in profiteering, the hallucination of sensual pleasure, revelry, extravagance and vanity. We all regret and repent for them. Please have them turn around and seek your forgiveness, and give them strength and wisdom to wake up.

Above all, we thank you for your presence in this house to protect and guide these children. Please come to each one of these young souls, who bows and confesses, have them grow healthy and strong, pretty and faithful, and make them the head of others."

This way Suk saw and heard good things in Christ, showing a good example to others every day. Never again was she ever lonely.

When she closed her eyes, she saw the smiling face of Jesus Christ and heard his sweet voice,

"My lovely one. You are my daughter. It is my joy to be with you all the time.

Whenever you are tired and lonely, come to me. I'll carry you on my back."

This gave her such comfort and strength.

On and off, Suk saw her mother in her dreams, and her mother's tender smile added joy and vigor to her days. In her vivid dream, her mother stood with a big smile in silence. Nevertheless she could hear clearly her mother praising,

"My dear Suk. Of course you are the head and not the tail. It is my greatest pleasure to watch you showing a good example to the world. You are watched over, and your good heart and your exemplary deeds are duly recorded in the book of life. You are a winner and I am proud of you."

It was so vivid that her smiling face appeared whenever Suk closed her eyes, missing her mother.

Pastor had never neglected searching for Jean, Suk's twin sister. He kept searching through the papers and listening to the radio even after the war's conclusion, but there was no knowing of her whereabouts. People, though they did not express openly, assumed that Jean was killed in that midnight air-raid.

Suk used to blame herself, grieving remorsefully,

"It was my fault. I could have made her clutch at Pastor's trouser, not his sleeve. The sleeve was too high for her to reach. It was my fault. I could have warned her to grip at it no matter how sleepy she was." Suk had the habit of reciting this whenever she missed Jean.

In 1958, five years after the truce was signed, Suk was a junior in high school and took the National Qualification Test to enter medical school as Sister Sun did in her junior year. At first Suk wanted to go to a seminary and work for the House of Immanuel just like Sister

Sun. However, Pastor and Madam Lady strongly recommended her to apply for medical school.

Pastor said that he had prayed for Suk and Yong to be doctors to help the poor who could not afford medical expenses. Suk and Yong were top-tiered honor students, and their outstanding academic excellence was well qualified to be admitted into any medical school.

Suk won first place in the entrance examination of the National Medical School across the nation and she was entitled to full scholarship. Yong was also admitted to the same school. The entire house, as one can imagine, was excited at the news that two orphans were admitted to the National Medical School. It was quite the miracle.

That evening they held a special thanksgiving service at church, but what was the tear shed for on this joyful occasion? It started with Pastor who broke into tears in the middle of his sermon, when he touched on the victims of the time, quoting the cruel death of Suk and Yong's parents in the wake of the fratricidal war and their miserable days thereafter, and the tears spread by contagious fashion, shifting the entire congregation into a wail of joyful crying and thanks.

Suk used to swear and pray to God,

"I will be a medical doctor to be your hand of caring and healing the sick out in the world. Please guide me so that I can concentrate on my study and watch over me until I finish."

As did Yong,

"I want to be a doctor to do good works for you my Lord, and to please Pastor, my spiritual father. Please place upon me the full armor of God so that I may take my stand against the devils scheme under any circumstance. Make me a dependable son of responsibility, a man of integrity."

Yong and Suk were a peculiar couple. The world may not have the ear to listen to their love song, but this couple had been singing their song from a time unknown to them, that it must have been planned from the start. They were having a spiritual communion, the communion of trust and love from the time their adolescence knocked on their hearts.

Each house consisted of two rooms and a wooden floor; one small room for the respective leader and another much larger room to accommodate roommates, and the wooden floor served a duel purpose for meetings and as a study.

Suk shared the small room with two other girls while the remaining ten girls were assigned to the larger room. Altogether 12 orphans and one leader were allocated to each house. Any girl that was on their menstruation period was temporarily assigned to the leader's room.

On the floor was a long table, designed to sit twelve orphans, six on both sides facing each other. A bookshelf on the floor was partitioned into five compartments in which each level of text and reference books were displayed.

Each house had monthly and weekly schedules formulated by the respective leader in consultation with twelve other roommates, regarding such matters as food service, cleaning service, washing service, and prayer service in turn.

The house leader conducted brief prayer services twice a day around the table; the morning prayer after breakfast and evening prayer before bedtime. In these prayer services, the leaders read daily bread having everyone memorize the verse.

Those on duty received meals from the central kitchen and served the table, while others did other duties by a system of rotation. In case of emergency, such as impending weather, the leader filled the time-gap at his or her discretion, usually conducting various indoor programs.

As Suk entered the house, everyone gathered to sit around the table on the floor. Suk took the head seat and announced,

"If everyone is ready, open to hymn number 377." All in the house chorused instantly.

"When we walk with the Lord. In the light of word,
What a glory He shed on the way! While we do His good will,
He abides with us still, And with all who will trust and obey

Trust and obey, for there's no other way

To be happy in Jesus, but to trust and obey"

As the song ended, Suk continued,

"The word for tonight comes out of First Corinthians, Chapter ten, and verse twelve. If you are ready, let's read in unison."

"So if you think you are standing firm, be careful that you don't fall" And then,

"Whose turn is it to pray tonight?" She asked.

"Me." Sunja stood up. She was the youngest one in this house. Until the age of six, orphans were kept in the House of Grace, acting as a nursery, and then assigned to an appropriate house. Sunja opened her mouth to pray,

"Heavenly Father, thank you for having our sister Suk passes the examination to go to medical school. She is always the best. I pray this in the name of Jesus Christ, Amen."

Suk answered,

"You did a good prayer. Thank you. You may sit down now. Remember we shouldn't forget in our prayer to ask Jesus to come to us and give us good words, and help us to listen and obey the words. Do you all understand?"

"Yes, sister Suk," all replied.

Then Suk delivered a short message for three to four minutes on the scripture verse they had read together,

"The message for tonight was especially for me. God warned me not to be arrogant as I earned first honor in the examination, but to be humble. Likewise, when you get 100 percent with your test, you should not slacken down but rather study harder for the next test."

"We understand and thank you for the words, sister Suk," they all responded.

Suk closed the service in prayer,

"Dear Heavenly Father, thank you for your precious words. We want to obey and live by your words. We want to become a great person like Esther, Sarah, Deborah and Ruth to please you, and to please Pastor and Madam Lady. We promise you we will not become arrogant but humble and obedient. We pray this in the name of Jesus Christ, Amen."

"Amen." When all responded, Suk added,

"Anyone who had not finished today's homework should finish it before going to bed."

"Yes, we will, and goodnight, sister Suk." They were dismissed for the day.

Yong also returned to his assigned house, the House of Barnabas. Every Sunday evening all house leaders had a meeting with Pastor in regards to next week's schedule.

The following day, exciting news arrived to the House of Immanuel. It was a notification from a local medical school that Yong had passed the entrance examination and was the first place winner.

"Yong must have applied to this school without our knowledge. Look at this," Pastor handed the notice to Madam Lady. The notice stated that the applicant, Yong passed the examination with the highest score.

Reviewing the notice, Madam Lady said,

"It's a big relief for us. Yong has always been a thoughtful young man. As you know, it is going to be a hefty burden on us if we were to send both Suk and Yong to Seoul, not only financially but also physically in many ways."

"When did we ever have enough money to do anything? Since they are smart and self-reliant, we may have to support them only for the first few months, and then they will find a way to work their way through college. Especially Suk was given full scholarship. Let us not worry. Our God will take care of them," Pastor disagreed.

After breakfast, Pastor called Suk and Yong to his office for a meeting,

"Let's bow our heads." Pastor prayed,

"Almighty God, thank you for this meeting. We have urgent business to discuss in your presence. Please listen to us and guide us to your will, and have us obey you. We pray this in the name of Jesus, Amen." He then addressed Yong,

"I have surprising news for you." To this, Suk and sister Sun raised their heads with blinking eyes. However, Yong seemed a little uneasy, casting a glance at Pastor.

"Yong, I have a notice from the local medical school." Facing Yong, he kept on,

"You are the first place applicant. Here it is." He put it on the table before Yong.

Surprised at the news, Suk exclaimed,

"What?" She opened her eyes wide. Madam Lady intervened, saying,

"There is nothing to be surprised about! God saw our situation and He arranged this for us." Then sister Sun snapped in,

"Yong, did you really apply to that school?"

For the first time, Yong raised his head with an embarrassing smirk.

Then, Suk turned pouting,

"Oppa (oppa is an affectionate respectable term for elder brother), why did you do this behind my back? Did you really do this?"

"No, I didn't mean to cheat anyone, but as our financial situation indicates, if we both were to leave, our family will be pinched. I didn't mean to hurt you and I will never do it again if this offended you."

Suk then burst into tears. Madam Lady handing out a handkerchief to Suk, soothed,

"Stop crying, Suk. He didn't mean to cheat on you. He took in consideration of the financial and operational situations of the House of Immanuel. Try to understand."

Suk stopped sobbing. Pastor opened his mouth, facing Yong,

"I highly appreciate that you deeply care about our house, but if you really care of us, you should go and start with the best school in this country."

To this, Yong stood up and said,

"Pastor, you are our father. It's not fair to burden all other sons because for the sake of one. Furthermore, I am your eldest son. I can't leave this house now. Suk's situation is different from mine. Of course her role as a model to our 122 brothers and sisters is indispensable, but I will try harder to fill her place. I believe I can kill two birds with one stone, if I choose the local medical school here."

Sister Sun butted in to confirm,

"Yong, did you plan to continue looking after these boys even after you enrolled to the local medical school here?"

"Of course. I traveled to the medical school yesterday. It took only forty minutes by bicycle. I also heard that some of students transferred to the school in Seoul after the first two-year prep course."

Then all of sudden, Suk stood up and exclaimed without a second's remorse,

"Pastor, I have a big favor to ask you. If you buy me a bicycle, I will go to the same school with brother Yong."

The meeting had concluded. The fact of the matter was that if both Suk and Yong were gone, the House of Immanuel would have had serious problems. Especially for the little orphan's chorus which Madam Lady and Sister Sun had prepared a touring performance around the world. Yong and Suk were vitally needed in the House of Immanuel.

As usual, Yong embarrassed Suk with surprising news. Yong was a broad-minded thoughtful person. He was in a way like a chess master; he could envision four to five moves ahead.

He had as much character as he did height; Yong was almost another head taller than the fine figured Suk, and statuesque with broad chest and handsome face.

When they happened to be alone, their conversations were either about God's word or the House of Immanuel. The most pleasant time for them was the time shared biking together to and from school. They waited until their lunch break at school to meet up and eat together. During their lunch break, they would revisit the daily bread they had learned at pre-dawn service.

Today, Yong opened his mouth first,

"Suk, the daily bread for today was really intended for me:

'Be like-minded, having the same love, being one in spirit and purpose. Do nothing out of selfish ambition or vain conceit, but in

humility, consider others better than yourselves. Each of you shall look not only to your own interest but also the interests of others.'"
To this, Suk praised him,

"Yong Oppa, in that respect you are great, however, I took today's words to be aimed at me."

"No, no, you are almost perfect. You can't possibly be any better. Besides, you are a woman. Therefore, I will always take good care of you, okay?" Yong asserted.

"I know you will and I thank you for that. That's one of the main reasons why I thank our Lord. Especially when you recite the daily bread, I feel the comfort and peace in my heart," Suk confessed.

"Do you? If so, let me recite the bread for today. Let's reiterate it every minute so that you may be donned in comfort and peace every minute."

"Go ahead, brother Yong. What was given at the predawn service yesterday morning?"

"Wait a minute, the bread for yesterday, not for today?" Yong seemed fumbling in his memory.

Then Suk started,

"Let me do it.

'Have a life worthy of the calling you have received. Be completely humble and gentle, be patient, and bear with one another in love. Make every effort to keep the unit of the Spirit through the bond of peace.' How was it?"

"Excellent! I also felt the comfort and peace in my heart as I was listening to your recitation. Every word is alive and active and penetrates even to dividing souls and spirits. By the way, Suk, you want to concentrate on your studies until you become a doctor and then you are going to serve the poor and the sick, right?"

"That's right, brother. I'll fulfill my promise with our Lord."

"Of course you will. But um... when are you going to get married?" Yong asked with obvious hesitation.

Suk, blushing of innocent shyness, whispered,

"After I become a medical doctor, then I will come to you and Pastor about it," and dropped her head almost instantaneously.

"The same is with me. I have a couple more goals to accomplish before I will come to you and Pastor as well. Yong the Second goes to senior high next year and Yong the Third will be a 4ᵗʰ grader. The first goal is that my brothers and other children in the House of Immanuel remain straight in Christ without swerving to either side, and the other goal is to keep myself straight in Christ so that I won't disappoint you before the world and before our Lord, Jesus Christ."

Suk still drooping, thanked,

"Thank you, brother Yong. I'll pray for that." She thanked to God for such a wonderful brother and she reassured to please God and Pastor together with Yong.

As time went by, many years ahead, it became an annual event in the House of Immanuel that two or three orphans took the National Qualification Test and entered the National University on the heels of Suk and Yong. A feat made possible due to Pastor's constant prayers for bestowed spiritual eyes on top of the physical and intellectual eyes to every single soul that was brought into the house. The moment the children were brought in the house, they no longer became orphans. They became members of a larger family in Christ.

In March 1960, Suk and Yong finished their two-year prep courses and both students were admitted to Stanford Medical School through the arrangement of Pastor Jonathan in Denver, Colorado. Overjoyed at the news, Pastor handed out the admission papers to Yong, who was entering the office,

"Hallelujah! Yong, we have good news here!"

"Good news, Pastor?"

"Yes, really good news! You and Suk are both admitted to Stanford!"

"Oh, that news..." To Yong's insipid answer, Pastor wondered,

"What's wrong? Is there anything against your grain this morning?"

"No, not in the least, father." Yong hesitatingly uttered.

"You guys made full scholarship. Not only that. If you do a good job, they might allow you research funds. Isn't this wonderful, Yong?"

Yong absorbed deeply in thought, paused a moment and then,

"I am sorry to say this, but I am not going to take the admission now. I will stay here four more years. It won't be too late if I take it four years later. I, the eldest of all, just can't leave this house like this. However, Suk is different. Please have Suk leave alone this time and I will leave when she comes back."

Surprised at his determined remarks, Pastor was a little fluttered,

"Did you say that you are not going to take the offer? Any person of normal sense would exult over this, but you reject it?"

"But I am not any person, Pastor. I am your eldest son, father."

Overwhelmed by his sincere attitude, Pastor half heartedly pleaded,

"I understand and I highly appreciate your true heart toward this place. Nevertheless, this is a blessed opportunity God had in store for you, and you should take it. I urge you, Yong."

"But Pastor, it was God who made this decision of not taking the admission this time. Yes, I asked God to help me to become a doctor, but not necessarily an American doctor. Please let me be a Korean doctor first, and then later I can go abroad to learn more.

Confessing the truth, the reason I applied to Stanford together with Suk was to test myself, and I think I made the right decision. What is more demanding to me is how to remain as the eldest of this house and serve our Lord and serve you and all the brothers and sisters of the house. Therefore please leave this matter up to me, father Pastor." As usual, no one could sway his firm determination.

"Brother Yong, you are not coming with me this time, are you?" Suk asked with serenity.

"It is fantastic just to imagine us flying together, and what a blissful moment it would be! But look at the situation here," Yong said in a persuasive tone.

"Well, if you don't, I won't go either," she resisted.

"Yes, you should. I did this to have you study there in peace and with little distraction. When you come back as an American doctor, I will take your place. Nothing would be too late. What matters is His will," he insisted.

Suk knew Yong better than anyone else. She was ready to give in,

"You are very thoughtful and I adore you, brother Yong!"

"Thank you, Suk, for your understanding and cooperation with me. One thing we should cherish in our hearts is Romans 8:35."

Suk brightened up and recited sprightly.

"Who shall separate us from the love of Christ? Shall trouble or hardship or persecution or famine, or nakedness or danger or sword?"

Yong instantly followed up,

"That's right. I pray the bond between you and I along with the House of Immanuel would be as strong as our love with Christ so that we can hand in hand get past any hardships."

"I do too, my respectable brother Yong," she reaffirmed.

For a full month before she left for the United States, Suk searched extensively for Jean through the mass media of daily papers and radio stations. This time, she printed hundreds of thousands of personal letters to Jean, and circulated them among schools and churches in the country, which read as follows:

My Dear Sister Jean,

On September 31st 1950, the year the Korean War broke out, our mother and father were murdered under the arbor tree, Byukchon village, Cholwon.

You and I clung to their cold bodies and cried out day and night for three days.

The following year, On January 2nd 1951, you and I were among the refugees on the run, along with our Pastor and his family. At dawning, we passed by Uijongbu when we were suddenly thrown into a series of air attacks aimed at approaching Chinese armored vehicles. Since then, we have been lost to each other. I visited the Byukchon village only to find out that the village now was within the Demilitarized Zone, which was inaccessible to us.

Our pastor and I have searched for you, but we haven't heard anything at all. Now, a month later, I am leaving for America.

Jean! My dear Jean! Where are you? Answer me upon seeing this letter. I am mailing out this letter to all the schools and churches in this country.

> Your sister Suk
> Missing you so much
> The House of Immanuel
> Busan 00-4325

A few days before departure, Suk and Yong visited to Yung-do Island.

"Suk, you have been outstanding the past ten years. It is quite striking to see those youngsters follow your step to be good sons and daughters in Christ."

"Brother, I haven't done anything special for them. It was truly the grace of God and Pastor's constant prayer for them to grow healthy and strong in faith."

"I agree, but without you and your exemplary obedience and love."

"No, no! To be honest with you, brother, I had no choice. It was not that I was good and obedient." Yong halted his walk and held her in both hands and praised,

"That's it. Look at the beauty and the humility in you. Your inner-self, attributing all glory to God! God is so fair that he gives his blessing equally upon every being on earth. You took it with thanks

97

and obedience, while others took it with arrogance and disobedience and abused them." Yong then pulled her in for a heartfelt embrace.

"Brother Yong, you didn't understand me. I had no choice."

"What you are saying is that you had no choice but be humble and obedient. That's why you are so beautiful and graceful in heart. Didn't you know that you are a striking beauty? Who has such an attractive elegant look and figure as you? On top of that your inner being is incomparably genuine and pure. Confessing you the truth, I have been apprehensive for coming closer to your inner beauty lest I should smear it like a finger mark on clear precious marble." As Yong confessed his pure heart toward her, Suk blushed, saying,

"Brother Yong. I am not that particular. I am just bland and ordinary. Through your heart, you are beautifying me." So saying, Suk dropped her head.

This time, Yong approached her seriously,

"I hope you understand why I broach on this subject."

"Tell me why, oppa!"

"When you go out into the world, most people are not righteous-minded. Their heart is deceitful above all things and beyond cure. Remember that most people live according to their sinful nature and have their minds set on natural desires.

They seek sensual pleasure and satisfaction. They are bent on selfish interests. They are apt to turn away from God to pursue their own interests. These people are mostly arrogant, questioning God's whereabouts and his existence. Jesus called them wolves. They often disguise themselves as sheep to satisfy their hunger and thirst, but they can never be satisfied."

"I'll do my best to watch out for these people and steer away."

"Suk. It's not enough to just 'watch out'. You should fight them off. They will rob the beauty in you and destroy your soul, stealing the spirit of our people. When your body is sick, you may find a good doctor. However, for our soul and spirit there may not be a good doctor. Be on alert when you are left alone. Our enemy the devil prowls around like a roaring lion looking for someone to devour."

"Yes, oppa, you know me. I promise that I will stand firm and resist them. Please be rest assured."

"I wouldn't have to worry this much if I were to accompany you. So far, we have been doing well before our God, but what would happen to the House of Immanuel. I mean to our Pastor and the brothers and sisters that depend on us. The answer to my prayer concerns was that you go alone this time and I stay here until you return as an American doctor."

"It is very judicious of you. I read your heart, oppa," agreed Suk.

"When Jesus sent his twelve disciples out in the world, he said he was sending them out like sheep among wolves. Now sending you alone on this long journey, I feel the same. Please promise me not only to watch out but also fight them off. It's not going to be easy for you, a fragile woman."

"No, not really, I am as strong as you. Besides, when Jesus is with me, how can any wolf dare to attack me? You know the Holy Spirit armors me with the spiritual power to discern sheep from wolves." Suk continued after a pause,

"Oppa, now may I express my heart?"

"I am ready, Suk."

"Oppa, you are really great. You are sometimes too perfect. That's why I adore you. I thank God, do you know why?"

"Well, tell me why."

"Alright. You have been my guardian to keep me in the garden of God. You are the one who guarded the chastity and purity of our relationship before our God and before the world. You placed me in your eyesight before anything. That's why I adore and respect you more than anything in the world. I trust and depend on you. To me, you are the most precious one in the entire world. I have to confess this to you.

I will definitely concentrate on my studies the next four years, and I will rush back to you the moment I finish the course. I pray for you and I so that we may do the intern course together wherever our God has planned."

"I know you will. That's why I am always happy."

"I am too. I am the happiest girl in the world."

Walking back and forth on the Yungdo Bridge, the two held hands tightly. Though it was not chilly, Yong embraced Suk at the hint of a gentle breeze from the sea.

On their way back home, Yong asked,

"Suk, your subject of special study hasn't been changed, has it?"

"No, I am going to stick to it. I believe one of the reasons why we are born as women is to bear children and raise them well in Christ. I am going to specialize in this field." Then looking up at Yong, she continued,

"Oppa, you are going to major in pathology and microbiology to eradicate the root of all diseases. I am proud of you and I am moved at your grand plan. It is exciting just imagining it."

"I am, too. Let's realize our dreams in the name of Christ."

"That's more than okay, oppa. Make sure you know that I am always with you." Suk was walking, leaning slightly on Yong.

There was not a single word from Jean.

The night before Suk's departure, the House of Immanuel had a farewell service. Pastor again wasn't able to swallow his tears, turning the entire congregation into a sea of tears when he testified in his farewell sermon all the miracles he had experienced.

Blessing upon Suk, he proclaimed that,

"She is always with our good God. Her way is wide open and prospers in abundance. She is freed from deficiency, discomfort and fear. She is guarded as the apple of His eye." Pastor also spoke highly of Yong's decision in juxtaposition with Moses' decision in the desert. Then applause and exultation almost pierced the ceiling.

When Suk bid her final farewell, all 122 brothers and sisters of the house burst into tears. Suk cleared her voice,

"Dear brothers and sisters. The four-years will be but a brief moment. My dear Sunja will be twelve by then, a fifth grader. Let us work hard to be healthier, stronger and wiser in Christ in four-year time. Can you promise?" Suk shouted.

"Yes, sister Suk." Everyone responded.

"In the meantime, be nice boys and girls to Pastor and Madam Lady, and take good care of yourselves. One last thing! Please pray for me and I will pray for you."

She concluded her farewell with the gesture of having both her thumbs up, signifying that everything will be alright, and they returned her gesture.

In March 1960, Suk left the House of Immanuel for America to become an American doctor. A month later, on April 19th, students across Korea rose against the government in the wake of a rigged election. A year later, the May 16th 1961 Military Coup d'état followed the student uprisings.

On the other hand, in the same year of the 1961 Coup d'état, Suk's twin sister, Jean, was ruined as a hopeless prostitute. Now let us hearken to Jean's story.

5.

Sorceress

Some ten years ago when Suk was frantically crying out, "Jean! Jean!" stamping and writhing in the middle of the refugee procession, Jean was dumped unconscious on the edge of a huge bombed hollow.

As a series of air bombings were poured upon refugees on the run, some were heaved up and burst in mid-air, without feeling a second of pain. Many others were scared to death yet were still alive. Jean was thrown into the air by a blast then plumped down on the edge of the bombed hollow.

Her head fell on the belly of a dead man and she was stricken unconscious. She fell into coma for some time. Layers of clothes she had on were drenched in sweat. Through the freezing cold, she was sinking into the depths of slumber, then she heard murmuring nearby, faintly she was coming back to her senses. The murmurings sounded like her dad's sweet calling ringing around her ears.

As her ears opened, she heard the foreign language of the Chinese red army. She opened her eyes in the twilight. A cold spasm sent jerks from the scruff of her neck down to her spine. As she came to her senses, she tried to sit up but her bottom half wouldn't move as her legs felt so hefty.

She struggled hard to sit up, wriggling about, but it was all in vain. After awhile she tried again and this time, she could move to her side. At the moment she barely turned, she shrieked,

"Umma, Mamma!"

Right in front of her opening eyes was a gory scene! A man's head with two eyes wide open on the bust! To make matters worse, she was resting on the ruptured belly of the man! At the horrible sight in the twilight, she fell into a dead faint, screaming, "

"Umma, Mamma!"

The wintry sun nonchalantly sunk behind the western hill. Freezing air was ready for frosting the mountain fields all over, and in the sky flocks of sea gulls were cawing away 'caw-caw', as if asking her to wake up. The caw-caw sounded like her mother's call, 'Jean- Jean' and Jean instinctively woke up. She gathered herself to sit up but her legs still refused to budge.

Dusk fell quick and the darkness spread. Presently, twinkling stars appeared frozen in the dark sky. She closed her eyes and exerted all her strength to pull herself but she experienced severe pain in her left ankle. She clenched her teeth and turned over on her left side. This time she made it.

She started crawling with clenched fists, dragging her aching left leg. At the thought of an emergency, strength gathered to her shoulders and her clenched fists. Pitch darkness was a big relief to Jean as it draped her eyes from seeing the horrible sights of mangled dead bodies.

Communist red armies made a detour around the bombed hollow, and their munching footsteps on the frozen barley field and their babbling were heard by her ears like the murmuring of people at the fortnight market.

Pulling herself out of the edge of the hollow, she struggled crawling on both fists along the highway and before long; she came across an ox-cart country road. She felt about and touched the oxcart tracks. A light of hope flashed upon her mind as the oxen track reminded her of a village somewhere nearby.

She shifted her body onto the country road and kept crawling on like a lizard for some time. Exhausted, she sat up on her right hip to catch a breath and then, tried crab-walking, picking herself off the frozen ground with her right fist and buttocks, with her left hand pulling her left leg. It turned out to be much easier and faster. She snickered, self-reproaching,

"Why didn't you try this first?" She felt she would be able to crab-walk miles like this toward her sister Sun and Suk. As she came to her senses, she recollected,

"Yes, that was Pastor's gory head on the bust. He was after all right ahead of me."

A stroke of fright seized upon her.

"What could have happened to Suk? What about sister Sun? Most probably I am the only one who survived the air-raids." She fell dizzy in terror and closed her eyes, wanting to rather die than live on. She couldn't breathe and opened her eyes only to be stricken with fear and horror.

She sat still for awhile and then, came to think of Joseph who was thrown into a cistern. Wasn't Joseph scared? Yet, she was dead scared. She couldn't move and her mind was racing back to the scene,

"That was Pastor's head. Then, what could have happened to Suk, my only sister?"

Another surge of fright seized upon her and she couldn't stand it. She desperately wanted someone nearby, another human, someone who could share her breathing and someone to talk to. Then she thought she shouldn't be horrified like this. She jerked herself off the fear and resumed crab walking.

The oxcart road was divided into two paths; one was to the Jipyong village and the other narrow lane was bound to Kumchun Buddhist temple at Ochul village. The Ochul village was heavily bombed and destroyed when the retreating northern armies concentrated there in the wake of the U.S. Incheon landing.

At the dividing point was a bird watchtower. When Jean hit the point, she was hopelessly exhausted from picking her frozen way all night through. The first cockcrow was shrilling through the darkness of Jipyong village and presently the eastern sky was dawning. At the sight of the watchtower, she crawled in it with a big relief to catch a breath, and immediately she fell to the ground, exhausted like a log.

As the day was breaking, refugees stirred bustling up. Some were villagers but most of them were from the north. These refugees passed by Jean under the watchtower, snorting out,

"Another dead! Come on. Beat it. We have no time!"

Another group followed them. They must have been a schoolteacher's family, judging by their attire and their babbling talk about 'Principal.' They had passed by Jean without even glancing at her.

The icy sun burning in the eastern scarlet sky lost its fever and hung in there, opaquely frosted. Then three or four female monks were trotting down along the narrow lane. Seeing that they all clutched at tight packages, they too were on the run southward. At the sight of Jean, they approached her, put hands together unanimously, mumbled a short prayer, made a flat bow to Jean, and then took off.

After they left, a haggard old lady was approaching from the village and at the sight of Jean, she fell head over heels, cursing,

"Alas, what a maiden ghosts this is! To be smitten by five death roles!" The old lady swooped upon her,

"Wake up, you little one! Don't get frozen to death. Wake up!" She tugged on Jean's left leg. "Ouch!" Jean shrieked awaking in pain.

"You, a mean vulgar! Shriveled at the frozen ground to be a frozen ghost? Now wake up!" Again she pulled Jean's left leg.

"Ouch! Grandma, It hurts!" Jean grimaced, sitting on her right buttock.

"What a nice figure you are cutting! Even without shoes! Where are you from?" She demanded.

"I am not sure, mama. In the air-raids yesterday, our pastor, the madam lady, sister Sun and my only sister Suk, were all killed. That's all I know," she sniveled.

"Oh, my heavens!" The old lady ticked her tongue, heaving a sigh and continued, "But you can stand up, can't you? Try it." So saying, she tried to help her up.

"Ouch! It is painful to death!" Jean groaned. The old lady grimaced at Jean's futile attempt, accepting her pain,

"You must get out of the cold. Come on my back!" The old lady squatted and turned her back to Jean.

This lady who was above fifty years or older was so stout for her age that she carried Jean on her back with little problem.

The cottage at the entrance of village was this old lady's. She was a well-known sorceress in the region; a diviner who told fortunes, healed the sick, and entertained ancestors in communion with spirits in heaven and on earth.

The old lady believed that the sanctuary room should be cleansed to invoke departed spirits in and the table for the invited spirits should be unsparingly prepared for offering.

Invocation and conciliation services were divided into twelve phases; such as the invocation phase to call in the departed spirit, the singing and dancing phase to please the invited spirits, the hearkening phase in which the invited spirits would impart messages to the diviner, and the farewell phase to send the invited spirits off.

Old Lady laid Jean on the floor of her sanctuary room and cooked grain porridge for Jean. Then she brought in hot water to wash Jean from head to toe. When she came to Jean's left ankle, she startled and screamed,

"Look. It's swollen like a balloon! It's burning with fever, too. Don't move. I'll be right back." She hurried out. After awhile, she came back with a shaggy sturdy butcher who was said to be an expert in fixing fractured knees and ankles. Old Lady quickly brought in a basin of sap water for Jean to dip her swollen leg in.

The butcher, upon sitting down on the floor, picked Jean's ankle and examined closely, massaging the swollen area. Then suddenly he grabbed Jean's left leg with one hand and with his other hand he clutched Jean's left foot by the sole, pulled it forth in full strength, and then screwed it back into the socket of the ankle.

Jean shrieked,

"Ouch!" and quickly teared. It was a matter of a second. Now the butcher, soaking the ankle in herb water, pronounced in his base tone,

"Well done! You will be all right!" He stood up and resigned.

That night, Jean had a nice long sleep in Old Lady's sanctuary room.

The following morning, Jean greeted,

"Mama, I don't know how to thank you. My sister Suk and Sun might be at home by now, if they did survive. I have to leave now."

"No, you can't. Your ankle needs at least two to three days to recover!" Old Lady protested.

"But, mama, as you see, I can walk like this. I crab-walked all night on my buttocks, as I told you." To assure Old Lady, she demonstrated how well she could walk.

"But, my little one. Why don't you stay just one more day? It is a day's walk to Byukchon village. If you start early in the morning, you may get there before sundown."

She soothed her.

That night, Jean told Old Lady what had happened to her since the war broke out six months ago. Old Lady, deeply sympathized with her, made an incantation to invoke her gods, and announced,

"Your sister Suk and Sun are not dead. They are alive!" Jean was gratified and highly exulted at the news.

Early next morning, Old Lady shook Jean awake, handing a couple of boiled eggs and steamed potatoes, she said,

"Come back, if you can't make it." She also put out a pair of her rubber shoes for Jean's travels.

Jean passed by the bird watchtower and limped along the oxcart road when the eastern sky was dawning in scarlet. Old Lady was a meticulous and good-hearted lady. Jean wondered why she was alone. What about her husband? She regretted that she had not asked these questions to the lady.

She looked upon the sky in which skylarks were peeping and piping like rolling jewels. Suddenly she had a fit of shouting,

"Umma! Mom!" Sorrowful sobbing gushed out. She cried out unrestrainedly, "

quickening her steps as the sun was peeping its grandeur upon the eastern hill. It seemed that just one bout of sobbing was enough to set her on a brisk jaunt.

In no time, she came to the highway. Looking forward to seeing Suk's excited face, she became light-hearted and her sorrow seemed gone afar. Looking back at the bird watchtower she just came down from in such short blissful moments, she recalled,

"The same road, the same distance! How frightful and how rugged it was that night! I struggled against the fear of being licked off by a horrendous ghost on this icy road, crab-walking throughout the pitch dark horrible night." She heaved a deep sigh.

When she stepped on the highway, the sun was up on the hill and the Chinese red armies were seen from the highway, marching in formation southwards. At the first sight of aircraft, they fell flat on both sides of the highway and played a silent death. The moment the aircraft disappeared, whistling peeled through here and there, and soldiers stood up to dust off their trousers and reformed to continue their march.

Sometimes the aircrafts didn't just fly by once but they came back over and over to pour bombardments upon the soldiers. Anyone among the soldiers who was scared and ran away would be doubled up without fail and rolled over to death. Even those who played dead were killed.

Jean walked in the opposite direction, facing the soldiers coming down, deliberately keeping her distance not because she was afraid of them but because she was afraid of the aircrafts.

When the sun crossed over its zenith and hung in the middle toward the western hill, Jean was climbing up the pass, which she sometime ago came down with her mother, looking down upon the city. Again she had a fit of missing her mother and it could not be remedied.

She cried out loud and clear,

"Umma, I do miss you. Where are you, Mom?" Tears welled up in her eyes. She cried out to her heart's content, ignoring soldiers pouring down, louder and louder.

Jean was now fueled by Old Lady's revelation,

"Your sister Suk is not dead. She is alive."

For a second, Suk's excited face popped up in her mind, asking,

"Where have you been all these days, Jean?" Then she thought she would definitely cross-examine her, retorting,

"Where have YOU been all the while, leaving me in the lurch, Suk?" But then immediately she changed her mind.

"No, I would rather jump upon her, embrace her tight, and cry out to my heart's content."

She was determined to be backing home before sundown.

"It is only twenty more miles to go!" As she confirmed the distance, her fatigue was gone and her strength was renewed.

Finally she came to the concrete bridge at the entrance of the village. But what a weird scene awaited her! She couldn't hear a human voice from the village; a once bustling village now hushed like a ghost town. Not even a trace of the northern or Chinese armies that had terrorized the village with their menacing march was visible.

It really aroused an eerie sensation to see the village completely dead.

Jean recalled the day when she and her mother came down to see her friend, Boksoon following the complete devastation of the town in the wake of thunderstruck air-raids.

Horror struck her heart.

She crossed the frozen stream and headed towards the sheriff's office. As she approached the village, the uncanny sense of desolation deepened. The sheriff's office door was flung open as if it had been marauded. She then walked past the sheriff's office to pan the rest of the village.

Alas! She was consternated at the sight! The U.S. command post, the school and the county office were all gone. Some remains were half burnt and sooted black. She saw huge hollows here and there. It was as if she walked in on an apocalyptic dream.

With a ray of hope, she ran to Pastor's quarters and the bell tower. They too were gone, holding on was a tilted wall of the church. Chinese or northern armies must have packed into the church only to be annihilated. Jean doubled her fists and made a dash toward the cliff, and crossing the stream, she mumbled,

"Our house must be all right. It's in the woods." Hurriedly she climbed up the ridge in anticipation.

Yet, the once peaceful cottage suffered the same fate. The house was gone. She rubbed her eyes to refocus, only to confirm her nightmare. The house was completely blown away. The bamboo shrubs in the back, the water pump out front, and the thatched fence were all gone. Instead, she saw two huge exploded hollows with scattered bodies all over the front field. The pine forest in the back was burnt or singed in smudges. It was a horrid aftermath of a fierce battleground.

Jean fell to the ground. She lost all her strength. Everything was gone! She cried out and then whimpered,

"Umma, where are you? I'm asking where you are. Answer me. Now tell me what to do next, mom!" She shouted herself hoarse.

In the frigid sky, the blushing sun was ready to sink below the western hill. Fully exhausted, she looked upon the dark scarlet western sky. Then, all of sudden, the thick cloud poured sleet upon her face.

Drooping her head, Jean plodded down the ridge. She came back to the empty highway and then the dusk swiftly wrapped her up with pitch pall of darkness. She was shedding tears as they fell frozen on her cheek.

She felt her way out across the frozen stream at the entrance of village and she was trudging back the way she came. As night fell, Chinese armies gathered on the highway from nowhere and marched in formation to whistling commands.

Jean was mumbling in discontent,

"Stupid! What's the flare bomb for? Isn't this an opportune time for it? One flare bomb and a couple of aircraft would be good enough to kill all those soldiers. Then, I will make a dash right into the middle of them and dance wildly to get killed!"

Aircraft failed to appear that night.

In the night sky, the half moon was clearly illuminated. Soldiers were marching, eating biscuits. The smell drifted to her nose as she approached closer. She was hungry. She approached a soldier and put out her hand. The soldier handed out a bag of biscuits, babbling in Chinese.

That soldier was a goodhearted one. She took it and ate it. She followed the soldiers, eating biscuits for a while, still holding on to hopes of a flare bomb. This time, hefty sleep fell on her eyelids. She cursed herself,

"You. An empty shell! Now, do you really want to sleep?" She however could not shake off the drowsiness.

There was an empty cottage on the roadside. She entered it. It was an abandoned house. She pried open the room and fumbled for a piece of rug. She got it. She fell on the rug and instantly fell asleep.

When she woke up in the morning the street was open and empty like the house she had slept overnight. She searched every nook for something to eat. In the kitchen storage she found a basket of dried boiled potatoes. She tasted it. It tasted better than the biscuits. Jean left the house, latching the door back. She returned to the home of Old Lady around sunset.

"I knew you would come back," Old Lady received her with a great smile.

That night, Jean learned that Old Lady was a maiden sorceress. To her present age, she had never known a man. She also explained that when a person was entranced in spirit, he or she could hear and see what the flesh can not. She called herself an old She-Buddhist.

She had to keep herself clean to be ready to receive the spirit at anytime, and she was not to take any defiled things. Shaking the bells was to exorcise the devils and to invite in true spirits. She said,

"Only after you attain a spiritual state of perfect selflessness through frantic song and dancing, can you encounter the spirits." She also explained that to heal the sick, ancestral or departed spirits are invoked and offerings are made to them, then and only then, can they extract the devils out of the patient. Old Lady continued lecturing on how to sing and dance to Jean for days.

Jean had always experienced an eerie feeling, some queer erratic feeling when Old Lady tried to bewitch her through incantation. While Old Lady was talking, Jean was awfully displaced and she could not concentrate on Old Lady's teachings. At the beginning, she didn't know what all these were about, but as time went by, it was so suffocating that she couldn't even breathe, when Old Lady lectured her on sorcery.

Many fiendish apparitions appeared to Jean in a variety of forms; mostly in a form of an old snake, sometimes in a form of a pale woman with unkempt long hair, and other times in the form of an infant coughing out blood. The common theme that her apparitions had in common was that they appeared in the darkness. At such apparitions, Jean cried out in a fit of convulsion and she became totally oblivious of her mother or her sister. Jean was tellingly getting weaker and paler.

One early morning before dawn, the old lady shook Jean up and said,

"You are right, Jean. One is enough. I am going to release you." Ticking her tongue, she kept on,

"Not everyone can be a diviner, you poor thing." Babbling ambiguous remarks, she pulled Jean out of the cottage,

"Now you may go. Your sister Suk is alive. My spirit can hardly penetrate your wall." So saying, she turned around and locked the door in.

In this way, Jean was at last ousted from the old lady's cottage. Jean also thought that it was not right dillydallying every day, seized within the grasp of horrid phantoms. Strangely enough the moment the old lady turned around, Jean unbelievably felt free and cool. It was early February.

When Jean came out of Old Lady's tutelage, the entire region was covered with snow from the latest heavy snowfall, and there was no knowing what led north or south. The snow buried the road roughly knee high.

She strove her way out to the bird watchtower, clutching at the small package Old Lady clasped into her hand. She thought it best to shelter herself inside the watchtower until daybreak. She huddled into it.

According to Old Lady, about a half day's walk from the highway southwards would lead to a small city, and that city was always crowded with people as it was close to Seoul, the capital city. In this city she might be able to find a place to earn her meals in exchange for some chores.

Old Lady's ambiguous remarks,

"Your sister Suk is not dead. She is alive," had given Jean new hope and strength. Jean couldn't wait, fretting herself, and then questioning,

"Is she alive? How? She must have been killed. Even Pastor couldn't survive. Suk was right after Pastor. How could she survive? That can't be right." Then she would visit the flip side,

"Yes, she might have survived like me. If that's the case, she must be alone. Who knows, we might encounter each other by accident in that city? Be positive, Jean!"

Siberian freezing storms swept through the fields and the nipping cold gripped the watchtower. Her limbs and ears were tingled with frost. She would rather stumble through the snow toward the highway, facing the nipping wind, in an effort to regulate her blood. She slumped in the snow step by step along the roadside trees.

It was dawning when she made it to the highway, groping through the snow covered oxcart road. Then from a gorge on the left hand side, swarms of soldiers gushed out. These soldiers in unison covered themselves with white aprons around their necks.

At the sight of an aircraft, they would lie flat on the snow-covered ground with the white aprons on. As they got on the highway, they started jogging, flying the white aprons. Their babbling words were foreign to her.

Coming down the hill with the soldiers ahead, Jean could see the contour of the city Old Lady had mentioned. At the entrance of the city lay a school building. The soldiers disappeared into the school. Passing by the school she proceeded inside the city.

The city seemed deadened like an empty tomb. The heaven, the earth and the city were all frozen hard. The city was practically a haunted house. All the stores in the market place were tightly closed. The town office was empty. She just wanted to talk with someone after her long struggling journey in the snow.

She recollected that sometime ago, she and her mother had knocked on the closed radio shop violently and repeatedly to get it opened. Now she stood at an empty grocery store. She started pounding the closed store, shouting,

"Open the door please. Would you please open the door, please?" She kept on pounding and shouting for nearly thirty minutes, when suddenly a bucketful of cold water was dumped upon her from beyond the fence next door, ranting,

"You, damned witch! Are you crazy to turn this town into shambles? Get out of here, Now! If you invite the barbarous Chinese soldiers to this place, you know what's going to happen to us, don't you? Beat it. Otherwise I'll pour another bucketful on your dumb head! A bad omen! Damned witch!" The man was heard spitting on the ground and vanished.

Astounded at the cold water and ranting, she was frozen dumbfounded, and yet she was relieved to hear a human voice. She was tempted to resume pounding the door to bring that man out, but at second thought, she turned around in fear of another bucketful of water.

The dumped water began freezing on her. She thought she might as well go straight to the Chinese soldiers in the school. Then she caught a sight of a bell tower. She hurried to the church. The church was tightly closed welcoming no visitors.

Coming out of the church she saw a thatched house with the gate ajar at the end of the alley. Missing so much the human touch, she stealthily approached the house and called,

"Is anybody home?" No one answered.

She entered the house and into the master room. There was a thick rug laid on the hot floor. She felt the floor. It was lukewarm. Had this house been resided? Seeing an ashtray and a long tobacco pipe placed on the upper floor, an old man must have occupied this room. Jean decided to squat on the warm floor and wait for the unknown old man.

— — — — — — — — — — — —

As the sun set, darkness fell quickly. Jean was crushed with overwhelming sleep and exhaustion, and fell in a dead sleep.

Early in the morning, a thunderous ranting bombarded upon her forcing her to quickly collect her senses,

"Who is this wretched witch? What the heck is this? Beat it! Right now!"

Startled at the ranting and kicking, Jean leaped quickly to her feet. There stood a giant droopy-faced drunken old man looking down upon her with upturned eyes, bawling more like lamenting,

"Yah, my first and second sons and their families were all beaten to death by the red! My daughter, her husband and their kids were all bombed to death! So what! What an ugly dog bone are you to creep into my place? Do you want to get crushed to death?" Jean frazzled by the situation and frenziedly took flight.

The old man was a former horse cart driver throughout his life. He had four boys and girls. During the war, all his children and grand children were brutally killed or had been bombed to death. He then turned demented as a drunkard. A few days after his verbal assault towards Jean, he was killed in an accident by an army vehicle.

Since Seoul, the capital city was turned over to the Chinese and northern armies, fierce fighting continued along the new Pyungtaek-Samchuk resistance line.

Thus again, Jean was thrown out onto the streets in the freezing cold. She was quickly made a street bum. Now she had to beg for food from door to door in order to survive. She heard Seoul was the largest city and that it was much easier to beg for meals because more people journeyed the streets. She was headed for Seoul.

It was not easy to be a beggar especially in wartimes.

Once she was hauled out like a hog and her only pan was almost smashed under the foot of a mad restaurant owner, and in another incident had a young bully snatching her pan away and hitting her over the head with it, leading her to almost faint.

In time of war, most people were tense and easily irritable as they lost their regular income, and they had to sustain their livelihood with whatever they had left in their hands. They were stressed out with imminent problems of life and death.

Through repeated harsh treatments and inexpressible persecutions, Jean learned how to get by as a beggar. To survive as a beggar, one had to be smart enough to pick and choose the correct timing and host, and then rise to the situation.

Jean surveyed the land first and then located a house as a target, which may afford charity. Hanging around the targeted house, she waited patiently for the time when the entire family including children sat around the table for meal.

Before they picked the first spoon, she would beg for a morsel of rice loud and clear, whining in hunger. It was a lot of work but it paid off. Jean had better luck in rural or suburban areas than urban areas, because suburbanites were much nicer than urbanites.

For shelter, she would find a vacant stable or cow shed. Sometimes she slept in an open shed under straws or dried pine needles. In a few weeks time, Jean became an every inch ragamuffin. The old Jean and her bright figure were gone. When her stomach twisted in hunger, she took flogging or any kind of maltreatment as a matter of course, and bowed with both hands together,

"Thank you, mama. Thank you, sir."

She had an appalling knack for adapting to new environments. She shuddered in a stable or cowshed in the freezing cold throughout the night and sprawled in sleep under the sun during the day. When she was awake, she sat on the sunny side and pulled off her clothes to hunt countless lice, or shake them off.

Seoul was a large city. She entered a residential area, but every door was tightly locked and there was no way to get inside. Once she tried begging from the outside, knocking the door for hours but no one cared for her troubles.

Neighbors passed her by as if she were nonexistent. She then relocated to a business zone and begged at a restaurant only to be dumped upon with trash and nearly mauled. War may have sharpened the citizens' atrocity. She quickly found it was a much harder task in Seoul to fill one's belly.

She searched through trash dumps and there she could replenish her empty stomach. Then at night, she would suffer through ripping stomachaches and terrible diarrhea lasting for days.

One night, she came to the Seoul railway station for shelter. She saw a restroom in the lobby. Though the station was closed, there stood northern army sentry on guard. She sneaked in the restroom and for the first time she saw herself in the mirror. She was frightened at her own appearance!

She touched the faucet. Warm water gushed out! Someone had left a bar of soap on the sink stand allowing her to wash herself for the first time since she left Old Lady's home.

At the corner of the lobby nestled a group of children. It was incredible that the northern army sentry tolerated them. They probably connived at them due to sympathy of the freezing cold outside.

Many of the children shared similar situations, such as; my father was a communist, the communist beat my father to death, my parents were air-raided on their run south. Therefore, they could easily make friends with each other. Truly birds of a feather flock together.

Their immediate concerns were how to fill their empty stomachs and where to sleep. They banded together to counter these concerns and managed to get by. To them, how their father died, where their brothers or sisters were, further what the teacher said at school, still further what the pastor said in church, and furthermost what their appearance was like, were all trivial.

These children got their heads together to discuss on how to get what they needed such as soap, combs, and sweets. It's all the same, whether begging or stealing, to end up being railed or mauled. If that's the case, why not just go ahead and grab whatever they needed? These boys however were dauntless and good-hearted.

When Jean came out of the restroom, she was a treasure among them. They treated her in a gentlemanly way. It may have been that these children may have seen their sisters or mothers in her.

Everyone treated her cordially. Many of the children called her 'elder sister' with the exception of one who was a couple of years older than Jean. He called her 'younger sister.' Since then, Jean didn't have to go out begging the streets, for these children made it their duty to bring food for her.

These dauntless boys were in the middle of a serious conspiracy.

"I am talking about that old lady, who runs the candy stand on the burnt lot next to the South Gate," one boy repeated.

"Are you talking about that limping lady?" Asked another boy.

"Yeah, I know the lady you are talking about, the fat lady who limps like a tumbling doll at the candy shop, right?" The third boy verified.

"Though she is lame, we have to watch pedestrians passing by. Otherwise they may seize you! Timing is important. When there are no pedestrians nearby and the coast is clear, you may just break in and run away with an armful. What do you think she can do? Follow you, limping?"

"You are right. This is about the right time for the game. We wouldn't lose anyway. At worst, we might be strangled but we'll never die."

Three boys agreed to take the brunt of whatever consequence delivered to rob the sweets stand. Their strategy was for two boys to attack the stand when no one was nearby and to pick a box or basketful of candies.

In case the limping lady came out after them, and if somehow the two boys were in danger of being caught, then the third was to raise hell in the candy stands to keep the lady from chasing, or the third would rob the stand and escape in the opposite direction.

That night, Jean ate a lot of candies and dried cuttlefish for the first time since the war. These boys hunted for anything Jean needed such as soap, comb, nail cutter, even shoes, not to mention providing her with three meals a day. She was treated like a queen bee and they were her little busy bees.

Then, something happened to Jean, probably because she didn't have to beg for food anymore. She grew restless of life and bored to death. She lost her appetite and slowly became ill.

Finally her condition worsened and she couldn't wake up. In the station lobby, the boys moved her from one place to another not to be detected by the sentry. Once, they moved her deep inside the Duksoo Palace. Truly these boys looked out for her best interest.

She fell unconscious for days. The boys somehow found porridge and fed her. Then one day, she opened her eyes and woke up, but she was no longer the old Jean. She was born again as a street beggar in complete oblivion of her past. She became virtually no more than just one of them deserted on the streets.

Jean, once in awhile came to think of her sister Suk, but sadly that didn't mean to her more than a pair of shoes these boys had stolen for her. Sometimes, God's words such as do not steal and do not covet the possession of others, which teacher Sun taught so vehemently, floated upon her mind. Then, she quickly brushed it aside, ridiculing it as nonsense.

From bad to worse, Jean began to defy God, provoking,

"It's not worth even a bowl of rice. God is dead! You with a full stomach call God and He will fill your ears, but to the cold and the hungry, God is deaf! He may pour another bucketful of cold water upon you when you cry for help in the freezing cold." Thus Jean turned away from God. Jean had changed.

6.

Barbed wire Entanglements and Uncle Hello

Fierce fighting staged along the resistance line, Pyungtaek thru Samchuk, for almost three months. The fierce winter with its relentless freeze had now changed its demeanor as if apologizing, and was greeted with a warm colorful spring dress.

In this way, spring unmistakably came in time and knocked on everyone's heart. As days got warmer, roadside trees cracked twigs and shot out buds. Spring haze of warm waves undulated in the fields, arousing and tickling golden bell shrubs and wild flowers into bloom.

As the weather changed for the better, so was the vicissitude of Jean.

Delicate stimulus of adolescence instilled in and was ready to knock on her innocent heart just like a wolf stalking a sheep that had been deserted in total confusion and disorder for months.

As the month of March marched in colors, air-raids abruptly increased in frequency and gravity. The U.N. forces finally spear-headed the new resistance line, and the Chinese and northern armies were in rout. Air fighters and bombers intensified their assault and dropped bombs in sheets on the thoroughly dilapidated ruins, and the roaring of guns was approaching closer. Yellow trousered soldiers herded back in retreat northward. In pursuit, aircrafts swarmed in to riddle them with shots and fright.

On March 15[th]1951, U.N. force's tanks and armored vehicles rolled toward Jean's hideout. Jean and the boys ran to the scene to hooray and exult themselves. Jean didn't know why she should be jubilant. She just followed suit of those who came out of deathbeds and hurrahed. She just shouted as others did.

Then, all of a sudden, she came to think of her parents; her mother and father's gory figures floated in her mind. She was coming back to her senses. She came to think of Jack, the American soldier who had taught her English.

"That's right. I set forth with a travel bag on my head, clutching at the end of Pastor's left sleeve, and while on the run we were in the midst of an air-raid. Pastor and Madam Lady were killed in the raid. The Old Lady said sister Suk and teacher Sun are alive." She was recollecting her past piece by piece, as if awakened from a dream.

"I have to find Suk. I have got to find her!" She had been disillusioned for awhile but now her objectives became clear.

Since that day, the Seoul railway station lobby was being crowed with refugees from the south. North Korean sentries had retreated back north sometime ago. Not only the railway station but the entire city of Seoul was being crowded with returning refugees.

The entire city had been completely pulverized like bean flour except historic relics such as the south gate, the railway station and Duksoo palace. On the city that was leveled to the ground, people crowded overnight with firm determination to start anew.

The station lobby was warmed with the heat of crowding people. The boys were happy as pick-pocketing became a much easier endeavor. Across the railway station, scores of tents were pitched up on the ruins overnight, and the following morning all kinds of eateries were lined up under the tents.

Like bamboo shoots after a rain, shanties and tents popped up across the city, starting with old market places such as the south gate and east gate markets.

That night, the first refugee train pulled into the station. Refugees were crammed and packed in passenger and freight boxes. On top of the train were also crowded with refugees. Their faces were blackened from the smokestack of the locomotive panting through tunnels. When the train pulled in, those on the top were all black with rolling white eyes.

The refugee train crawled its way into the railroad station at a snail's pace, either because of overloaded passengers or as a precautionary measure to those on top of the train hanging on like an acrobat monkey dangling at the end of a thin line.

Many refugees coming out of the station heaved a big sigh of relief,

"I have survived!" and then made a beeline to the eateries across the street.

Jean's posse of boys was excited for many reasons. Begging for food became much easier and pocket picking was much less riskier than robbing a store. They got their hands on whatever Jean needed and made her happy.

She washed herself clean, combed her hair neatly, and changed shoes. When she came out, the boys exclaimed,

"Wow! How pretty! She is fantastic!" The boys exulted in turn.

The oldest yet shortest, named Yongpal, stood behind them with arms akimbo and shouted,

"You kids, shut up! One more yell and I'll kill all of you." He pulled Jean out.

Yongpal's birth name was Soo. Yongpal was his nickname.

Soo was from Paju and his father was a police officer. When the war broke out, his mother was in her last month of pregnancy waiting any minute to give birth. Their family could not seek refuge, waiting for her time.

Later his father was caught and executed by the red-banded comrades. It was days after Soo's father was killed that his mother labored at home and gave a birth to a boy, however, the baby didn't make it. He died the day he was born leaving the mother completely sapped of life.

No one could give her urgent care. She couldn't have even swallowed a spoon of seaweed soup. Soo was a 6th grader at that time. His neighbors and relatives had all gone on refuge. Soo lost his composure and became eccentric when his mother fell unconscious and passed away.

He couldn't stay home alone as he hated seclusion. He hated the village. At last he left his house and the last six months he had become a vagrant, hanging around the Seoul station.

Soo took Jean along toward Namsan hill. He asked,

"Jean, you are telling me that you have to go back home?" Jean had been telling them that she would go back home ever since the refugees returned to crowd Seoul.

"Yes, I have to. My sister Suk and Sun might have returned home, or might be on their way back home as I am now ready."

"But you told me that the village and your house were all bombed and burnt out, didn't you?" Soo asked.

"That's right, but the last time my village was bombed three months ago, teacher Sun had the U.S. engineering corps help rebuild the school and the country office buildings. She would do the same when she gets back with my sister Suk."

Soo was absorbed in deep thought and was walking up the hill without a word for awhile, and then opened his mouth,

"If that's the case, you have to go, Jean. If you go, I will leave here as well."

"Where to?" asked Jean.

"To my hometown, Paju. Our house must be there as it was. Then I will come to your place," Soo pronounced.

"To my place? Do you know how to get there?" Jean questioned in surprise.

"Hey, I am an earthworm. I can find anywhere. I promise that I'll come to your place, but I'll check out Paju first, okay?"

Though Soo was one year older than Jean, he took good care of her as he would have done for his deceased mother. He remembered that he frantically ran about to get the seaweed soup for his dying mother. He felt his mother's warmth in Jean and he would do anything to assist her. Therefore he goaded the other boys to run about to get whatever Jean needed.

When Jean was excited and thrilled at the things ushered her way, Soo stood behind with arms akimbo, self-complacent, watching that she overjoyed on the spree.

Jean looked relieved when Soo promised her to come to her place. She asked anyway,

"Really? Then I will look forward to seeing you at my place. You promised, didn't you?"

"Sure, I did. I will come to your place for sure. I promise," he reassured.

Both fell in silence for a moment and then,

"Jean, it was really nice when I carried you around on my back. Especially while I was carrying you to Duksu Palace, my back was warmed with your tender warmth and I didn't want to get you leave my back. I was a weird freak, wasn't I?"

"I was unconscious at that time, you told me."

"That's right. You were in a coma, but you came back and I was beside myself when you opened your eyes to recognize me, and I was so grateful!"

"Oppa, it was I that should have been grateful, not you!"

Jean called Soo "Opppa" for the first time, bestowing respect and admiration towards Soo.

When Soo first met Jean, strangely enough he felt motherly warmth in her. He often talked to himself, pondering,

'If I had carried my mother on my back to our relatives and there remote place, could she still be alive?'

"You just called me 'Oppa.' From now on, I am your Oppa, okay?" Soo seemed to be much gratified and then continued,

"Jean, if that's your decision, you had better leave early. You are not a beggar, are you? You were more like a warm stove to us when we returned cold from begging," He confessed.

Truly Jean had never been cut out for begging.

Realizing now is the time for her to leave, her eyes wetted warm and thanked,

"Soo oppa, I do thank you for your unsparing care of me. You are truly an angel to me. You just promised to come to my place after you stop by Paju. Please keep your word. I will wait for you, oppa."

"I will and I do promise." He fumbled around his pockets for whatever money he had, and,

"Jean, that's all I have left after I bought your shoes."

Jean declined, saying,

"Thank you indeed, oppa, but let me be on my own feet from now on. When I am geared up, I can do as good a job as you can. Instead I would like to have chachang noodle with all boys this evening, if you can afford."

That evening, Jean, Soo and the posse of boys had a farewell party on chachang noodle and fried pork. It was a delicious and delightful farewell party. Jean set out for a lonely homecoming journey late that night.

Early April, the night air was ideal for walking on a journey. She didn't accept the money Soo offered, as her declining was the only way for her to express her thanks to the boys for what they had done for her. Now, she would keep walking and beg on the way for food whenever she was hungry, and squat anywhere to have a nap whenever she was exhausted.

These boys were courageous in how they managed to survive. The world dumped them into the valley of death, yet they undauntedly strived out of it. The world taught them to be honest and obedient yet turned its head away from these kids, who were left to steal and conspire against others as a mode of living. Jean was shedding tears reminiscing of those poor boys.

The full moon's shine exposed the dismal contour of field and mountains afar, lending landmarks and destination goals for Jean. Fortunately, refugees were seen in groups here and there on the highway to assist her travels.

She stood on top of the last hill toward Uijeongbu. She turned around to take a final look at Seoul, visualizing the boys now slumbering like shrimps under the dim light of the station.

Coming down the hill, the highway stretched straight all the way to Uijeongbu, she plodded her way down the last hill among the refugees, and then went along the straight highway.

As the twilight lifted, a village loomed up at the foot of a hill. In the middle of the village were a brick house and a step-on pestle mill. Approaching the village, she saw an empty thatched shed at the entrance. Behind the shed a sizable village was seated.

Jean was hungry and exhausted from walking all night through. It was too early to beg for meals. She thought she would have a rest inside the shed and wait there. Then she saw a farmer coming out from behind the shed.

As she came closer to the shed, dogs barked boisterously from the village. She was an arms distance away from the shed, when she saw a big dog dashing toward her like a darting arrow. She was terrified at the sight when the dog jumped and swooped upon her. She fell down in a swoon, shrieking,

"Umma!"

The dog ferociously bit her thigh and then jumped on her shoulder, snarling outrageously.

At the nick of time, the farmer caught sight and made a dash to the scene. He flung a stick at the dog, shouting,

"The damned dog! Get out of here!" The dog gave in, whining its tail down and ran away towards the highway. It was a stray mad dog.

The farmer helped Jean up and asked,

"Are you all right, Miss? Shake yourself off."

Jean gathered herself. She felt a tinkle in her thigh but she thought she could bear with it. The man bent over to help her up.

"Thank you, sir." She thanked him while staggering up.

"It could be much worse. Go straight home and ask your dad to take you to a doctor." After the farmer's last statement, he quickly wondered,

'Whose daughter could she be?' Trying to figure the father-daughter connection, he resumed his way to the mill.

Jean staggered to her feet,

"Thank you so very much, sir." However, she couldn't take a step. The man, looking back at her, asked her,

"Are you all right? It could have been much worse." With that he kept heading for the mill.

Jean barely made it to the shed and lay flat on her back to catch her breath. The wounds of the dog bite started aching, accompanied with cold shivers that seized upon her. Her mouth dried up quickly. She tried to stay awake, pinching her thigh. She was afraid she would sink in the depths of death if she were left alone.

"I got to go the village and get some food to gather myself. Jean, wake up!" She urged herself as she struggled to sit up. Her cheek was burning in fever and her hands had swelled. She barely made her way out of the shed and staggered toward the brick house behind the mill.

Her attempts were futile; she couldn't muster the energy to make it. She collapsed and fell to the ground, shuddering in spasms. Then the farmer who was coming out of the mill caught sight and rushed to the scene, tossing gathered wood off his back, and said,

"What's the matter? You can't walk?" He picked her up in his arms and hurried toward the village.

At the first cottage on the corner, he pushed the thatched gate in, yelling,

"Mother, help! Look at this." An old lady came out of the room and shrieked,

"What on earth is this? Isn't this a maiden?"

"Yes, mother. She was bitten by a mad dog."

"Did you say she was bitten by a mad dog?"

"Yes, the mad dog! I saw it. What can we do?"

"So, she is bitten by a mad dog. She must have been bitten badly. Bring her in and lay her down on the lower floor."

She searched Jean's body and quickly located the wounds. She unclothed Jean swiftly and turned her over to expose the wounds on the rear thigh, and then ordered her son,

"Go and get some manure, radish and yellow phosphor. Quickly!" She then bent over with her mouth wide open and sucked the wounds with all her might on the thigh. She kept sucking hard as veins started to expose themselves through the skin, and then she spit the blood into a urine bowl repeatedly.

When she sucked all the bad blood out, she plastered the wounds with mashed raw potato and bandaged with a linen cloth. Heaving a big sigh of relief, as if she completed a task right at the nick of time, she ran into the kitchen to cook grain porridge. She scooped the porridge into Jean's mouth, murmuring all the while,

"Healing Father, have mercy on this poor little one. You raised the dead. If this little one was to blame for, please forgive her and save her. I pray this in the name of Jesus Christ."

Soon her son walked in,

"Mother, I got every thing you asked here."

Then Jean came back to her senses and opened her eyes. Jean took the porridge the lady prepared. The lady said, heaving another sigh of relief,

"It's done. Well done! For danger is over. Our good Lord saved her."

Jean covered the wounds with herb plaster the lady prepared and drank the medicine.

In a few days, she could get out of the bed.

After she heard Jean's story, the old lady embraced her, saying,

"So, that's what you came across since the war broke out. You, a poor little one." She sobbed for awhile and then released her from her embrace,

"Do not ever thank me. I just did a little of what I am supposed to do. I agree with you that you should find your sister and teacher Sun to start anew as soon as possible. They might be home in your village by now."

"Thank you, grandma," Jean whispered.

"Let thanks be to God. Trials from God are worth ten times more than gold. Our God will be pleased to know that we value the trials before anything." Pausing a moment, she continued,

"However, let's not be too hasty. We have done our best to work antidotes into the wounds, but you cannot be on the street as you are. You need at least a few more days before you can resume your journey back home.

"But, grandma, I would like to leave tomorrow. I can't wait. Please understand me."

"I know how anxious you are to see them, but look at yourself. Your body can't follow your mind. I am just as anxious as you are but no one knows what's going to happen to you the next day. I think you have to learn how to be patient and wait for the right time. There are so many hills and valleys you will have to cross to Cholwon."

The lady persuaded Jean to stay until the wounds were healed enough to permit Jean to walk comfortably.

That evening, the village pastor and a few other members of the village church, who had just recently returned from refuge, visited the old lady's and collectively prayed for Jean. Jean was now aware that the old lady was a good Christian lady, she immediately thought of her own mother in comparison.

The village the old lady lived in was almost as large as Jean's home village. Several days later, the old lady and her son gave Jean a hearty send-off.

Jean was choked up with her unutterable gratitude toward the old lady and her son. They were truly angels habiting earth. Jean wondered why God let these wonderful angels live in a destitute state in a small cottage. How could it be that an abundant unsparing love flowed like a river from such a poverty-stricken home?

Seeing that there was no other man, the old lady must have been widowed and her son must have been either a old bachelor or widower. How could they be so caring and peaceful? In wartimes, people tend to be aggressive even leading to hurting others to get ahead. What made the old lady and her son so bountiful in serving others? Do they lack common sense? Do they lack in being ambitious to be rich like others?

Jean couldn't suppress her unknown sadness as she was shedding tears, clutching at the package of roast rice and potatoes, which the old lady handed over, saying,

"It may take a couple of days for you to get your home village. Take this when you are hungry on the way."

Jean wanted to turn around to say another goodbye but she didn't want to hurt the lady's heart by showing her teary face. She set forth to the highway, dropping her head in silence, grateful for such hospitality.

Truly love and grace can not be purchased with money. Respectable character and adorable personalities are not necessarily from education, social status and wealth. For most it may probably be the opposite. Who is waging the war? Isn't it the ones that are highly educated and powerful who masterminded such wars?

The lady didn't have much, but she gave a lot. She wasn't well educated but her words were as precious as jewels. She was old and weak, but her embracing arms were as strong as those of muscular wrestlers. She was not a trained physician, but her herb medication prescribed through her genuine heart and dedication was the elixir of life. In a word, she was a quiet practitioner of love.

It was almost a month since Seoul was recaptured and the throng of refugees on the highway had greatly thinned down. General Macarthur who became the Korean national hope to oust the invading red army to the northern border of the Apnok River was replaced by General Ridgeway to command the U.N. forces in Korea.

The road to Pochun through Uijungbu was open and empty. Once in a while, U.S. army trucks sped by, swirling up dust winds. Farmers were seen transplanting rice on the rice paddy and women busy sowing seeds on the field. Swarms of aircrafts no longer traveled the skies. People were starting to believe that the war was over. Nevertheless the bloody battle along the 38th parallel line was daily intensifying.

Jean will have to make a lonely journey all the way to Pochun, from Pochun to Woonchun, and then, from Woonchun to Cholwon. From Cholwon she would plod on her lonely trail step by step, through miles of hills and valleys of rocks and stones back to Byukchun village.

The last four months, this fourteen-year old girl had experienced shuddering nightmares. As she recalled those days, horrid scenes were fleeting away on her mind like a kaleidoscope, such as: Pastor's gory head flat on the bust with goggled eyes.

The serene sorceress who turned away, saying,

"Go and search. Your sister Suk is not dead. She is alive."

The tough yet tender hearted Soo, confessing candidly,

"My back was warmed in comfort, while I was carrying you on my back to the Duksu Palace."

The old Christian lady's genial face, admonishing,

"Learn to be patient and wait for time in hope," and finally the exulted rejoicing Suk jolting upon her, screaming,

"Jean! Where have you been all these days?" Which she had envisioned more often lately and she would retort in her vision,

"You are ugly, Suk! You are no longer my sister! Where have YOU been?"

Rehearsing the above experiences and dreams helped her forget how tired her legs were becoming. At last she came close to her home village.

When she was almost to the broken concrete bridge of the stream, she exclaimed,

"Who are they that dare to stand in my way and block my path!?"

At a distance, barbed wire entanglements were stretched across the road and grim-faced American soldiers stood there with guns, blocking the way.

"Why on earth should it be this spot? I can't take one step further!"

Stunned at the sight, Jean lost words in frustration and despair.

Jean firmly determined to take death and approached a helmeted soldier, stammering,

"Hello, uncle. Hello. Look there!" She pointed in the direction of the arbor tree.

"Please, let me go there, uncle. Right there under the arbor tree, my father and mother were beaten to death, and above the tree was our house on the ridge. My sister Suk must be there waiting for me. Please, uncle, please." Jean rubbed both hands together, begging and beseeching on her knees and kept mumbling, sniveling in tears and drippings.

The American M.P. gestured with both palms sunny side up, raising his shoulder with the head tipped aside, signaling 'what can I do?'

Nonetheless, Jean kept on,

"Please save me, Uncle. Please send me home. My home is right there, as you see. Otherwise, I'll be dying here."

Her tormenting plea and supplication knew no end, just like a bewailing daughter over her dying mother, repeating a scene that crushed the hearts of twin daughters.

"Right over there. Under that arbor tree, my father and mother were murdered. Right behind the tree, on the ridge was our home. Uncle, please. Can't you see me begging like this? Can't you, Uncle?"

She entreated in a frenzy of despair, mumbling and sniveling. This time, the American MPs, facing each other with the same gesture of raising shoulder, tipping head aside, signaled to one another, "What can we do?"

All the while, Jean had rolled to the ground to demonstrate her determination,

"Let me go, or I'll die here!" crying out,

"I just want to go to see my mother. I have no other place to go. Otherwise I will die here!"

American soldiers left her wallowing in the dust. The sun was lingering ready to set in the west. One of the MPs came out of the barracks with a box of rations. He came to raise Jean up and dusted off her hair and shoulders. He placed the box in her arms and whispered to her, gently stroking her hair, and then turned around and went back to the barracks. The setting sun shot out streaks of scarlet ray through cumuli of clouds like baneful stings, and then cooled off.

Well over midnight, the surrounding MP barracks was serenely silenced to the droning of generators in the compound. At a distance Jean crouched on the ground for a nap under the flickering beam of floodlights from the entanglements. Once in awhile, gunshots shook the dead of night, and the awakening of soldiers on duty were heard.

Jean could not leave the barbed wire entanglements, since she decided to wait for her sister Suk here.

The Soviet delegate to the U.N. proposed for armistice, and the war went into the phase of limited warfare. In other words, the Korean War was brought onto the negotiation table between the two powers. The situation was unpredictably unstable and volatile all along the front line.

Jean roamed about the MP barracks as a derelict, skipping meals. She quickly became gaunt and a haggard ragamuffin. Whenever she came across an American soldier, she restarted her plea,

"There, right there under the arbor tree, my father and mother were mauled to death. My sister Suk must be waiting for me there." By then, American soldiers stopped paying her any attention, assuming that she had gone nuts.

One day Jean suddenly came to think of Soo.

"Did he say to Paju? He would carry me on his back."

She rose up resigning her hopes of waiting for her sister Suk, and set off for Paju.

The sun for the month of June was brilliant, and the air was still with little breeze. Summer was just around the corner. Jean was plodding back the way she came up some time ago. Whenever she was tired, she flopped to fall asleep. This time in her dream, she saw Suk killed in the air-raid.

She hated walking alone on the empty road. She hated the open field.

She hated the desolate countryside. She simply missed human habitat. She believed that Soo would wait for her somewhere, as Soo promised her that he would come to her place after he stopped by Paju. She kept trudging along the road, now in search of Soo, not recalling when she had her last meal.

Who said, "Human life is tough." Jean filled into the role of a lengthy tiring vagabond from Chulwon to Paju, from Paju to Seoul, from Seoul to Uijungbu and from Uijungbu to Donduchun solely in search of Soo.

She was still alive, alive in faint memories of this and that. Her body was hopelessly incapacitated from hunger and thirst, and further from frustration and despair. What could be the difference between man and animal? It may be that human pain and agony overwhelms the human desire to survive. That's right. Sometimes devils overwhelm the spirit. Jean was not an exception.

As proposed by the Soviet delegate in the U.N., on July 1st 1951, the first round of armistice talk was held at Kaesung. On October 25th, they moved the conference site to Panmunjum. On January 17th 1952, the military demarcation line was established as agreed upon by both parties. On June 8th 1953, war prisoners were exchanged. Lastly, on July 27th 1953 the armistice was signed to conclude the three-year-and-one-month brutal war.

7.

Partisans and Prostitutes

One nipping cold morning, two ladies were talking in the inner room of an inn named, 'Happy Inn' which was next to the beer hall, 'Sing Sing Club' in Dongduchun.

"I helped her to take a bath. She has an unusually nice figure," a lady who seemed to be a maid of the inn spoke, mopping the floor.

"Does she? She could be frozen to death by now if it wasn't for you," another lady at the lower hot floor responded, striking the match to start on a Yankee cigarette.

Puffing the cigarette, the lady continued,

"Did you say you found her at the bottom of the chimney stack?"

"Yes, ma'am. Maybe that was the only place she could shelter herself from the freezing cold. As the briquettes kept burning in the furnace all night through, the lower part of the chimneystack was warm. Her hands and feet were badly frostbitten. That girl reminded me of my lost Kumsoon! So I picked her up and brought her in."

Kumsoon was this maid's granddaughter. The maid came from the south with her granddaughter, Kumsoon, whose parents were killed by the communist. They were on the verge of starvation, and they heard that people can eat off crumbs from the soldiers' table in the U.S. military bases.

This lady set out for the frontline in the north, looking for any U.S. soldier base. Tragically, on their way north her granddaughter became ill. The lady carried her granddaughter on her back, begging for food but one day the girl died on her back.

Kumsoon's father, the lady's only son was drafted to the punitive police force to mop up communist partisans based in Chiri mountain ridge. Because of his being drafted for the police force, when the war broke out, the entire family was killed except Kumsoon, who was at her grandmother's home at that time.

As the maid mentioned of Kumsoon, the old lady cut in,

"Here you go again. Stop that song! I mean reciting your granddaughter Kumsoon and the southwest punitive police force. I know your son was drafted for the punitive force and later was killed by the red-banded comrades."

"I didn't mean to bring up that story, Ma'am, but that girl resembles my Kumsoon so much." The lady was already choked in tears. Rubbing away at her eyes, she continued with a serious face.

"This girl is ideal for an errand girl. She can deliver meals and hot water to the thirteen wanton girls' rooms (thirteen prostitutes) and also run and fetch items for them from the grocery store."

"Do as you please. I'll leave that girl up to you."

As the conversation ended, the old lady indulged on her memories, heaving a sigh; the heart-sore memory of the partisans and the southwest punitive police force, and the further heart-breaking story of each one of the prostitutes.

To tell you the origin of partisans, we have to trace back to the earlier period of our history. We had a chaotic transitional period in our county from the time of liberation from Japan in 1945 to the time of both governments being established in north and south, during which time the leftist and the rightist wings staged blood-shedding confrontation.

The northern communist government was led by the 33 year old Kim Il Sung from Russia and the southern government by Syngman Rhee from America. While there was only one party in the north, in the south were 260 different parties and organizations mushroomed.

Taking advantage of social disorder and confusion in the south, the leftist infiltrated espionage agents into south through the South

Labor Party and Democratic Youth Party to instigate rebellions against the southern government.

On April 3rd 1948, people rallied in Jeju Island in protest against establishing the southern government in separation of the northern government. Then U.S. military government mobilized the police force to suppress the rally and arrested a large number of demonstrators.

This ignited an all-out people's uprising, and the people assaulted police stations to rob and to equip with weapons. And now those demonstrators turned into armed mobs to attack the right-wing organizations. The military government dispatched 1,700 men of police force to the scene and reinforced it with the 9th Regiment of Jeju National Defense Guard stationed in Jeju Island. (National Defense Guard was the former body of Army)

During this mopping-up operation which lasted for four months beginning November 1948, 130 villages of the 160 villages on the island were totally destroyed or burnt along with a large number of innocent villagers massacred. Almost 10% of the total population of the island, approximately 30,000 islanders were either killed or heavily wounded.

To further reinforce the mopping up operation, the government issued the order to dispatch to the scene the 14th Regiment of National Defense Guard stationed in Yosu.

Now the leftists in the Guard, including the company commanders, Kim Jihee and Hong Sunsuk rose against the government order and defected to assault police stations and other municipal offices in Yosu and Sunchon area, turning both cities into manslaughter-house for seven nightmarish days. Thousands of innocent citizens were brutally killed in both cities. This military revolt rapidly spread to Kurye and Kwangyang areas.

As the government force pressed on, the rebel army equipped with modern arms escaped into the adjacent Chiri mountain ridge to join with then south labor party partisans. Then Korean War broke out. UN forces made the Incheon landing to thrust into the back of the northern army and blocked their withdrawal route to north. The northern armies in rout withdrew into adjacent mountains to join up with already existing labor party partisans.

Now the partisans centering around the Chiri and Baekwoon mountains spread all over the southern peninsular except Kyunggi province, in which Seoul is seated, and established the liberation front to stage guerrilla operations all over rural areas in the south.

Consequently most of those rural areas were placed under the control of two different powers; at sunset, the southern police receded from rural villages and the partisan took over them, and at dawn, the partisans withdrew into mountains and the police took them back. Thus the police arrested communist sympathizers during day and at night the partisans took reactionaries away.

While fierce battles of limited war continued along the military demarcation line since 1951, the partisans were rampant over most of rural areas in the south.

To rise to the situation, the UN Command ordered the 8th Division of Korean Army, headed by Gen. Baek Sunyup, to take charge of the guerrilla mopping-up operation in the rear, and the police force engaging in the operation was reorganized as the Southwest Punitive Police Force. The army and police joint operations continued until 1955 and most of the partisans were either killed or surrendered.

Kumsoon's father, the maid's son was drafted for this police force, and later he and his family were killed by the partisans from mountains as reactionaries. And now, let's hearken to the story of one of prostitutes;

Throughout a pitch dark midnight rain that had been pouring in sheets, a woman was frantically splashing through a muddy rice paddy in the dark. Occasionally, strong mountain gales carried the downpour to slap the woman's face.

Whether she was sloshing in paddy or sloughing out of furrow, she couldn't tell. She was so pressed that she had no room to think about it. She was just struggling through. Once caught, she would be killed on the spot.

Up until six months ago, this lady was known in her village as a comely docile maiden who was obedient and faithful to her ill father. She was married at the age of nineteen to the only son of a widower welder in the upper village. Though the groom was poverty-sticken, he was handsome, and he promised her that he would look after her sick father and her three younger brothers.

About two months after she was married, the war had broken out. When the northern armies arrived, the husband, being fed up with his family's impoverished conditions, joined the so-called revolutionary movement and participated in the people's committee and people's court, to mend change. He was bent on land reform to deprive the rich of the land and share it among tenant farmers.

About a month thereafter, the U.N. forces landed in Incheon and launched an extensive offensive. The battle was a turning point in the war, as the red army withdrew. Her husband ran away into the mountains to be a partisan. Since then, she was continuously questioned of her husband's whereabouts by the southern police during the day. At night, her husband and other partisans came down to the village on their revolutionary missions.

One early morning, the punitive police force enveloped the village and assaulted one of the partisan hideouts. The lady wasn't aware of the hideout in the village.

Astounded by gunfire, she woke up in a panic. She later discovered at the bottom of the upper village gorge, her husband's bloody body riddled with two shots, one in the head and the other piercing his chest.

In this surprise assault, a head partisan, the district chairman of the peoples committee was kidnapped and beaten nearly to death, and other partisans in the hideout ran away seeking refuge in the mountains.

At sunset, the punitive police force withdrew from the village with the kidnapped chair partisan. At nightfall, partisans came down from the mountains to take over the village. That night, the partisans took back with them three women of the village. Their goal was to goad the women into the mountain before the break of dawn as they had a grave mission planned for the women to perform in their hideout headquarters.

This lady was one of the three women. She was not afraid to undertake any secret mission planned by the partisans. It was that she couldn't leave her ill father and three younger brothers behind. Therefore, she risked her life and ran away from them while climbing up a steep mountain gorge in the down pouring rain.

With a fluttering heart, she barely made it back home that night.

Upon dawning, she packed up odds and ends and moved out of the village with her ill father and three younger brothers. She had been fed up with daily interrogations by the punitive police during the day and now she was no longer safe at night. Staying meant risk being beaten to death as a reactionary by the partisans. Besides she no longer had means to find food for her family in the village.

She had five younger brothers at a two-year interval, and two of them died of an unknown sickness. Her mother died upon the birth of the youngest, now four years old.

What remained of her family were three brothers, ages four, eight and thirteen years old, along with her ill father. She heard it was safe for her family in the city and she hoped to find work.

The family carried as much as they could: barley, beans, potatoes for immediate food and some clothing. The sky was covered with thick clouds of rain, roaring and bawling with frequent thunder and lightning. There was no light in the sky, not even a glimmer.

It was dark when they arrived in the city, Chonju with bags made heavier through the rain. For the first few days they sheltered themselves from the rain in an open shed in a mill and waited for the rain to subside. Behind the empty mill was a concrete bridge. They waited for the water to recede.

The rain finally stopped allowing the family to find space under the bridge to build a hut. Now that her family had settled in, she went off to find work. She was open to take whatever was available. On lucky days, she worked on a farm or a field. She would pick radish leaves and boiled them for sale by lumps in the market.

One day, she came across a golden opportunity in the market. The potential job was none other than the scavenger soup, kkulkuri porridge business. At that time, people congregated around U.S. soldier bases. Among them were scavenger contractors who collected and hauled trash out of the U.S. base. Scavenger soup was made out of items found within trash drums which were placed at each mess hall on the base.

These drums were filled with discarded or remnant foods at the end of each meal. When these drums were hauled out, they sold it by the bucketful. Vendors bought bucketfuls of food waste. They sorted out offensive things like cigarette stubs out of the waste food and then they boiled it again for sale by cups in the market place. They called it scavenger soup, kkulkuri porridge. Ironically the soup was sold as a nourishing food.

She started a scavenger soup vending business. She bought a bucketful and at times two or three bucketfuls at the trash dump and hurried back home to cook it over for sale in the market.

Her business was turning a profit allowing her to buy a small shanty in the city. She could also send two of her younger brothers to school. Her ill father improved a great deal when they moved into the shanty. They were very pleased that they no longer resided in the old village. But a year later, she was forced to discontinue her business. A strongman had an exclusive contract with the trash collector and monopolized the scavenger soup business.

Though her source of income was terminated, she still wanted her younger brothers to continue their education. She had her hands full as she also had to look after her father. For sometime, she could not find a way to support her family. In her mind there was no light at the end of the tunnel. Her life was losing hope and joy.

This lady's name was Kilja. The bottom of her rice pot in the kitchen was up.

Her two younger brothers went to school. She left her now six-year old brother and her father at home, picking up the bag of empty cans and bottles she collected for sometime.

Her collection of cans and bottles became her only source of hope that they might eke out another day with the money from the sale of the cans and bottles. The next day was her concern. She had to do something for that next day. She was well adapted to this kind of hardship in life. Under any circumstance, she always had the money to do manage to survive another day.

With the money she made from the empty cans and bottles, she bought a bag of raw potatoes and a dozen dried cuttlefish. She washed and boiled the potatoes. She prepared the potatoes and dried cuttlefish to sell on the vendor's stand at the corner of a street nearby the U.S. Air Force Base. She put the boiled potatoes in twos or threes on a clean tray and covered them with a mosquito net. She also displayed the cuttlefish next to the potatoes and squatted by the stand, waiting for her clients. Her clients were mainly shoeshine boys and other juvenile vagrants roaming about.

Once in a while, western-dressed ladies came by to purchase them in bunches. She tried to make as many friends as possible for her client buildup. She stressed on the cleanliness of her merchandise.

Different from the sweet potatoes, she paid special care to keep the cuttlefish from heat on sunny days and from the humidity on wet days. Maintaining the livelihood for her family day by day with selling potatoes and cuttlefish was not a big issue. The problem was that she could not afford lump sum payments for tuition, textbooks and school uniforms for her younger brothers.

In winter, she sold roasted chestnuts and potatoes instead of boiled sweet potatoes, but the return was so meager compared to that of summer. Even that was not an issue. They would skip meals to cut down the food cost to make it through the winter. They were well used to it.

It was the start of the rain season and customers would not come out during this time. Kilja squatted at her stand with an umbrella under the awning of a two-story corner building, waiting for hungry souls. She wrapped cuttlefish in papers to keep them away from moisture.

Money was important more than ever as the new school semester was to start following the summer break. A man, who came by yesterday, stopped by again today,

"How pathetic you are, lady! Spin your head. Just keep your eyes closed and you will make a ten-day wage! Can't you understand?" Kilja was temporarily disinclined to speak and asked herself,

"Should I follow his advice? Closing my eyes for a short while and I can make ten days work." She seemed hesitant, asking herself again,

"If I close my eyes twice, that will bring enough money for my brothers to continue school next semester."

Then the man shouted again,

"Oh, I can't stand this. I have a good idea. Let's do it this way." The man was in his thirties and shouted, asking,

"How much do you want for all the stuff on the stand? I'll take them all."

He handed Kilja a lot more than the actual price, and continued,

"Instead, you have got to listen to me. First of all, you go to the public bathhouse and take a good bath. Then, come to the 'Happy Inn' at the end of that alley. They will take a good care of you there. It's just a matter of you closing your eyes for a short while. Today I am not going to take away what you earn."

This man was a pimp whose financial resources dealt with prostitutes. He arranged intimate sessions and took a portion of funds. He continued,

"But the next time on, you'll have to share a little bit with me. I'll let you go without it today. Understood?"

The rain was now at a full down pour, perhaps to drown out the man's advice to Kilja. Kilja however heard the man well and to her it made sense. She decided to head to the inn from the public bathhouse. A couple of soldiers were seen coming out of the 'Happy Inn', cackling and giggling.

The lady in the inn greeted her in,

"Is your name Kilja?"

"Yes, that's my name."

"Have you ever been to a place like this?"

"No, this is my first time."

"Do you know about men?"

"I was once married."

"What about your husband?"

"He died."

The landlady surveyed Kilja from head to toe, concluding,

"You have a beautiful complexion. You are too good!" and shouted inside,

"This is a green bean. Do her hair and give her pajamas, and show her what to do."

"Yes, ma'am." The maid came out.

Thus Kilja was crossing the bridge to her ruin.

Later she came to the 'Sing Sing Club' and 'Happy Inn' everyday. Back at home she was believed by her family to have a good paying job at the Base Post Exchange.

What made Shimchung throw herself into the Indang water? (In our legendaries, a filial daughter named Shimchung was sold for the money to open her blind father's eyes and threw herself into the Indang Lake.) What about Kilja who finally gave up herself for the sake of her father and her three younger brothers? She did throw herself into the modern Indang water.

These women involved in the sex trade came from various backgrounds and situations. A shared commonality was that they took the plunge to the 'Happy Inn" for the sake of others, most likely their family. But in the water, there was not a Palace as in the legendary story. Instead, at the bottom of the water was a fathomless ruin of depravity.

In it, they licked and ate the sensual pleasure in the darkness. Once shoved in and slumped in this infernal slough, it was not easy for any victim to pull his or her leg out of it, since the darkness domineered over it according to its rules.

The soldiers who cackled and giggled to the dawning slipped out of each room, and the snorting sound of women was oozing through the sills, vibrating the door flaps.

Fierce fighting was daily intensifying along the 38th parallel line as the demarcation line was to be determined at the time of the armistice to be signed. Where American soldiers were stationed with barbed wire entanglements, people gathered for employment and scavenger soup.

Dance halls and other entertainment allies mushroomed nearby the military bases. U.S. military bases throughout the length of the war steadily increased in number to claim to be one of the top employers in the nation. Furthermore, those employed were looked upon as blessed ones with high pay.

As the town turned boisterous with gathering people, the land-lady of the inn quickly remodeled and added rooms and opened the business around the clock. In this way, pleasure districts spread under the pretext of recreation like poisonous mushrooms all across the nation.

These pleasure districts became unprecedented hot-beds of social evils such as debauchery, vanity and extravagance. Most people misunderstood them as a new trend of western civilization and bent over backward to not only accommodate but imitate them as well.

Vices fueled by debauchery, vanity and extravagance were new to them as the western civilization was, but they were surely not the core. On the contrary, there was no difference between western and eastern civilizations when it comes to moral and ethical standards. All mankind were the same in Christ.

Jean, who had been searching for Soo since last summer, lost hope as he was nowhere to be found. She became sick of begging for food. She was tired and exhausted of surviving. Finally she resigned herself to fate.

One nipping cold night, Jean happened to fall under the chimneystack of the 'Happy Inn' as she was on the verge of starvation. The maid of the inn found Jean on her way to a market place and brought her in.

Thanks to this maid's gentle heart and fond memories of her granddaughter spawned from Jeans likeness, Jean could finally fill her empty stomach and sleep on a warm floor for the first time since the war had broken out.

The days grew shorter and the nights stretched longer. The unyielding freezing cold made icicles thicker hanging on the eaves, and wet hands would be well-advised to approach doorknobs with caution as they would stick together longer than one's intent.

In this severe cold, it was like a dream for Jean to eat until she was full and sleep in warmth. What was even more exciting was that she was treated as a human being. When she took a bath in the warm water, she felt as if she was being born anew. Furthermore, the sausage and hamburgers, which she had never experienced before, tasted like heaven.

She was a little clumsy at the beginning, but in a few days, she became accustomed to her new environment. She picked it up quickly what she was expected to do. The inn maid was more like her mother in a way. The maid was extremely happy with Jean, as was Jean with the maid. Jean was recovering her lost weight fast and her eyes began sparkling in no time.

In a few months, a number of women moved into the inn. It was no longer a regular inn. It became an open house for prostitution. Of course, Jean didn't know anything about the practice of harlots. She started work, answering to yelling and she was chased by incessant chores in the swirl of prostitution all day long.

She was usually hectic when by noon; late risers among the women began yelling in turn for hot water, for towels, for defiled water to be taken out of their rooms. When Jean delivered the meal table, picky complaints of "not enough" showered upon her such as not hot enough, not cold enough, and not tasty enough, and they irritated her with constant fussy demands of this and that.

She also had to answer all the vexing yells from the maid in the kitchen such as "Hurry, take this, bring that back." Twelve legs would not have been enough to run around and meet every demand, but Jean made due with just two legs.

Somehow Jean managed to handle it with wits and speed. All the noise and fuss became a new rhythm in her life, and she well adapted herself to them. Then those women began hailing at her, commending,

"You are great! You did a good job. Take this." They threw tips or candies to her. Jean took all the tips and candies to the maid, and the maid would return some back to Jean.

Jean's main job was to change the briquettes of the thirteen furnaces to keep the rooms warm around the clock. In addition she had to clean up the rooms and waste, on top of waiting on the women and the maid. Her days were truly hectic.

Three years passed since the war ended. Jean grew in the swirl of hustle-bustle. Her once flat breasts swelled. Her thin hips grew chubby. Her original figure zoomed up. In fact, she grew into an attractive voluptuous female that even the women exclaimed at her in turn,

"Wow! Look at that girl! Check it out. Look at her breast and plump hips! She is more than sexy. Isn't she? She is fresh, too."

These women were least hesitant in enticing her into the way of debauchery by words and even by action. It was like a plant louse creeping on a fresh bloomed rose. Jean had to spend her sensitive adolescent years, the prime of youth in the mess of lewdness and debauchery, watching and listening to the shameless people who lost the light and enjoyed the darkness.

It was high time that Jean should have equipped herself with spiritual arms to fight off the devil's temptations through the power of daily bread of words and prayer.

She was relentlessly thrown into and left abandoned in the inferno! How could anyone expect her to get out of that slough all by herself? The only discipline she received was from the maid, railing at her,

"You! Don't ever be like those prostitutes!"

At the beginning when the maid was ranting at her, Jean did not know what it meant. Then one day, she noticed a white soldier went in a room to meet a woman, and then in the afternoon, another man went inside the same room to meet the same woman. This stimulated a strange sense of curiosity in her.

For the first time, she gave ear to the sounds coming from inside the room, while changing briquettes to the furnace. She heard a weird sound that stinged her ears and stifled her heart to a shock.

That sound fluttered her heart and quivered her in shivers, sending electrifying sensation to the crook of her knees. Her mouth dried up instantly and she was swiftly ready to give in to the impulse of the moment.

She felt urged to peep into the room stealthily, just once, only for a second, and then again and again. It was not enough. It was insatiable, and then she fidgeted herself into a fever.

This toxin was more like a swishing whirlpool by a serpent slitting the water with its head high up. At last, that serpent had trapped and coiled her with its tail. She was benumbed and the serpent was Satan.

Since then, Jean waited for the time to change briquettes to each room. She had to change thirteen different furnaces a day. She had ample chances of indulging in the darkness. Listening to the tickling and fondling play from inside, she went on a dreamy journey on the wing of fantastic illusions, sailing over the turbulent wave of queer pining groans and outburst of violent passion, and then sunk down deeper daily in the mire of destruction and ruin.

The more she listened and watched the scene, the more she thirsted for it. It was truly insatiable. The darkness shielded and darkened the pall of broad daylight, and the hunger and thirst for it were unquenchable.

Christmas and New Year celebrations were gone. People ate, drank, shouted, and enjoyed a lot. The freezing cold receded. The warm sunlight alighted on the front yard of the inn, spreading its wing of shimmering haze.

Jean's heart was swayed adrift for no reason, and started watching every movement and behavior of those women with keen interest. Two women were in a dispute on the sunny side of the front parlor of the inn.

"Hey, woman, get out of here! I don't want to hear the same old story. Our past is bitter, so what? What do you get out of reciting that we were poverty-stricken, we starved for days, and someone killed somebody?" A woman vented, puffing a smoke.

"Then where are you from anyway? Did you just pop up out of the ground or drop from heaven all at once? We can neither deny nor throw it away. That is our past." The other woman retorted.

"So what? What do you get out of it? I don't have tomorrow. My past is bitter. My future is pitch-dark and so I don't want to think about it. We all are pathetic prostitutes. Didn't you know that?"

That was true. These women in the dark had no past. They threw it away as it was aching and bitter. They did not have futures either because they didn't exist. Therefore, they often serenaded plaintively, "Please do not ask about my past..."

Those who lost their past do not want to think about their future either, because the future was a headache that drove them crazy.

They had only the present. In other words, they had neither remorse nor hope in life.

Even with the present, their concern was something tangible and visible. The invisible or the intangible became a lie to them. Therefore, even with the present, they were thoroughly calculative, self-centered and narcissistic.

To them altruism or self-sacrifice was an abhorrent lie. What made them so miserable? Who threw them into this satanic den? How much longer should they be left abandoned in that den?

Those who missed the light would eventually give up the light. They became so lazy that they wouldn't lift even their own fingers for their meals. Someone had to feed them.

They can't stand a little bit of discomfort. They can't wait for anything profitable. They should get it right away. They speak out whenever they want without hesitation. They openly seek pleasure, and when left alone, they are seized in sorrows and lamentation. Addicted to the wine and smoke, they are slowly dying, wailing a ballade of nihilism.

Pitifully Jean was unknowingly assimilating her way of life to that of those women. Their intolerant attitude of toying with Jean accelerated her propensity for following their suit.

One day, a woman in nude tugged her into her room, and Jean, stunned at the sight, broke away from her which sent other women in the house into a roar of laughter. Jean stopped running and turned around to laugh together with them. Jean was unusually quick to adapt herself to new surroundings.

Jean began conversing with these women. Soon she prattled with them fluently, calling 'sister' to any two or three-year senior and 'aunt' to married women. Tongues are powerful in forming up and acknowledging one's personality and character. Jean was rapidly changing to fit in searching for the dark mire of ruin in the broad daylight.

Among these women, there was always an exception like Kilja. Kilja didn't live in the inn, but she answered the call, standing by at the 'Sing Sing club' as a call girl. She had a shanty that she bought while running the scavenger soup vender business.

A young minister came and built a tent church nearby her shanty. At first, her youngest eight-year old brother was taken to the church along with other neighboring children. Then her twelve-year old brother joined them. Some time later, the eldest brother joined them as well. All three brothers went to church.

One day, the young minister visited them at home and found their father on his sick bed.

"What's wrong with you, father?" Minister asked.

"I have been bed-ridden for years. Since the youngest one's mother passed away upon his birth, I have never been out in the sun," he answered.

"Have you been to a hospital?"

"What hospital? We couldn't afford that. I am just waiting for the time to die."

"What do you mean by that, father? You should gather yourself and live long. I noticed you have many things to do. Your eldest son is only in the ninth grade."

"How nice it would be if I could live that long? However, as you see, it is too late for me."

Father turned aside, rubbing his eyes. The minister prayed awhile on his knees and then,

"Life or death is a matter up to God. Our Lord raised the dead. He is alive. He is omnipotent. Please open your heart and receive Him. Let's pray together. He said, 'Seek, and you will find, ask and it will be given to you.'"

The father, turning around, asked,

"Is it true? Would he heal a useless one like me?"

"Of course He would," the minister answered and continued, "If you find out why he came to this world in flesh, and why he crucified himself on the cross, and if you believe in Him, He will come to you and heal you without fail."

"But how can I find Him and how can I believe in Him?" Father asked.

"That's why our Heavenly Father sent me here to see you today. He came to this world to save us all from death. He crucified himself on the cross to heal you so that you may declare the praises of Him who called you out of darkness into His wonderful light. You have been in the darkness but now you are in His wonderful light. Do you believe it?"

"Yes, I will if I am healed."

"You will be healed if you ask Him to heal. You are already healed. Let us pray together."

Minister opened the Bible and read from the book of Mark, Chapter 5:25-34:

'And a woman was there who had been subject to bleeding for twelve years. She had suffered a great deal under the care of many doctors and had spent all she had, yet instead of getting better she grew worse.

When she heard about Jesus, she came up behind him in the crowd and touched his cloak, because she thought, 'if I just touch his clothes, I will be healed.' Immediately her bleeding stopped and she felt in her body that she was freed from her suffering. At once Jesus realized that power had gone out from him. He turned around in the crowd and asked, 'Who touched my clothes?' 'You see the people crowding against you,' his disciples answered, 'and yet you can ask, who touched me?'

But Jesus kept looking around to see who had done it. The woman, knowing what had happened to her, came and fell at his feet and, trembling with fear, told him the whole truth. He said to her,

'Daughter, your faith has healed you. Go in peace and be freed from your suffering.'

From that day on, the minister visited and prayed for the father everyday. One day, the father rose from his sick bed and declared,

---

"Praise the Lord, minister. I am healed! Each time you are here, my heart pounds hard and I go strong. My eyes are brightened and

I can see the blue sky now. As you prayed, He healed me, and I got the light back. Now I am in the light."

Father came to church with his three sons. The dismal shroud at home was lifted and the entire house was shone bright in His light. He was not only an attendant to the church but also a servant to the House of the Lord. The church congregation started praying for a job for the father.

Kilja who had degenerated to a call girl from a scavenger soup vender had been leading a miserable life with a guilty conscience, cheating on her family. When her father rose from his prolonged illness and became a Christian, she was exhausted from her dark double life.

Once the light shone upon her, she couldn't stand the darkness anymore. She might have been hanging on to a thin line; her filial duty towards her father coupled with her sisterly love toward her brothers that kept her from being thrown into the mire of ruin. Though she had been behind the light, she did not desert the light. Our good God will not break a bruised reed and will not snuff out a smoldering wick.

Kilja came to church to see the young minister, and confessed,

"Minister, I am a sinner."

"Sister, I am a sinner, too. We are all sinners."

"But can a sinner like me be forgiven?"

"Our good God heard your confession. He is pleased to forgive you."

"Do you mean that I am forgiven of all my grave sins?"

"Yes, sister. Look at the cross. Look at our Jesus Christ who shed blood to pay for all the sins you committed." Then, the minister read to her scriptures,

"But if we walk in the light, as he is in the light, we have fellowship with one another, and the blood of Jesus, his Son, purifies us from all sin. If we claim to be without sin, we deceive ourselves and the truth is not in us. If we confess our sins, he is faithful and just and will forgive us our sins and purify us from all unrighteousness.

If we claim we have not sinned, we make him out to be a liar and his word has no place in our lives."

He reaffirmed, saying,

"Sister, I am telling you again that our good God heard your confession. All your sins are forgiven. Believe it."

Kilja went up to the prayer house on Samgaksan and there, she went on fasting for days and nights. When she returned home, her entire family became born again Christians and their house turned into the Kingdom of God.

Kilja had been dealing Yankee goods for almost a year. She had outlets both in south and east gate markets. Her business was getting fairly settled. The young minister had found a job for her father as a mechanic assistant at a transit company. The eldest son now a senior in high school planned to study law to become a judge or prosecutor.

Kilja had a good reason why she chose the Yankee goods business. She was familiar with Yankee goods and she had secured a source to purchase from. However, her primary purpose was to testify how Jesus saved her and her family and to introduce Jesus Christ to those victims wandering in the darkness.

She demonstrated to them what a blessed living she and her family had, and witnessed how Jesus worked miracles for her and her family. She simply wanted to share the love, joy and hope with every one of them. In response to her testimony, most of those women gave her the cold shoulder while others openly resented her, calling her names. Nevertheless she never stopped witnessing throughout the seasons with great patience.

When Kilja first met Jean at the Happy Inn, Jean was hopelessly turned pitch-black wallowing in the darkness. She was deeply indulged in the sweet seduction of sensual pleasures. She waited for the right time to change the briquettes, and when the time arrived, she set all her organs in motion and stretched her fanciful pectoral fins to indulge in carnal pleasure, cruising through the dark waters of debauchery.

"Did you say your name is Jean?" Kilja asked.

"Yes, that's my name," Jean answered.

"To be on the right track at such a young age can never be overemphasized. It is the very first thing you need to have. There is only one right track in life. That is Jesus Christ. I'll ask the landlady to send you to church every Sunday," Kilja suggested.

"You are asking me to go to church?" Disinterested, Jean stood up.

"Yes, I am serious. You will listen to God's words and you will meet good people at church."

"Oh, that stuff! I did more than enough. Do you want to know something? The communist murdered my mother and father. And my only sister was killed in an air-raid. They are all gone. According to the ladies in this house, that church stuff is all a lie and I agree with them. Besides, I have no time to waste on such matters. Don't bother." Jean then left.

Kilja's heart was sore watching Jean running away. Kilja simply wanted to be one of the good hands for Jean as God's words have the power to raise the living from the dead.

8.

Those after Sinful Nature

Unexpected things may happen to those women in the 'Happy inn', such as the emergence of an old boyfriend who would coercively wrestle the woman out of the house, or some family emergency that forced the occupant to vacate the room overnight.

When a vacancy occurred, the landlady would contact the applicants on the list of reservations on a first come first serve basis and the vacancy was immediately filled. Jean was assigned to clean up the vacant rooms and make it ready for the new host.

As spring breezed in, Jean's mind became adrift. She was still captivated and entranced in thought from what she peeped in at the furnace last night. The landlady and the maid were busy in the inner room ripping off curtains out of a bolt of woolen cloth to change all the curtains in the house with a fresh spring color.

The maid shouted at Jean who was cleaning the vacant room.

"Jean, is it almost ready? The new comer just called saying she is coming now."

"Yes, ma'am. I am working. It will be ready in a minute." She was setting the bed, dressing table, and wardrobe in order, when someone walked in, greeting,

"Is anybody home?" A young man entered the inn with a young woman. It was a familiar voice. Jean turned her head toward the entrance, and then, in a flash her stomach turned completely upside down,

"Oppa. Isn't this Soo, oppa?" Jean screamed and then flinched a second at the sight of a woman, when Soo dashed at Jean with upturned eyes, shouting,

"Jean! Aren't you Jean? Oh my!" He jumped upon her and embraced her tight, tugging her head backward twice to take a closer look. They were stuck together for awhile, and then, Soo raised his head and exclaimed,

"You were here?"

"Yes, Oppa. I have searched for you all over!" She was stamping her feet noisily.

"I did too." They were stuck again, tightening harder.

The young woman with Soo snorted at the sight and walked inside the inn. The inn maid, coming out the room, asked,

"You must be Chunja. Come on in." Showing her to the room and continued,

"What happened to your pimp? Are you alone?"

"That's the guy." The woman answered, nodding in the direction of the entrance.

Catching the sight of the two embracing tight, the maid raised hell, bombarding names,

"That harlot has gone nuts. I knew her head was over her heels. She deserves five deaths. Go stuck like that and don't ever come near me, you lousy wanton!" She led Chunja in, smacking her tongue at Jean and Soo.

Soo pulled Jean out of the inn and was urgently searching for something; scanning his eyes here and there and then he found one.

"Yes, that is it!" He hastened Jean towards it and goaded her into it. It was another inn at the corner of the street.

This way, Soo could have his way with Jean. Jean had a poisonous sting to her conscience. As the pain repeated, she was benumbed to unconsciousness and was falling into a fathomless pit.

The debauchery in the darkness had the same effect on one's life as that of wine or smoke. Satan uses it as bait to fish men with its peculiar string of 'curiosity'.

Satan first gives a poisonous sting to devour a victim.

Who ever said the first puff of smoke didn't choke but rather was soothing? Who ever said the first sip of liquor didn't sting but rather smooth your throat? It all stings at first as death enters in the darkness. It surely does. Satan repeats the sting at the vital point to hook his victims. From this point on, the victim would be dying slowly, though seemingly alive. Satan may justify itself before God, saying,

"I warned them with repeated stings of pain, but they kept inching closer, offering their lives to me. I really had no choice."

Since that day, Jean's eyes were blinded to the light and in them; imaginable lewd and cunning schemes began quickening. It is said that what you see and hear will lead to a thought, and the thought will form character. What Jean saw and heard was sensual and lascivious, and her thirst for them was daily aggravated. In the dark world, evil schemes know no end.

The following day, Soo stopped by the Happy Inn to collect his cut of the money and was planning his return back to Paju with Jean. Jean, still engrossed in last night's fantasy, was satisfied all over and was beside herself with hilarity all the way to Paju.

Her comfort was similar to that of when one finds big relief. "I am saved!" explodes from the mouth of a dope addict who is given dope having been wallowing in dying thirst for it.

Jean on closer inspection realized that Soo was much different than the Soo she knew seven years ago. He was mature and adept in handling a woman.

The bus was crowded with country venders. Among them were western-dressed women loudly chewing their gum. Soo and Jean seated themselves at the very back of the bus, Jean expressed, leaning on Soo,

"I have gone crazy because of you."

"It's the same here." Soo complacently smiled and clasped her hand. They were about the same height. Jean however looked a little taller as she was slim.

"When I made a life or death journey to your place in Paju, you were not there!"

She pinched his thigh, pouting out her lips.

"Yeah, I sold that house some time ago."

That was true. When Soo returned to Paju, he roamed about the U.S. military base and came across a married woman. They lived together for awhile. As the woman suggested, Soo sold the house and ran a prostitution business together. Then one day the woman left Soo with all the money they had. Since then, Soo had remained a pimp.

"What did you do with the money?" asked Jean.

"I just spent it. It wasn't a lot to begin with." Soo was cool and self-composed. Jean was further attracted by his manlike coolness.

As the bus jolted, they touched and rubbed each other's thighs. Soo tightened his clasp; Jean felt her heart squeezed tight.

"I went to your place, too, but your place fell within the military restricted zone."

"You did?" Jean responded with a hint of exuberance.

"Yes, I did. I took the chance of waiting for you, but in vain," Soo answered.

"By then, I was probably exhausted at the Seoul station in search of you."

Now that they were together, they would never separate again, so each party pledged as corporeal instinct dictated. It appeared that Jean was excited at the thought of being fondled in his strong arms to her heart's content.

As a matter of fact, she was gloatingly relishing on an idea that she could play out coquetries with him every night just like the women of the Happy Inn, and have fun day and night. She was drenched in sickening fanciful dreams for herself under the guise that Soo would provide anything she wanted.

The bus was crowded as it stopped to pick up more passengers at each stop. A woman vendor with a basketful of peaches was pushed in toward the back, and at a jolt she let the basket fall off on the floor.

"My peaches! They are for sale!" She yelled just as quickly as she picked the peaches back inside the basket, when Soo shouted,

"Woman, how much is the peach?"

"One hundred won for two peaches, sir," the woman answered in a sweat, picking the peaches and continued,

"Give me a minute. I am almost done." She gathered all the fallen ones, and then picked two bald ones to hand over to Soo.

Soo passed one to Jean, saying,

"This one is really pretty just like you." He took a big bite to crunch it noisily. To Jean, the way Soo crunched the peach looked sexy and manlike.

Dusk fell on the street when they arrived in Paju. Soo took Jean to a basement tearoom of a two-story building in front of a military base.

"Oppa, why on earth to a tearoom, why not your place?" She asked.

"Oh, my place is messy. It's not ready to receive a queen. Wait here. I'll be right back."

"No, it's all right with me. I will come with you and clean up the mess," she insisted.

"No, not in the least. Didn't you promise last night that you would listen to me from now on? Please wait here. I'll be right back." He left.

Soo picked up two bouquets at a flower shop and then headed to a sweets store to buy a cake and candles. He hurried back to his place.

He sprayed perfume in the room, set the bed with a bouquet on each side, and then lit the candles. He turned on the record player to sing a romantic melody and decided to blow out the candles, choosing to rather light them in front of Jean. He took a few steps back to review his work,

"Oh, I forgot the drinks!" He then hurried out to a liquor store.

In the meantime, in the smoky hall of the tearoom, Jean gave ear to a different tune being played in the hall, a mournful song 'Island Village Teacher' by Yi Mija and another heart-breaking song 'Hiding tears' by Wiki Lee, moved her to tears. She was completely sold on the melancholy lyrics.

Soo returned and proudly announced,

"I am here to escort my queen!" Spreading both arms towards Jean.

Jean threw herself into his arms, shrieking "Oppa!"

.

When they arrived at his place, he picked her up by both arms, carrying her into the room. Once inside he lighted the candles on both sides of the bed. He turned off the lights and then turned on the record player.

The love song, "You are my Love and my Life," flowed out, confessing one's love. Jean was instantly mesmerized in ecstasy. She couldn't stand her pounding heart and confessed, gathering her panting breath,

"Oppa, I love you!" Pulling him in.

"I love you, too" They exchanged their violent passion, drabbling and smearing the name of 'true love.'

On their third morning together, Soo who got up early and brought breakfast and morning coffee from the sweets store the last two days was still asleep, snoring hard. He had drank too much the previous night. The way he stretched both legs with his fat belly wide open looked ugly and disgusted Jean.

Jean's stomach uttered a croak. In cases like this, the women of the Happy Inn would badger a little, simply saying, 'I am hungry' to make their partners spring up. The men would fetch an armful to eat immediately.

At last, Jean said,

"Oppa, I am hungry." Soo did not give her a response as he kept snoring. Jean tried again,

"Honey, I am hungry." She shook him. This woke him up but he turned aside, saying,

"Let me sleep a little more," as he commenced snoring.

This upset her but she gave him another thirty minutes. This time she shook him harder and pleaded,

"Honey, I am really hungry. Please wake up!" Now this threw him into fury and he bawled,

"Don't you have your own legs, girl? Why do you play like a leech?" He stood up in a fit of anger, kicked the door open, and went out.

Jean was astounded. She wanted to gather herself and walk right out, but she had no place to go. She chewed anger and waited. Soo returned with bread and coffee, and begged,

"Jean, I am sorry. I was out of mind. Forgive me."

Jean was pacified and tears welled up in her eyes.

Soo hugged her, but all of a sudden she was scared of Soo. The women of the Happy Inn might have raised hell and kicked him out, she thought.

Soo left after breakfast. The autumn rain was soaking the earth in silence. Jean was feeling tedious. She turned on the record player. It sounded dull like soda that lost its carbonation. She turned the record off and turned the radio on. Someone was talking about politics, which she couldn't understand. She turned off the radio.

"Not everyone can be this tedious. Yet it's much better than being hectic. I will pamper myself!" She mumbled. She looked out the window. She caught roofs dripping rain into a stream. It sounded monotonous.

Lying in the bed, she talked to herself,

"All I have to do is to lie in this bed, smoking and sipping wine like those at the Happy Inn. Wait a minute. I don't have any cosmetics. I'll have him buy some for me."

She was getting tired of being alone, when someone knocked on the door, reporting,

"Chachang noodle is here, ma'am. Put out the empty bowl at the door when you have finished. I'll pick it up." A deliveryman from a Chinese restaurant was at the door. It smelled good. She picked it up, snickering,

"He is all right. He hasn't forgotten me."

For the first time in her life, she was served, sitting with both legs folded together. She slowly ate it up, appreciating chew after chew. She put out the empty bowl by the door, wondering what Soo would bring for dinner. She assumed that most likely he would ask her to dine out.

The early autumn rain chilled her. She dug into the bed, thinking,

"And I will rest enough so that I may pleasure him all night through," she giggled.

The women of the Happy Inn slept almost to noon and when they woke up, they yelled for this and that to Jean, turning into quite the merry-go-round.

She felt that she could understand them now. Now Jean had to adapt herself to a new rhythm of life. For the adaptation, she missed a few things; how to play coquetries to melt man's heart, and how to pull the string to collect the catch in time. Jean recalled the tactics in which women of the Happy Inn collected extra tips such as cigarettes, whiskey, cosmetics or electronic items, which were later sold to Kilja for cash.

Jean observed herself in the mirror and exercised a coquetry. She was immature but she thought she could mold herself into a fox through practice. Coquetry is an asset necessary for women and it could be the glamour and fragrance of refined women depending on the time and place, she thought to herself. Watching closely her own manner and motions in the mirror, she realized that she had a lot to improve.

The following day, Soo came home early with a big smile, revealing,

"Jean, I bought what you asked for last night. I bought it by the set." He laid out in front of her a Revlon cosmetic set.

"Wow, you are the best!" Jean hugged Soo, kissing his neck.

"You are a fox! Get out of here," Soo shied.

"Honey, don't. I can't live without you," she uttered. Soo really welcomed her compliments. They embraced tight. Jean thanked Soo by putting into practice what she learned and witnessed at the inn for years. She thanked those nights she had changed the briquettes.

The following afternoon, Soo returned home with an English textbook and a few stationeries. Jean, bursting into joy,

"I can't live without you. You are the best. I will study English hard so that I may catch up with you." To this, Soo grimaced and remorsefully replied,

"Jean, you are wrong. My English is broken English. I don't even know how to write. Since you are a smart girl, you will pick it up quickly."

"Okay, honey. I once learned English from an American soldier named Jack. I will dig into it and surprise you."

Learning English gave Jean something else to do at home on top of her seductive training she performed in front of the mirror.

She set her heart on learning English, but the following morning she found herself rammed against the wall. No matter how hard she tried, she couldn't figure out how to sound out the letters. She came to the conclusion that she couldn't educate herself. That night Jean aired her complaints to Soo,

"Oppa, is there any place nearby for me to learn English?"

"What did you say? You said you could study by yourself."

"Yes, I did, but I don't think I can go any further without help. I tried all day long but I couldn't figure it out. Can you please find me a place to learn English. Let me learn first and then I'll teach you, since you have no time to study."

Soo took it seriously and pondered her proposition, drawing a conclusion, he believed that it was clear that she will be getting herself into trouble with the ability to speak English; he then cleared his throat,

"There is no need for that. Ignorance is a good remedy sometimes. You promised to listen to me, didn't you?"

"Yes, but I am going to hate you if you don't let me. I am too lonely when you are not around." Jean started fussing about, twisting her hips like a child who doesn't its way.

"Alright, alright. I'll look into it. I heard there is an English class on the way to the marketplace."

"Alright. I want to take that class, Oppa." Instead of wriggling, she embraced him tight and just like that he had given in to her demands.

It was not that simple for him to allow her to take an English class, because Soo knew that once Jean started speaking English, she would look down upon him. Besides, his income as a pimp was not steady, and therefore he might have to do something else to support her classes. Though he had agreed as she pressed on, he postponed it until one late evening when Jean asked,

"Oppa. You said you would look into it, didn't you?"

"Look into what?" Soo asked, trying to play innocent.

"Don't pretend as if you didn't know. What else can it be other than the English class? You are afraid that I might run away, aren't you? Believe me I will never leave you unless you force me out. Trust me, Oppa."

Soo was instantly convinced and relieved,

"Not because I don't trust you. I have been quite busy lately, that's all."

"I trust you, Oppa. You are a man of fidelity." She hit the vital point of a gangster. Gangsters live and die under the mantra of fidelity. Integrity was the principle of their faith.

The following day, Soo came home early,

"Jean, you promised me not to run away no matter how well you speak English."

"Of course, I won't budge an inch until you force me out, I promise. Have you found out anything new?"

"Not only found it but I also registered you for it. Follow me. They have a new class starting tomorrow. They told me that a well-known instructor from Seoul will teach the class."

Jean followed him. The sky was high and blue. On both sides of the street to the marketplace were lined up with Yankee merchandise vendors. A lady at the entrance asked passerby's if they had dollars for exchange. A man was on a sewing machine embroidering nameplates and unit marks. Another man was drawing a portrait of a western-dressed lady.

A common characteristic of these vendors was that they didn't carry much merchandise on display. Some had a few necklaces and trinkets in a display case. Noticeable was the large volume of people either loitering or roaming around the marketplace.

At the entrance of the marketplace was a two-story building. At the basement of the building was a tearoom, named Milky Way. The English class was to be held in that building. Soo and Jean pushed through an unmarked door, having no sign to confirm what was conducted inside.

"Come on in." A middle-aged gentleman sat across the door.

"This is my girlfriend that I just registered for," Soo introduced Jean to the man.

"Thank you. Please come on in and have a seat." He offered a sofa on the right hand side and introduced himself,

"My name is Chang. Jean is your name, am I right?"

"Yes, that's my name," Jean answered.

"We are waiting for two more students. Originally I do tutoring, but due to increasing demand, we are forced to form a class." To this, Soo seemed a little uneasy.

"We don't want tutoring. You said you have a new class starting tomorrow," Soo protested.

"You are very right. This class starts with three students, but if new students come, we will screen extensively before we invite them to this class."

"That's all right with me. How long does it take to study Englsih?" Jean asked.

"Well, it is up to the student. Learning the basics is very important in English. Have you studied English before?"

"Yes, about seven years ago. I learned a little bit from an American soldier."

"How old are you?" The teacher asked.

"I am twenty years old. I am going to turn twenty-one in a few days," Jean answered.

"Twenty-one years old. I think you'll make a great student."

Two women entered the office desiring to be students. They looked very similar to the women of the Happy Inn. Upon seeing the women, Soo stood up hurriedly to dismiss himself,

"Jean, I am leaving," and left the office as quickly as the words uttered out of his mouth. One of the women asked the other,

"What brings that guy here?" and then facing Jean,

"Are you his friend?"

"Yes, he is my friend. Do you know him?" Jean asked.

"Oh, yes, I once had a deal with him," she answered cheekily.

The teacher Chang opened his mouth,

"Let's get the ball rolling. Since you are all beginners, we are going to start with the basic. Remember that we are studying the living English, when I say living, I mean how to converse with others in English." One of the women cut in,

"Of course, we are not here to learn about Shakespeare. We are here to learn how to write such things like, 'Honey, I love you.'" The other woman interrupted, swearing,

"You bitch. Shut your mouth, when teacher speaks." The teacher continued,

"Listening is not enough with English. You have to talk a lot and scribble a lot."

The first woman asked,

"The basic English you just talked about. How long does it take to read and write it?"

"Well, it depends how hard you study day and night. It takes three to six months to cover the basics, I would say.' The woman continued, giggling,

"How can anyone study English day and night? We should work at night to make money."

"Well, when I said day and night, I meant you study at my class during the day and at night you practice and rehearse what you studied in class. That way you study day and night. Otherwise, your English will never improve."

The woman continued,

"I think you are right. Suppose we finish the basic course in three months. At the end of the course, should we be able to write in English, 'Honey, the day after tomorrow is my father's birthday. Can you buy me two cartons of camel cigarettes tomorrow for his birthday present?'"

"Yes, you may be able to do so. Remember that through your willingness you are in control of how much you learn."

"Of course, I know we should study day and night."

"If you work hard, you may be able to answer yes or no to any question in English."

"Well, that's good enough. Let's get it on!" The second woman urged. These girls seemed excited at the thought of reaping even before planting.

In this way, these three women started learning English formally for the first time in their lives. The English teacher printed out daily textual sheets for his students. In the first month, they mastered four different characters of the alphabet and phonetic symbols. Jean's interest in the English language increased as the days went by.

She also picked up new techniques and coquetries from the women in her class.

These women took sensual pleasure and technique as an art. They would say,

"Art is art. It's a human creation. You must be creative to become a good artist. A good artist keeps on digging into the human nature. I mean that sweet sinful human nature."

To Jean, this art of seduction sounded like a fantasy and played like a juggler.

It was a flame. Once the flame was snuffed out, she felt chill and hunger. The longer she met the acquaintance of these women the more she shielded the fire from being extinguished. Who called the dark world a fathomless pit?

From what Jean learned from these women, Soo turned out to be very green behind the ears in bedroom activities. She often wondered how another man could pleasure her, fueled by the talks of men who were great in bed that these women openly talked about so often. Jean slowly started opening another door of carnal sin as she associated with the women in her class.

One evening, Soo returned home late and declared,

"Jean, I have to go now."

"At this late hour? To where?"

"I have an urgent business matter to take care of."

"But why at night? Are you going to leave me alone tonight?"

"I have no choice, Jean. I have to go way down to Pyungtak."

"Can't you tell me why you must leave at such a late hour and travel that far down?"

"When I come back, I will explain in detail," Soo pouted regretting that he even brought it up. He continued,

"I am doing this simply for you. I'll do just one big bang!" and he hurried out.

Jean was finally resigned to sleep at the break of dawn, tossing about on her bed all night through, when Soo returned totally exhausted,

"Are you still sleeping?" Soo shook her up. Jean mumbled with her eyes closed,

"I am just about to sleep. Come into bed." She pulled him in.

"Jean, look at this. I did one score as I told you." He pulled a bundle of cash out of his pocket.

At the sight of money, Jean opened her eyes out of delirium.

"What kind of money is this? Did you say you did one score? Did you rob anyone?" She sat up and asked in astonishment.

"No, I didn't rob anyone I just unscrewed..."

"Unscrewed? What did you unscrew?" She held the bundle of money tight.

"I unscrewed gasoline out of the military pipeline way down at Pyungtak."

"What is the pipeline, Oppa?" She released the money bundle.

"I am talking about the oil pipeline to the U.S. military base. I was almost killed." Soo laid flat on his back, completely exhausted of energy.

Jean had never seen such a large bundle of cash before. She ironed out each piece of bill with her fingers and put them in a drawer. Soo was already snoring.

Jean went out for bread and coffee with a new air of confidence. She felt she was apart of wealthy elite.

She talked to herself,

"With this money, I would be able to have anything I want, such as rings, gold watches, necklaces, pretty dresses and shoes. Then I'll be fully equipped like the women in my class." Suddenly she came to think highly of Soo,

"Surely, Soo is a brave and smart man. Soo went all the way down south to Pyungtak. He guaranteed no one would dare come all the way up here to catch him. He also said that gasoline flowed like a river through the pipeline, so who would know if a small amount went missing? I agree that no one would be able to detect this smart man way up here. He is such a smart guy!"

She knew it was just a matter of time before she could spoil herself with material things that the women in her class adorned, now that she access to money. Afterall, Soo did say he did it simply for her. She had it in her mind that to make it even with Soo all she had to do was to make him feel good and happy one or another. Her morals were looping down in a funnel headed to despair.

When she returned home with bread and coffee, Soo was still sound asleep. Jean picked up her school bag and headed for class. Entering the classroom, she greeted,

"Hello teacher. How are you this morning?"

"I am fine, thank you, and you?" Teacher replied.

"I am fine, too. Thank you." Jean answered sprightly.

Her classmate jeered at Jean, ridiculing,

"What's wrong with you, Jean? Have you eaten something wrong this morning?"

"No, not in the least. I ate only donuts and coffee." Jean answered triumphantly.

The teacher interrupted,

"Jean is doing fine. She has no other person to practice her English with," he encouraged her.

"Thank you again, teacher."

Jean was talented in English. She practiced what she learned to herself in the mirror. Outside of the classroom, she studied the textbook Soo had bought for her, lending her an advantage over the other women. Therefore she was always praised and encouraged in the class by her teacher.

When she came home with hamburgers for lunch from school, Soo was still asleep. She pulled the drawer to verify the money and talked to herself,

"Wait a minute. What I need immediately are a necklace, earrings and a ring. If I get the earrings, where shall I get my ears pierced? I also need a handbag and a pair of shoes. Of course I need a good dress to go along with them. I will badger him rough tonight. He said he made the score all for me. I know he would listen to me if I squeeze him hard," she giggled.

The following morning, Soo pulled Jean out of house in a hurry, jollying,

"Ear piercing? It can be done at any jewelry store. You don't have to go to a doctor for that. I will take you to a jewelry store to pierce your ears now. While you are there, you may pick up anything you want, okay?"

Jean was exhilarated as they were on their way to the jewelry store hand in hand. Soo also had an unwavering air of confidence as he acted more manlike and was bragging exultantly,

"From now on, we should be classier. While we are out, let's check out the price of electric stoves, toasters and coffee makers. How do you like them?"

"I heard about electric stoves and toasters, but I have never heard of a coffee maker. What is it, Oppa?"

"Well, let's talk about electric appliances first. There are many kinds of stoves and toasters. Let's take a look at all the different kinds. You have to learn how to use them. Otherwise, you may end up with burnt toast and that ruins the machine. About the coffee maker, it is a coffee machine to brew coffee. Do you remember the coffee you had in a cup at the tearoom?"

"Yes, I do. When we have a coffee machine at home, we wouldn't have to come out to get it from the coffee shop, right? How nice it would be if we had all these appliances at home! We would just put butter or jam on the bread for breakfast and eat it with homemade coffee. It is a thrill just to imagine it!"

"We can also fry eggs and cook anything we want on the electric stove," Soo added, but Jean repelled the idea disgustingly,

"No, I don't want to learn to cook yet. We are still on our honeymoon. For the first year I don't want to do any culinary work. Besides, I am fully occupied with facial makeup every morning and English class you know," Jean protested.

"I got it. Whatever you say. You are the boss."

They walked inside the jewelry store at the intersection of the street. For the first time in her life, Jean was shown to the glittering showcase of jewels. Every single item was brilliantly shiny. She was so fascinated that she didn't know what was what. Everything was just fantastic and she wanted to possess them all.

The storeowner cordially and nimbly led Jean to a chair and played with her earlobe for awhile, and then,

"A little pinch!" So saying, he pierced it with a click,

"Did it hurt you?" It was just a matter of a second. Jean goggled her eyes and asked,

"Are you done? You didn't give me a chance to get hurt, did you?" She then turned her other ear to him.

Putting on the earrings, the man said,

"Keep these on for a few days so that the pierced ear may be healed and left open." Jean smiled and said,

"Yes, sir. I will. You are the expert!" This time, Soo joined to admire her,

"You look nice. You are strikingly gorgeous with them on."

"Thank you, oppa. I am truly happy." She played the fox, exciting Soo.

"While you are here, why don't you pick a ring and a necklace?" Soo offered, leading her to the showcase.

"Really? You are the best! How can I live without you?" She followed Soo.

"Of course, I am serious. Pick anything you want." Captivated, Jean felt as if she was walking on a cloud.

"I like this one and that one," Jean announced, pointing at a ring and a necklace.

The owner picked up the two items quickly and put them on Jean's finger and neck, and drew the mirror closer to her. Jean shone bright, looking at herself in the mirror.

"Oppa, Do I look pretty?"

"Oh, yes, you are gorgeous. I love you." Now facing to the owner,

"How much is it altogether?" he asked the owner.

"The ring is a little too big for her finger. I'll make it ready by tomorrow."

Soo ran short of money to pay off all three items, he countered,

"I'll pay off the balance tomorrow when I pick up the ring"

"No problem, Mister," the owner replied.

Jean walked out of the store as a different person. She believed money was everything. She had fallen victim to the lust of money and the material world.

"Oppa, thank you for the gifts, and I'm sorry you ran short on money."

"Don't worry about it, Jean. I am your oppa, right? I am always ready to give you anything you need, okay?" They were extremely happy that day.

When Jean entered her English class, everyone in attendance was shocked at her new appearance.

"Jean, you look glamorous today. Have you pulled a big score somewhere?" asked her classmate.

"Yes, I did. Does it hurt your stomach?" Jean bragged.

"I beg your pardon! You'd better watch your mouth, you dirty little one!" She was on the cusp of attacking Jean.

"Hey, look. I am no longer inferior to you. Except that you are three to four years older than me. Now I have everything you have." Jean was adamant in her stance and ready to counterattack.

The woman started back, saying,

"I agree. That girl had some kind of wind, either good or bad," returning back to her seat. Jean was now on equal footing with these women. If only she was proficient in English, she believed there would not be another woman that she would not be on par with.

One late evening, Soo came home late.

"Jean, I have to go down to Pyungtak tonight again. I'll be back tomorrow morning. Lock up inside and sleep tight."

"I will. You are not going alone, are you?"

"Of course not, a few other boys are coming with me. There are others that are waiting for us down there, as well. Don't worry about me."

Jean locked the door and studied her English textbook that Soo had bought for her. Now that she mastered the phonetic letters, she could read most words, and she also learned how to consult with the dictionary.

The other women in her class were learning the sounds of the letter and working on the printed worksheets. Jean was moved up to an advanced class and even in the advanced class; she distinguished herself as a quick learner.

Everyday Jean picked up new words that she had run across and added them to her vocabulary bank. She also memorized entire pages, sentence by sentence, of the book Soo bought her. The teacher made special tapes for Jean to study at home and she completely memorized them. No one could beat her in the class.

Jean never revealed to Soo her deep interest in English and her progress made in class. She was afraid that he might not permit her to attend class, if he knew how much she had learned.

What frightened her the most was how Soo looked smaller to her everyday, and she was extremely cautious not to reveal such feelings toward him. She wanted to keep things rolling as they were for she was in a comfortable state.

She was stepping up her zeal in studying English. She was highly recognized and praised by others in the class for her natural knack for English. Jean was engrossed in her popularity behind Soo's back. However, her popularity was always accompanied with deception.

The following morning at dawn, Soo returned home, burnt out. When he jerked out a bundle of cash, Jean hugged him, expressing,

"Honey, I love you," yet it was no longer from a burning heart as before. It became just a matter of formality. Nevertheless, Jean was grateful to Soo for everything he did for her, but she couldn't deny the fact that Soo looked belittled as days went by.

In these days, even the English teacher admired her,

"You do know you are true eye-catcher, don't you Jean? You are much more beautiful than Miss Korea. I have come across many female students, but I have never seen such a beauty like you. If you add English to that striking beauty, you will be really something, something fantastic!" Other times he would send a serpentine glare at Jean.

Those women, who were so haughty in the beginning, now seemed frigid before Jean. She was so popular in the class that no one dared to compete with her. Jean's pronunciation and her command of holding a conversation were unique and outstanding among other students. When Jean returned home from her afternoon class, Soo was sound asleep.

"Oppa. It's time to wake up. It's already three o'clock in the afternoon."

"Okay." Soo extended both arms with eyes still shut. He wanted to be hugged.

Jean closed her eyes and hugged him.

"I love you, Oppa."

"I love you too, my queen. I am your slave." He stammered over a few words.

Both closed their eyes and hugged.

Soo ate the hamburger and coffee Jean brought, and revealed,

"I was almost killed yesterday when the gasoline jutted out and flushed out on my face like thunder." Stunned at his remarks, Jean exclaimed,

"You got be careful, Oppa! You were almost engulfed with the disaster!"

"It wasn't my fault. This stupid guy put the pipe in the wrong way."

"What happened, then?"

"What happened? What do you think happened? The gasoline flooded all over."

"Wouldn't someone track you down, because you left large amounts of evidence there?"

"Well, how can anyone come all the way up here? Don't worry too much. There are times we have to risk our lives to survive, you know."

"I am afraid that you will get hurt."

"Don't worry. I'll be all right. Let's get out of here to pick up the things, ok?"

Soo stood up to get out of bed.

When Jean came out with Soo, she didn't wear makeup in fear that she may attract men's attention, which could irritate Soo with their sidelong glances. She experienced quite often that when she came out with a western dress and makeup on, passersby would cast awe-stricken glares at her, captivated by her beauty and glamour.

Noticing Jean coming out with casual attire on, Soo yelled at her,

"Hey, this is our first date in awhile. Look at your apparel."

"Oppa, we have a date everyday, don't we? Why are you so particular today?"

"Honey, have you forgotten what is today?"

"Today?" She fumbled a minute and then, sparkling her eyes,

"Yes, Oppa. Today is my birthday! How did you remember my birthday?"

"Well, we celebrated your birthday at the Seoul Station, didn't we?"

"Yes, we did. We did with all the other kids there. I can't believe you remembered my birthday! Wait here, I'll be right back." She ran back to her room. She hurriedly put her makeup on and put on her best dress and high-heels.

At the sight of her spruced up, Soo exclaimed,

"Wow..." He was so excited that he lost his words.

"What's the matter with you, Oppa?" These are things that you bought for me. Isn't this what you wanted me to be," she pouted.

When she wore high heels, Soo was terribly shortened in height. Compared to Jean, Soo looked like an errand boy. He was a little discomforted, but who asked for this? When they were out on the street, people glanced at her and surprised such a beauty existed. Equally shocking to them was the man whose arm she was wrapped around.

American soldiers on the street openly hailed their cheers towards her. A U.S. Army jeep passed by and soldiers in the jeep hoorayed and whistled to her.

Entering the alley to the market place, Soo finally suggested,

"Jean, let's stop by the tearoom. I am not comfortable."

"All right, oppa. I am a little thirty, too." They entered the Milky Way tearoom.

In the smoky packed tearoom, vacant seats were not readily visible, especially on a Friday evening. The tearoom lady came out to lead them deep inside to a back seat. As they walked through the tearoom led by the lady, those in their tables raised their eyes in a stunned look at Jean. Cigarettes fell off the lips of gasping mouths at the sight of her beauty. Many of the male patrons were accompanied with western dressed ladies that sat across the table.

An American soldier had his gaze fixated on Jean when she first entered the tearoom with Soo, and when she passed him by, he stood up suddenly and acclaimed at her,

"You are wonderful! You are gorgeous!" A girl across the table stood up and shouted at the soldier, calling him names and quitted the room. The soldier, coming back to his senses, put his hand on his forehead, apologizing,

"I am sorry. I am sorry. I thought my girlfriend was walking in the room! She reminded me of my girlfriend in America!" and followed after the ranting girl.

So far, Soo could handle the glances and admirations directed to his girlfriend from strangers, until Jean seated herself, facing the door and the English teacher was coming down the stairs with a lady having finished teaching his night class.

When he saw Jean in the back, he cracked a big smile and approached her, speaking in English as usual.

"Hello Jean. How are you?" He approached extending his hand. Jean was a little hesitant and extended her hand to shake, responding,

"I am fine. Thank you and yourself?"

"I am fine, as well. I am glad to see you here."

"I am glad, too. Thank you." She responded.

Soo knew intuitively that this fluent exchange of formalities couldn't have been done over one or two bouts of practice.

This brazen faced teacher signaled to the lady he came with to 'wait a minute' and then sat across Soo to start praising Jean.

"In four months, Jean turned out to be the best student in our class."

Jean across the table batted her eyes at the teacher repeatedly, signaling him to stop, yet the teacher kept on indifferently,

"I have been teaching English for the last ten years, but I had never come across such a quick learner as Jean. We call her a genius. She is not learning English with just her head. She is studying the living English with her heart and lips. She is great!"

Soo's face blushed in red and stood abruptly, repelling,

"If that's the case, she is no longer needed to come to class!"

Stunned at his remarks, the teacher stood, expostulating,

"Not in the least. There is no end in studying. I just wanted to convey my honest appraisal on her progress. If she keeps on this way, her success in life is in the bag. She shouldn't discontinue the class. It's not right to keep a jewel buried in the ground."

To this, Soo resolutely declared,

"Jean quits the class starting tomorrow!" Now facing Jean,

"Get up, Jean. Let's get out of here!" He pulled her out of the tearoom.

As Jean was forcibly pulled out of the tearoom, she resisted,

"Oppa, what's the matter?" Soo perked up, gasping,

"Don't you know why, or are you stupid?" Soo growled back.

Jean pulled her hands free and shrieked,

"What's wrong with you, brother? Why are you so mean to me?"

This infuriated Soo to the top of his hair, and he came to bully her with a menacing look, shouting,

"What did you say? Repeat. Do you want to get hit?" He clenched his fist and was about to hit her. Jean was shocked, she shrilled,

"Oppa, what is this all about?" she shrieked again,

"Are you crazy?"

Then a man passing by halted and approached Soo, warning in gentle tone,

"Hey, young man. Talk. You can talk, can't you?"

He grabbed Soo's clenched fist and stopped him from striking Jean.

Soo lost control of his anger and threw a punch at the man, yelling,

"Do you want to die? Otherwise get out of here!"

The man was nimble and agile and swiftly ducked and caught the punch, grasping Soo's hand and bawled,

"I warn you to be quiet, unless you want to die," the man threatened. With both hands in the man's grip, Soo jerked his head that headed the man's jaw violently.

The man released Soo's hands, and smoothed his jaw. The man was no longer amused, spitting on the ground,

"That's too bad!" He picked Soo and flung him down to the ground. He followed up with a barrage of punches and kicks, until Soo was stretched out nearly incognizant.

Jean was frightened and stopped the man, pleading,

"Please don't. Stop it please!" The man spit on the ground, venting on,

"This little rat! He must want to die. He had better know who I am." The bully turned around shaking off both hands to symbolize that he was finished. Then he turned around again and approached Jean,

"I didn't hit him first. He did it. Bad luck!" He then walked away. This man was a notorious gang-leader who had the entire frontline territories under his control.

Shortly thereafter, Soo came back to his senses and was barely able to stand. He managed to wobble back home, when the bully appeared again from nowhere. He said,

"I am a man of honor. Shakeup and stand straight, you little rat, otherwise you will be killed," he warned Soo.

Soo, who had been blinded by his rage, now recognized the man, and played a rat before a tomcat, casting downward.

"Do you know who I am? Don't you know the 'Raw Persimmon?' That's me."

"Yes, I do know you, big brother," Soo answered meekly.

The man suddenly turned gentle and kind,

"Which way is it to your place? If you can't walk, I will carry you on my back." He turned his back toward Soo and squatted.

"That's alright. I can walk." Soo wobbled.

"Why don't you lean on me?" He helped Soo to the house. When they arrived at Soo's place, Raw Persimmon questioned,

"Is this your place?" He asked and facing Jean,

"Do you stay with him?"

Jean didn't answer him, and rather asked Soo,

"Are you all right, oppa?" She helped Soo to their room. The man looked back at Jean with a look of bewilderment and left, shaking his head.

As Soo lay on the bed, Jean went to the drug store. She cleansed the wounds, bandaged with medication, and gave Soo medicine to swallow. Through a swollen mouth, Soo mumbled to Jean,

"I hope you wouldn't ask to continue to take the English class again. I let you go there because you said you were lonely. I didn't send you there to make Miss Korea out of you."

"Who said that learning English makes you into Miss Korea? You were heated up in anger for no reason today," Jean whimpered.

"For now, no more English class, all right? I also hate your makeup and I don't want you dressed up like this ever again. I want you to stay inside. You are not allowed to be an inch outside! You got it?" Soo yelled.

Jean was at a lost for words. She thought it was not a proper time to settle this matter. She shut her mouth and asked herself,

'Can you handle this? Yes, I can. His anger will be melted away like ice cream on a hot day. He is a simple man. I can always make him agree and have him suit me perfectly. Why not? I'll get what I want at any cost.' Her burning desire to possess intensified.

9.

Gold Digger

A snowstorm swept through the town. Another cold front was approaching with Siberian sleet ahead. In the nipping cold, people scurried home on the frozen streets, chased by a wintry night falling close behind. It looked as if the unabated nipping gale was to swirl in the night-sky throughout the night.

Three days ago, Soo kissed and bid farewell to Jean,

"I'll be back first thing in the morning," and left home late that evening.

In the first night that Soo had left, Jean, for the first time, felt better without him. As she was getting tired of Soo's clumsy bedside manners, compared with those she stealthily observed at the Happy Inn.

On the second day, she wondered if anything serious had happened to Soo, and she came to think of her English teacher, though a bit too old for her, would do a better job at night, judging by his broad jokes and naked approach to her with sly winks lately. Besides, this man made ten times as much as Soo made, just for teaching English.

On the third day, she thought something serious happened to Soo. During her lunch break within English class, she shared funny jokes with her teacher in his office and her heart throbbed a little. When she came home, Soo was still missing. No one knew about his whereabouts. She just spent her last dollar on lunch that day.

Her room was packed with classic furniture such as a lacquered wardrobe with mother of pearls studded on, a sofa, colorful light stands, a foreign-made bed and dresser, a variety of foreign cosmetics, a radio and record player, electric stove, toaster, coffee maker and many other items of luxury, while people out in the world could not afford even a soap for washing their face.

She also had a table and a bookshelf filled with English books and a dictionary. She had almost everything she wanted. All she had to do was simply press the water tap and water gushed out. Soo was the water tap. Even with the English class that Soo was so adamantly against, she never missed a single class, and now on top of it she was about to take a music and dance class in a few days.

Where could he be? Fretting herself, she, for the first time wondered if he ran away from her as he was fed up with her pomp. If that is the case, he could have told her, or at least left a note before he made his run. Or something might have happened to him! Then she was obsessing over delusions. Could it be that he was in a fight and got killed. Or he might be hospitalized with a serious injury.

Jean throughout her life witnessed many strange deaths. She saw swollen bodies beaten to death. She saw men blown up and busted into pieces in midair. She saw people howling murderously and the next minute falling like flapped flies.

Many times in the past, she regained her strength simply at the thought of still being alive. What's the meaning of life? To her, it is to breathe, to possess, and to enjoy with song and dance, and thus to satisfy the craving peripheral nerve cells.

Once filled and then emptied, it becomes desired; hence her life became an addiction. For those in the darkness who turned away from the light, the meaning of life was nothing but what they saw and heard in the darkness.

She was now resorted to sell an item in her room for food. It was difficult for Jean to part with anything in her room as all the items were indispensable to her. She asked and answered herself,

'What about the recorder? I can't sell it because I can't play my tapes without it. What about the record player? I can't. It sweetens my ears with sad songs when I am lonely. Then what shall I sell? How about the rings and necklaces? No, I can't. They should be always on me to illuminate my glamour. They are truly indispensable. Then what? Soo's Parker jacket? No way, it's going to be the first item he will look for when he gets back. Well, then this must be the one!'

It flashed in her mind. It was the Zenith radio. It was more of a decorative item for both Jean and Soo. When turned on, it raised hell with international and domestic noise, which she was not interested in, and sometimes it trumpeted all nonsensical rambling such as a housewives corner and all other humbugs through the Christian broadcasting.

She believed she made a right choice. She was very hungry as she had been surviving off of dry foods and sweets in the pantry room. She picked her overcoat off the coat hanger and was about to leave the room, when someone entered the house, calling,

"Excuse me. Is anyone home?" It was a familiar voice.

"Who is it?" Jean asked, opening the door. She was surprised at the bulky figure at the door. She flinched back and exclaimed,

"Who the hell is this? What do you want?" It was a man, the same man that almost smashed Soo on the street sometime ago and called himself "Raw Persimmon."

"It's severely cold outside. May I come in?" He walked in with no hesitation as if he were invited and visiting his peers. He already entered the room, steaming clenched hands with his mouth blowing warmth. Once again he blamed the weather, squeezing and blowing both hands,

"It's nipping cold, isn't it?" and stood at the corner.

Jean was forced to offer,

"Have a seat," pointing at the sofa. He took the seat, spitting words with a searching glance around the room,

"Better than I thought! You have everything, not a single item missing. That's why the boy did that! Now I see what made him do so." He pulled a cigarette and lighted.

Jean got goose skinned, and repeated to herself the man's last statement, 'Now I see what made him do so.' He must have news about Soo.

Jean asked offhand,

"If you know anything about Soo..."

"Of course, I do. Otherwise, what do you think I came all the way through this freezing cold for and now face a beautiful girl like you?" The words slithered out of his lips. Jean, in a pressing tone, asked again,

"Where is Soo, and what is he doing?"

"So, you don't know where he is, and you want to know it! I feel for you." He was slow and dignified.

Jean urged him to spit out the information in an urgent tone,

"Please tell me! Where is he and what is he doing?"

Finally the man narrowed his eyes and in a ridiculing tone, he mocked,

"Where he is… she wants to know…. Where else but in jail?"

He puffed it out, puffing at a cigarette.

"What? What did you say? He is in jail?" She was stunned at the words.

"Yeah, he is in jail. He deserves it. Yes, he is in prison."

Jean was shocked and drew closer to peer into his eyes, and pleaded.

"Mister, please tell me why, why was he put in jail. What did he do wrong?"

"You don't know what he did!" He was still in a derisive tone.

"No, I don't know. Please tell me why he is in jail." Jean was growing impatient.

The man bowed his head down and closed his mouth. Then slowly raising his head to Jean, he cleared his throat and said,

"I am not married. I am not a married man." His answer was totally irrelevant to her question, but he was serious. He narrowed his eyes again and kept on,

"You are a very pretty girl. I am not a married man. I am single." He kept his stare on Jean.

"What do you mean by that? It doesn't matter whether you are married or not. I just want to know why Soo is in prison. Please tell me why?" She pleaded again.

"Why he is in prison and what he did wrong, I'll tell you, but before I answer your question, I want to clarify my marital status. I am not a married man and I am single." Then he stood up before Jean, and placed his hand on her shoulder.

The moment she felt his hefty hand on her shoulder, an awkward sensation electrified down to her knees. Jean closed her eyes. Then an idea flashed in her mind,

asking to herself,

'Jean, you are almost twenty-two years old. You are no longer a girl. You are a woman. Are you going to be swallowed or to swallow? Of course, you can, can't you?' Then she mustered strength and asked,

"All right. You are single. How shall I call you then?"

At this, he cracked a big smile and gloatingly drawled out,

"Oh, I have been waiting for this moment. You may call me anyway you want, my lovely one. How about Oppa?"

"Certainly. I will call you Oppa. Now tell me why Soo is behind bars."

Raw Persimmon turned soft and mushy suddenly, and said,

"Yes, things are squared away the way I have wanted for so long. We make a good match, don't we?" He seemed very much relieved and continued,

"He was caught stealing gasoline!"

"Gasoline?" She had suspected so. She then asked herself immediately what she should do next. Then Raw Persimmon cleared his voice again and added,

"If that was all there was to it, how nice it would be! Unfortunately, he killed a man, as well. He is a proven murderer!"

Stunned at his words, Jean was speechless and almost fell forward. Raw persimmon caught her quickly and soothed, tapping her shoulder,

"Pretty one. You know nothing. That's the game of life. It happens as often as three meals we have each day. I am sorry to tell you that he will get a life's sentence and die behind bars."

Jean was lost in though at his announcement, but somehow in the depths of her heart, she felt relieved. She was overwhelmed with a strong pity towards Soo. Jean burst into tears.

She was crying out for some time when she felt warmth in someone's arms. Raw Persimmon embraced her tight. The surge of maddening sorrow, which had to do with her own self-pity than from the loss of Soo, seemed to have subsided on its own.

Her empty stomach croaked. With her face down, she conversed with herself,

'I have to live. I have to live on alone. Yes, I'll have to live on all alone… but I don't want to give up my lifestyle. Wait a minute… this man that calls himself, Raw Persimmon, must be a big ring leader. I will grip this guy. I will hold him in my grip. How? Men love sexual immorality, debauchery, orgies, drunkenness, and above all coquetry. I'll give him what he likes. In return he will give me what I like, gold. What's wrong with being a gold digger?'

She raised her head with eyes closed. He released her, trying to caress her with both hands. Jean, pushing his hands away, whimpered plaintively still with closed eyes,

"Oppa, I am hungry!"

This sprang him up outright, and he howled in astonishment,

"You haven't had dinner yet? Oh, poor little one! Wait a second. I will fetch something for you." He kicked the door open and ran out in the nipping cold.

Jean was blank and dizzy. She gathered herself and touched her hair, rubbing her eyes. She sat at the dresser and started powdering her face, muttering,

"Life sentence? Killed a man? Die behind bars? So that's the end. The end is the end. It's a reality. I can't do anything about it. We call it an end."

Life is transient in nature. As fallen leaves are ignored and forgotten, so too are people that pass by, they become ignored and forgotten. They are not only forgotten but also they are forsaken. Life is merely a stage for a spring dream. Dream is a dream, good or bad.

Jean's old days fleeted away in her old memories; her times as a panhandler begging for food door to door, having been chased by dogs, having been bitten by a mad dog. She was often thrown onto the dusty ground and people passed by, she was simply ignored and forgotten.

Raw Persimmon came back with a deliveryman. He brought a variety of foods and whispered in more ticklish terms than Soo,

"Jean, I didn't know what you like. If you don't eat, you'll die. Forget everything and now is the time for you to eat and be pretty again, okay?" He pulled Jean by her hand towards the food.

Raw Persimmon was twice the size as Soo, yet his tone was soft like fur and tender like a marshmallow. His manner was dolefully corny and mushy. Thinking all wolves are the same, she sat at the table, inviting him slyly,

"Aren't you going to eat?"

"Oh. That's a kind offer. As a matter of fact, I haven't had the dinner yet." He was jumpy.

"Let's eat together. Come on!" She invited.

"All right." He sat across from her on the table.

"I didn't know your preference, so I just picked up whatever was available."

"I can eat anything. I am not picky with food," Jean assured him.

"That's good. Let's eat together." He pushed all the dishes under her nose.

Jean snickered in heart. Why is he here tonight? Is he here to deliver the news of Soo? She could read through his mind. She had the advantage knowing that he wanted her to love him. She pondered, he looks strong all right, but I shouldn't play loose.

"Oppa, are you going to sleep here tonight?" She flung the bait.

"Jean, where can I go in this nipping cold? Let me stay overnight here, please." The way he was fussing about was more of a tumbling bear than of a strong guy built like an ox. His playing so mellow looked so funny to her.

She learned at the Happy Inn and knew that all wolves are the same, yet she expected a tough guy like him would play a little tougher. But quite on the contrary, he acted like a fur seal, and his motions were slithery like arms of an octopus. Seeing his mannerisms, she shouldn't be sold out that easy.

"You'll find an inn or a motel out there," she feigned innocence.

"Do you really mean that?" He protested.

"Of course, I mean it. Am I a toy to you?" She then murmured,

"Though I don't expect a lifelong matrimony, still I don't want to be licked once or twice, and then kicked to the curb." She was starting to make him melt.

"Jean, do you think I am here for a toy. Frankly speaking, I have fallen in love with you since I first met you in that scuffle with Soo. I have never forgotten you ever since." He vented out. Jean playing her games, manipulating emotions, demanded,

"That's your pickup line! You can use that on anyone but not on me. I am different. Please get up and move on!" She sternly pressed him out. To this, Raw Persimmon went down on his knees and begged,

"Jean, you are totally wrong. I swear. Trust me that I am crazy about you. I gave a lot of thought to this matter. To be honest with you, I was almost about to plot against your boyfriend Soo. When I heard that he was thrown into jail... He saved me a lot of time." Suddenly Jean ran into a fit of fury, and shouted,

"Don't ever utter a word of Soo in front of me!" She warned.

"Okay, Okay. I got it. I won't say a word of him. I promise, but everything is true, it's true that I love you. I'll definitely treat you as my queen. Confessing the truth, I am here to take you." Raw Persimmon put on a serious face.

"Take me? To where?" Jean asked.

"Wherever you want to go, I'll go with you. The town of Uijungbu where I stay has a big U.S. base, too. Can you come with me?" He was serious.

Jean felt that he needed a little deeper sting to commit himself to her and changed her tone,

"Oppa. Think it twice. I am a very greedy girl. I plan to take music and dance classes. I can't drink plain water, I need black soda instead. Also I can't stand the smell of the bean and pepper paste. I live on sausage, hamburgers and other western foods. I am a very expensive girl. Can you fill me up with all of these?"

To this, Raw Persimmon coming closer to her like a cub toward her mother bears, panted rough,

"Of course. It goes without saying. I'll take full charge of it. I will make you more than twice as happier, and I will leave everything up to you. You can do whatever you want, I promise." Jean wouldn't miss this critical moment and squirmed in a motion of giving a child the breast, pronouncing,

"But you have to know that I am a gold digger. I need gold!"

"Hey. That's what I want you to be. I have gold mines all over."

"Are you serious?"

"Of course, I am serious. I swear on my name!"

Now Jean thrust herself and dug in his chest, playing the coquette,

"What shall I do, if you break your words?" Then Raw Persimmon swore to God, embracing her in his arms,

"It'll never happen. I tell you what. You can kill me if I break my promise."

"Oppa, that's cruel! How can I kill you, Oppa?" Pounding his chest, she fussed and continued,

"I'll run away. I can't stand anyone who is a liar," Jean declared.

"I am just saying." He defended and at second thought,

"Yes, you may. You may run away in case I don't keep my promise, okay?" and pulled her again in his arms.

Jean had mastered her craft of playing coquetries with men, having men reveal their hand even after the cards were dealt was her specialty. The incident with Raw Persimmon was simply practice. Jean agreed to move to Uijungbu as the Raw Persimmon suggested.

The following morning, Jean asked,

"Oppa, are you going to buy me anything I need there?"

"Of course I will. Let's start a new life together. Get rid of all things you have here. I'll buy you a whole new set there in Uijungbu."

"Then I will sell all the furniture here and with the money I'll trade for a diamond ring and a necklace."

"That's a splendid idea. Throw away all that you have. Let's get out of here; I will buy whatever you need."

"Oppa, I was about to sell all these things, and with the money I planned to trade them for better ones."

"But, Jean, that's a stingy idea. Sell them or give them to someone. I'll buy a whole new set, as I told you." They both went to the jewelry store.

Raw Persimmon was two-times thicker than Soo. He was bountiful and generous. He picked out more expensive jewelries than those Soo had bought for her. He was also surprisingly meticulous and incredibly generous.

"I'll open your personal account today." They went to a bank nearby and he opened a new account for her with a hefty deposit. He then told her,

"I'll leave today for Uijungbu and come back in two days. In the meantime, get rid of all your old items. I'll send you someone to help you as soon as I get there."

Around sunset that day,

"Is ma'am sister home?" The helping hand that Raw Persimmon promised to send was at the door.

"Who's this?" Jean asked.

"I am sent by the elder brother, Raw Persimmon."

Jean came out to open the door and she was surprised. She expected an errand boy but to her surprise, a mature man as big as Raw Persimmon himself stood at the door.

"Please come on in." She let him in.

"Yes, ma'am sister. Treat me nicely and command me. Otherwise I'll be severely called to account for it. Is there anything I can do for you?" He was submissive.

"I don't think so. I just got rid of all the old furniture, but thank you."

"Ma'am sister, don't be polite to me. My name is Pig Nose. Call me Pig Nose."

"Um...sure," she blinked at Pig Nose, who looked older than her.

She ventured herself to play a mistress to him. And it worked perfect. Now he seemed to be relieved and comfortable.

"Ma'am sister, I feel wonderful and I will do whatever you order me."

"Where are you going to sleep?" she asked.

"Sleep? I made a reservation at the inn across the street. If anything you want, you may call me at the inn. However, I will make a round of checkups every hour until you go to bed." Jean was impressed and asked,

"In this freezing cold, you plan to check on me every hour? You don't need to do that. I'll feel uncomfortable," she rejected.

"But, ma'am sister, I don't mean to knock on your door every hour. I'll patrol around you. That's what's I am assigned here for, so that you may rest in peace and comfort." He then bowed to her and quitted.

She couldn't believe her eyes. She was born again as a different personage overnight. She was quite thrilled. She asked herself,

'Is there any reason to shake this off? No, I would rather leave it this way, and live in luxury and wealth.'

She enrolled in music and dance classes on top of an English class since she moved to Uijungbu, and she kept adding the number and enlarging the size of diamonds and jewelries to be a perfect Queen of the Night, in Raw Persimmon's underworld. She was satisfied and happy day and night.

Raw Persimmon was much simpler and more naïve than Soo in many ways. To him, Jean was like a comet in the night sky, especially with her excellent English and her striking beauty. He was always enamored and slobbered over her, and she knew how to make him flabby and happy day and night. Pig Nose waited on her around the clock as her driver and personal bodyguard.

10.

Haughty Harlot

Two years had passed since Jean moved to Uijungbu.
Raw Persimmon's territory around the U.S. military bases in Dongduchun and Uijungbu expanded over Yongsan, Incheon and Bupyung military bases and lately way down to Pyungtak and Osan bases.

RP (Raw Persimmon) had all the entertainment and amusement facilities such as bars and dance halls in those areas under his firm control, and coercively collected monthly dues from each region's head gangster. His organized ring and its territory increased steadfastly and further consolidated under his so-called the principle of integrity.

Any dishonest or disobedient gangsters were brutally punished, beaten to be crippled or worse, even to death. He also controlled over foreign goods markets around US military units. On top of it, he secured licenses with appropriate military bases as a janitorial and trash disposal contractor to gain free access to them.

Jean played an important role in winning the contracts with her strong handle in English coupled with her glamorous approach to sway the scepter. Consequently everyone in the gang including RP looked upon her in awe, especially when she was freely gibberish with ranking military officers on the base. Lately she spent more time on the military base in the capacity of a registered contractor than she did on the outside, as she had many American friends on the base.

At home she was untouchable. She was turning to be an arrogant tyrant.

Usually Jean and RP slept in late in the confines of a large bedroom in their mansion. Her room was softly lighted with rows of fragrant candles. Every nook and corner was accentuated with lust and lewd rhythm, arousing sensual pleasure to such an extent that no one could pass without sexual urge, taking another step further down to the steps of immorality.

About the time when the couple stretched out of bed, two to three maids were usually fretting about outside for their call. When RP made his way out ahead of sleeping Jean, he picked up his clothes off the waysides of the bed and tiptoed out stealthily. The maid led him to his bath. He would say, giggling,

"Jean is the best." He would tell PN (Pig Nose),

"Leave her alone and be quiet. Don't disturb her."

"Yes, sir." PN made sure the bathroom was ready for him.

After bath, RP would sit at the dinner table. He would eat his breakfast quickly, while PN and two other maids on foot watched over him, waiting to be directed. RP finished off his coffee and spoke to PN. PN was not only RP's right hand man, but also Jean's personal driver.

"Did you say that Jean doesn't like being on the outside?" Jean didn't like interacting with people outside of the U.S. military bases. She preferred the company and to have her food and drinks at the officers' club or officers' mess halls.

"Yes, sir. When she attends outside clubs, girls gang up and raise hell against her. Even the Yankees dancing with other girls would dump their partners and come to our ma'am sister, asking for a hand."

"Then what happens?" RP asked wondering if he had anything to be worried about.

"Ma'am sister is pretty adamant in turning down the Yankees and would never get herself mixed up with those kids. Therefore, she chooses the officers' club on the base."

"That's the problem. Those Yankees lose their senses before Jean," RP concerned.

"But, sir, you have nothing to worry about. She is great in handling them. She wouldn't dance with anyone. Sometime ago, the old commanding officer approached her for a hand, and she flatly refused him. I was impressed." Yet, RP seemed very much worried,

"Keep a good eye and good care of her. I will count on you, Pig Nose."

"Of course, master. Leave it up to me! No one can cheat on my watch, sir."

Whenever RP was to leave for a business venture that would last over many days, Jean would accompany him. However, on shorter trips like today, she would stay behind so that she may gain a good night's rest. PN would stand by, watching over her every minute.

When at last Jean stretched out of her bed, one woman dashed to the kitchen, while the other slid the bedroom door open and greeted,

"Are you up, ma'am?"

"Oh, I had a good sleep." Jean, sitting up, asked,

"Today is the collection day for the Bupyung area, isn't it?"

"Yes, ma'am. That's why RP left early this morning and he said he might be arriving late tonight."

"How many men left for Bupyung?"

"I noticed RP and three others, altogether four men left, ma'am." As Jean put her pajamas on, the maid scurried to the bathroom to make sure everything was right and ready, and then asked Jean,

"Is this going to be a short one or a long one, ma'am?" She was asking if Jean was going to take a short simple bath or a long relaxing hot bath.

"I am alone today. Fetch me some juice later." Jean answered and went in the bath.

The maid made a dash to the kitchen and informed to the kitchen maid,

"She is going to take a long one."

Jean would raise hell if her food was too cold or too hot.

The room maid hurried back to the bedroom to change the sheets and covers, put things order, picked up all the filth and trash, and slid open the window for ventilation.

She then ran back to the kitchen to pick up a glass of orange juice, rushed back to the bathroom, and slid open the bathroom door and reported,

"I have the juice here, ma'am." At this, Jean on the commode suddenly screamed,

"You dumb girl! What do you do with your hand? Can't you knock the door first?"

This scared the maid into dropping the juice onto the floor.

"Look at this!" Jean shrilled again still on the commode,

"Beat it! You ugly one!" The room maid was fired that day.

Jean came out the bath, ill tempered and called for PN,

"Take me in and I'll have breakfast there." She spit her words.

"Yes, ma'am. I'll have the car standby at the door." He hurried out.

When Jean mentioned 'in', she meant inside the military base. She could go in and out as a registered contractor, but in her case, the MPs at the gate would simply whistle her in with a salute as her car approached. She was a widely known beauty among officers on the base, catching the eyes of the commanding officer, along with purchasing and contracting officers. They were attracted by Jean's striking glamour and personality.

U.S. military personnel measured their Korean counterparts by their English capabilities, and no one spoke better English than Jean in the organization. Her refreshing pronunciation and sweet tone were good enough to captivate American soldiers. Her years of strenuous efforts have paid off, and this perked up her arrogance and added to her pompousness.

Her glamour and power influence reached all across the territories which were under the RP's clenched first. To expand his territory, RP knew exactly who to contact and how to shake it up. Following an initial overture, he would always put Jean in, knowing

Jean would get in touch with the appropriate commanding officer and the purchasing & contracting officer to pick up the contract.

Thus Jean was indispensable in expanding RP's territory and Jean knew his strategy. As territory expanded, Jean's influence grew larger and stronger. As a matter of fact the hegemony of the organization was divided into a dual-partnership; RP ran the territories for he did the grunt work that Jean could not. As far as the military contract business was concerned, RP could neither push in nor pull out without Jean. He was stuck in her firm grip.

Jean and RP had a very peculiar relationship; RP couldn't do anything without Jean's approval, and to her he played a puppy. Jean couldn't envision such a luxuriant pompous life without him, and to him she played a fox. Somehow RP was pliant to Jean who was indomitable to RP, because even though RP held their territory in his fist, he couldn't speak a word of English. English was quite the commodity.

RP who spent most of his days out and about monitoring his territories before he had met Jean, now his time was spent at home, tied to Jean's apron. He seldom left the Uijungbu area.

As Jean entered the officers' mess hall, PN stood at the entrance, watching her at a distance until she came out. As she seated herself at a table, Major Thompson, the purchasing & contracting officer raised his hand at Jean, entering the hall.

"Hi, Jean. I was right on time," Major Thompson greeted.

"Hello, Major. I'm glad to see you," she greeted. They sat across from each other at the table.

"How have you been doing?" He asked.

"I have been doing fine. How have you been doing, Major?"

"As usual, no particular fun, you know the typical bachelor's life."

"You must be kidding," she giggled.

"Am I? But I mean it." Major looked serious and then,

"I have been searching and waiting for a beauty like you," he snickered. The Major was a handsome brunette man in his late thirties.

"What would you like to have?" He asked.

"Are you going to pay for me? How lucky I am! But next time allow me to return the favor, alright?"

"Sounds fair, I'll be looking forward to you treating me with something delicious. What's today's special?" He scanned the menu,

"Meatball and chicken for today."

"I'll order the special," the day's special satisfied her order. Major called for the waiter and chose likewise, ordering two specials of the day, then faced Jean,

"I mailed out the invitation for bidding to all registered contractors. Have you received it yet?"

"What sort of bidding was it? I haven't received it yet," Jean replied.

"It is regarding the obsolete heavy equipments and scrap irons."

"Is that right? This one must be big enough to invite all contractors from Seoul, I'm sure."

"You are right. I sent invitations to all of them."

"What kind of equipments will be offered?" She asked.

"It includes three or four broken jeeps and a couple of old trucks. There will also be a lot of empty shells, old tires and barbed wire entanglements."

Jean was excited at the number of broken jeeps. She pledged, 'I'll get this one at any cost,' and openly asked,

"What shall I do to get it? I think I have to make this one."

"Of course, you can get if you tender a good bid for the best price, not too high or too low."

"If that's the case, the right price is well within your discretion, isn't it?" She pressed.

"Well, isn't that what I am supposed to do?" Major smiled at her with a cute wink attached.

That night, RP who left early in the morning for Bupyung and Incheon for the collection of dues returned home late at night with a flat nose, breathing heavily.

"Why are you so late? Is anything wrong?" Jean worriedly asked.

RP dropped his head without a word. Jean following behind, asked again,

"Did you collect the money? What's wrong?" She pressed on.

"Wait a minute. Let me have a drink."

Jean selected a can out of the refrigerator and handed it to RP.

Now RP, leaning on the chair with an extended drink of beer, mumbled,

"Something fishy I noticed down there. I couldn't collect the money today." He sighed. Jean was pent up with impatience.

"What did you say? Why couldn't you collect the money, Oppa?"

They were talking about monthly dues that the RP's gang imposed on each entertainment and amusement sector. Each district head of the gang was responsible for collecting the dues, and RP would pick it up every month. RP was absorbed in thought and silenced.

"What was so fishy?" Jean demanded. RP finished off his can of beer and mumbled,

"The time has come." He heaved a deep sigh.

"What do you mean by that? Didn't they have the money ready for you? I am almost choked. Tell me quickly!"

"You are right, I lost it."

"Lost what? I don't understand," she shrieked.

"Calm down, please. I'll give them a few more days, then I will crush them all!" Jean was alarmed and stood up, screaming,

"Tell me in detail. Don't bear it to yourself. I want to know whom you are going to crush!" Finally RP opened his mouth.

"The east gate gang! I heard sometime ago that those kids from the east gate peeped into our territory in Bupyung. I warned them a couple of times before, but this time they assaulted our territory and plundered every piece of our dues, knocking door to door of our clientele."

"What happened to your men? Where were they while the intruders were plundering our clientele?"

"That's the problem. Our men were outnumbered and beaten to pieces. Some of them were seriously injured and others scattered all over."

"Scattered all over? What do you mean by that?"

"Don't you understand? We lost the fight and our boys ran away not to get killed." RP was furious with anger.

"We can't just sit here and allow our territory to be stolen just like that, can we?" Jean cried out.

"That's why I was late today. Three of our men had their ribs and arms broken in the fight. I had to take and hospitalize them. One good thing was that none of our men were killed. I spent a lot of money for the wounded, far from collecting the money."

"So, what are you going to do with the Bupyung and Incheon territories? You are not going to give them up to the east gate gang, are you?" She enquired.

"Not a chance! I have invested a lot in them. Besides, if we leave them alone, they will quickly attack on our territories in Osan and Pyungtak, and eventually they will creep up here."

"Then what's your counter measure?" Jean asked.

"Well, I'll meet their boss and settle the case peacefully. Otherwise, I'll have a bout with him. His name was... wait a minute. I can't remember, but I heard he is a step-son to the president, Syngman Lee. He goes in and out of the Blue House (President's residence) like it is his own house. He calls his gang, 'division,' and his men call him the 'division commander.'"

When RP mentioned the stepson of the president Syngman Lee, one of the east gate gang leaders, Jean came to think of a terrorist rioting incident at the National Assembly which shook up the nation some time ago, and asked,

"Is that the same man who led gangsters to occupy the National Assembly and forced the Constitution Reform Bill pass through, blocking the opposition party? Also didn't he lead his gangsters to forcibly disperse the gathering of the opposition party at Changchun Park. I remember hearing that in the news. I remember hearing the gang leader was the step-son to the President."

"You are right, but that was his predecessor. The guy who masterminded terrorizing the National Assembly was Jung Jae Yi, who had a tie with Vice President Ki Bung Yi. Now his successor, Hwa Su Lim heads the east gate gang, and he led the plundering riot in our territory in Bupyung and Incheon today. This guy has ties with President Syngman Lee. He just drives me crazy!" RP vented his pent up frustrations.

"So what are you going to do with him?" Jean asked in anxiety. She knew the opponent was strong and formidable.

"What am I going to do? Well, I have just told you, I will try to talk him into settling the case peacefully. If it doesn't work out, then I will have a bout, life or death confrontation." RP was firmly determined to stand firm against his intruder.

Jean agreed that once Bupyung and Incheon switched hands, it would only be a matter of time for Osan and Pyungtak to fall off as well. Then the intruders would attack Uijungbu and Dongduchun in no time. It was imperative that they stop and crush Hwa Su Lim and his gang at any cost before it was too late. If a duel was to decide the outcome, Jean would definitely side with it.

"How old and how strong are they?" Jean asked.

"I am not sure. They recently started pushing their weight around. They cover the east gate market and its vicinity areas. We started first and we cover the largest territory in our country. They are young but they can be just as strong as us. So far, we just let them eat their portion, while we ate ours. Once in a while, they would sneak onto our territory and we would let it slide unpunished. But this time, they plundered our backyard!" RP was infuriated and continued,

"Since we had local fists organized in each area, no one could shake the foundation. Yet they put together an army of gangsters to break us into a big mess." He groaned. Jean was unswervingly adamant and further reprimanded,

"When they first started gibing at us, we should have gagged their mouth. Now what's the use of crying over spilled milk? You said we have a stronger foundation and networks across the nation. I think we should pull every string in our power to check them from further intruding our territory, don't you agree, Oppa?"

203

"I agree. Therefore I might be busy for some time and I may not be home. You asked me not to leave home under any circumstances. That resulted in neglecting local control, inviting upon us this huge problem. All thanks to you."

"Oppa, what did I do?"

"Didn't you ask me to come home before sunset every day?"

"No, please don't pass the buck on me. Do you mean all these problems are because of me?" Jean retorted pungently.

"I think so. Anyways, I shall be out for some time to get these things straightened up. You are coming with me aren't you?"

"But we have a big case here, too," Jean drawled out haughtily.

"What is it?"

"As a matter of fact, I met the purchasing & contracting officer at the officers club today."

"So, did he buy you lunch, again?"

"Yes, he did. He is a very nice person." RP clenched his teeth as that irritated him.

"I'll kill you if you mess around. I noticed the way he looks at you. It's freakish."

"Oppa, have you ever seen anyone not freakishly looking at me? Don't worry. As long as I have you, I won't be tempted."

"I am not worried. I just warned you. You know that the commanding officer and the purchasing & contracting officer were both captivated by your beauty. Watch out for them!" RP cooled down and remembered,

"By the way, what is that big case you mentioned?" He asked.

"It's about bidding. He said he mailed out a formal invitation to all registered contractors on scrap irons," Jean answered.

"What are the scrap irons this time?"

"Three or four broken jeeps, a couple of old trucks, a lot of bullet shells, and some barbed wires," Jean recited.

"Three or four broken jeeps?" His sunken thin eyes sparkled.

"Yes, and two or three obsolete trucks, as well."

"Wow! That would be a bonanza if we can get them. Broken jeeps and trucks can be sold on the spot. Is it going to be an open or closed bidding?" RP was very much interested that his attention had moved away from Hwa Su Lim and the east gate gang.

"Oppa, with open bidding we'll have a slim chance because all the registered contractors are invited. We should go for a closed bidding."

"Yeah, but can you make it a closed bidding without sleeping with the contracting officer?"

"Well, we should work it out some way. That's why I can't leave here, Oppa."

"When is the scheduled date for bidding?"

"He said it is written on the invitation, but it's going to be sometime next month."

"Wait a minute. Do they have old tires as well?"

"Yes, they do. We can talk about the bidding when we receive the invitation, but the Bupyung and Incheon case should be resolved immediately," Jean suggested.

"You are right. I am going to get hold of Hwa Su Lim and straighten things out. At worst, I am ready for a final scuffle, life or death. I'll break his neck either way!" RP declared.

"You say that he has ties with the President?" Jean seemed worried.

"It doesn't matter. When I slug, he will be slugged. When I squeeze, he had better be squeezed hard. Leave him up to me. I'll twist his neck, for sure." He gloated.

"I know you will, Oppa. I trust you. We shouldn't back down under any circumstances." Jean reaffirmed.

"I hear you. I'll run down to Bupyung first thing in the morning and reinforce our group there, and then I will go down to Osan and Pyungtak to fortify our position against possible infiltration. It's going to take at least three to four days to wrap things clear and tight. Don't worry, I will straighten it out."

"I know you will. One thing I advise you is to think before you throw your punch, okay? I'll wait for you, though I can't spend a night without you." Jean seemed assuaged of the situation.

"I hear you, but right now I want to forget everything that has happened tonight."

"Me too," Jean replied as she tickled him to bed.

The following morning when RP arrived in Bupyung, the territory was virtually turned over to the east gate gang. The east gate boss summoned all the local gangsters and bribed them by readjusting their sharing ratio from 40/60 to 60/40, a ratio far more favorable than RP's, to whom the local gang submitted 60% of their total monthly collections, keeping 40%. The chain of control did not end there, as the east gate boss replaced two local heads with two men under his control from the east gate gang.

RP was infuriated and confronted one of the new leaders,

"Do you want to die?" He grappled and wailed his displeasure at the new head. The new head allowed him to express his displeasure, saying,

"Let's be patient and reasonable, boss. If you hit me, I'll be hit, but that won't solve the problem. To solve your case you should either talk with our chief or scuffle with him, isn't that how it goes, boss? Before matters got to become this bad, why didn't you reply to our chief's call? Now if you want to throw your punch on this watch dog, go ahead, but it won't make any difference, boss."

"What? He called me? When?" RP never heard of it but was convinced by the sincere tone of the new head.

"Yes, boss. Our chief sent messages to you not only once but twice. Our chief couldn't understand your reasoning when you said you couldn't come down to meet him because of your beautiful wife." RP couldn't understand what he was talking about.

"What are you gabbling about?" RP raised his hand to throw a punch and then dropped, thinking the boy was right. It wouldn't make any difference kicking a watchdog. For the first time he regretted Jean.

"I have been hallucinated for years because of that fox, leaving things up to those unreliable kids. Those boys needed my constant leadership and care. She is the cause of fire!"

Frustrated at how the situation played out leaving him with egg on his face, RP madly drove toward the east gate market.

In the meantime, Jean woke up late and soaked in freshly prepared soap water, having the maid wipe her back. She picked up a cigarette and lighted it on the stool in the bathroom. Inhaling smoke, she was absorbed with thought concerning Hwa Su Lim, the head of the east gate gang.

She daydreamed, 'He is the head of the gang and he is known as a stepson to the President, Syngman Lee. He is the one who shook down our territories in Bupyung and Incheon. I wonder if RP can break his neck as he gloated. If not, how long can RP stand? It could be just a matter of time for them to take over Osan and Pyungtak. Then we will be at their mercy. RP will be a dead lion by then. Oh, my, I have to do something to protect myself!'

She woke out of her illusion, at the sound of her maid's voice,

"It's done, ma'am." The maid who was wiping her back helped put her pajamas on. Walking out, the maid reported,

"Ma'am, the breakfast is ready for you."

"Bring the breakfast table in. I'll have a short breakfast here," Jean ordered.

"Yes, ma'am." Quickly the maid brought in the breakfast table.

"Leave it there," Jean said as she sat in font of her dresser to powder her face, delving back into her wild thoughts.

'Judging by the situation developed thus far, this game is almost over. It might be a good idea for me to meet this east gate gang leader in person. It's going to be exciting! Who can stop him from being yet another wolf?' She snickered, and then her thought quickly alighted to Major Thompson.

'I am getting tired of these people. They all look like idiots. When I get rid of them I will glide into Major Thompson's arms. He is a very attractive gentleman and he is after me. Wait, he will be gone when his duty is up. What if I married him? Only if he were single but he is married. So what? In a country of free sex, I might be able to have an exciting life as found in fairy tales. That sounds befitting. Next time I will invite him to lunch in a desolate spot. There I will give him my smooth touch and see what he thinks of my fancy idea.' She giggled, looking at herself in the mirror of the dresser.

While she was on the imaginary wing, her food was cooling off.

"Is anybody out there?" She shouted.

"Yes, ma'am." The kitchen maid slid the door open.

"Take this out and warm it. I am coming to the dinning room." Jean handed the maid the breakfast table.

"Yes, ma'am." The maid withdrew the table.

As for the maid, finding a job that paid this well was almost next to impossible as to snatch a star out of the sky. All she had to do was to play dead and be submissive towards Jean and receive her paychecks on time. To her, hunger wins over humiliation, insult, and even maltreatment. Jean understood the maid's philosophy, she did not sympathize for the maid rather the maid's philosophy heightened Jean's arrogance.

RP pulled out of his car at the east gate division headquarters. A rugged faced thug quickly approached him and bowed, asking,

"How can I help you, sir?"

"I am from Uijungbu."

"Yes, sir. May I guide you to the drawing room?" He led RP inside.

"Thanks. I'll follow you." RP followed the man.

There were two doors on both sides of the staircase. The guide opened the door on the left hand side first, stopping RP short from coming inside. RP upon inspection of the room mumbled to himself,

"Oh my! There are too many boys in the room."

The guide held the door open giving RP ample time to search the room. Some twenty robust youths with rugged looks were gathered inside the room. RP flinched at the sight and intuitively sensed the guide's hidden motive. The guide sensing his message was understood then opened the door on the right hand side and led RP to an empty sofa in the room. RP took a seat at the sofa.

"What would you care for, coffee or juice, sir," asked the guide.

"No thank you. I am here to see your boss," RP responded, suppressing his anger.

"Oh, our boss is not available. He was scheduled to meet our President in the morning and then he would be heading for Pyungtak through Osan." This distorted RP's face,

"To Pyungtak through Osan?"

"Yes, sir. That's what he said." RP leaped to his feet and stormed out, declaring,

"I am Raw Persimmon. I'll catch him at Osan."

"Yes, I know who you are. You wouldn't miss him there, sir," the guide answered.

"In case I miss him, tell him I was here."

RP was on the verge of going berserk, and his heart nearly exploded at the thought that the east gate gang leader was on his territory without his consent. He pressed the pedal hard, gasping harshly,

"I'll catch him and break his neck!" He dashed like a darting arrow, gnashing his teeth.

Three days had passed and not a single word from RP. Jean called in Pig Nose,

"I want you to run down and catch him. Tell him to call me at home. It's high time he should have called me."

"Well, ma'am sister. Out in the field, things are not easy. As you know, long distance calls can only be made at the post office. It won't be easy for RP in the field to get to a post office, especially when he has his hands full."

"But I have a bad omen. Leave right now. Tell him that I have an urgent business to discuss with him."

"Aren't you coming along?" PN asked.

"No, I am a little tired. I'm going to rest at home all day."

Jean knew that the east gate gang controlled the east gate market, which is the trading and financial center of the country, and they had ties with President, Syngman Lee. It was very likely that RP may have turned into a sour persimmon overnight, should his gang collapse. It seemed to her that there were two ways for RP's gang to survive; one was to surrender to the east gate and the other was to pledge an all out war. That was the reasoning on why she sent PN to get RP back as soon as possible, to discuss her two survival methods. She was simply impatient just to sit and wait. She wanted to see the conclusion.

Late at night, PN returned with a flat nose.

"Come on in," Jean called.

"Ma'am, sister. I am sorry that I don't have good news."

"No good news? Did you find RP?"

"No, I couldn't. There was no knowing of his whereabouts."

"What do you mean by no knowing? He said he would get to the east gate market through Bupyung."

"I know, ma'am sister. When I went to Bupyung, I couldn't see any of our members there. It was fully patrolled by east gate kids. They said RP stopped by and left three days ago."

"That's what he told me three days ago, before he left here," Jean recollected.

"Then I headed for Incheon. The same was in Incheon, fully seized by the east gate gangsters. Our members were nowhere to be seen. These guys from the east gate grabbed my neck and threatened to kill me. I barely escaped from them to Osan."

"What you are saying is that Bupyung and Incheon were completely turned over to the east gate gang? Tell me what else?"

"Then I went down to Osan. To my frustration..." PN squeezed tears and whimpered.

Jean couldn't stand it and shouted,

"Cut it out Pig Nose! Keep on!"

"Well. None of our members were there either. Osan was also fully controlled by the east gate gang. One of them grabbed my neck and punched me. I took flight and barely escaped from there too."

"Are you saying that Osan was also turned over to them?" She screamed.

"Yes, ma'am sister. Osan is completely in their hands."

"I can't believe this! Where on earth are all our men?" She screamed again and continued,

"How was Pyungtak? Have you been there, too?"

"Ma'am sister, as you know, Pyungtak is a very small unit. Of course, I ran down there but the situation was the same. I couldn't come close to it. I could only verify at a distance."

"So, all our territories are completely stolen, but what happened to RP?" Where is he?" She was frustrated and shrieked out her pent up anger.

"When the guy grabbed my neck in Osan, I asked him if RP was there. They told me he was not there. RP was at Bupyung for sure and he was on his way to the east gate. I think he was last seen at the east gate, but I couldn't confirm it."

"So you couldn't stop by the east gate, could you?"

"No, Ma'am. It was too late. Besides, they wouldn't let me in."

"Alright, I heard enough. Go and hit the sack." She released PN.

According to PN, the RP gang collapsed hopelessly. And RP obviously disappeared either inside the east gate or on his way to Osan three days ago. First off, Jean had to find out RP's whereabouts. She now had a real reason to get in touch with the east gate leader.

The following morning, Jean went to the east gate headquarters. She arrived with only PN by her side. A rugged man received and guided her to his boss. Jean felt a chill at the rigid environment of the east gate headquarters. The division commander, Hwa Su Lim, was at his office. He was a bulky man and was sitting at his table perusing a pile of documents when Jean was showed in. He raised his eyes at Jean and politely invited,

"Come on in and have a seat, please." He then resumed screening his papers, talking to himself, "No, that can't be right," shaking his head.

Finally, he stood up and took a seat across Jean.

"I am sorry to have kept you waiting, ma'am." His dignified manner was more of a commanding general than that of a gang leader.

"I am here in search of my missing husband, Raw Persimmon," Jean addressed.

"I heard he was here to see me some time ago and left here for Osan, as I was in Osan on that day," He answered.

"So you haven't met my husband yet, have you?" She asked with a searching glance at his expression.

"No, I haven't met him yet. I sent messengers on a couple of occasions, as I had urgent business to discuss with him. I am still waiting for him." He looked serious. He was an outright speaker. Jean couldn't detect any trace of deception in his remarks.

"Then I have to report to the police. I haven't heard from him for the past three days." Jean searched his expression.

"Of course, you should have done so already. If I can be of any help, I would be more than happy, ma'am." His answer was clear cut.

Judging by his tone and posture, Jean gave him the benefit of the doubt. She concluded that he was a man that had no reason to be afraid or to hide anything from her.

While Jean met with the boss, PN, the pig nose was speaking with the guide.

"What time was my boss here that day?" PN asked.

"It was around 11:30 in the morning," the guide answered.

The time collaborated with PN's estimation as RP left home at 7:00 in the morning. The rugged faced guide continued,

"I led him to our office and offered him a drink, but he didn't want anything to drink, and asked me about my boss. When I told him that my boss was scheduled to be in Osan and Pyungtak, suddenly he stood up and left our office. He looked very upset."

"Our bosses may have crossed paths then," PN suggested.

"Not likely, my boss was in Osan until four o'clock in the afternoon. If your boss left for Osan as he said, he had more than enough time to get hold of my boss there in Osan, but they never met. Perhaps your boss never made it to Osan," the guide explained.

"That means my boss disappeared on the way to Osan that day," PN concluded.

Jean came out of the office and projected towards PN's direction,

"Let's go to the police bureau."

Jean filed the missing report to the police with identifying details of RP, such as his resident ID, driver's license number, and vehicle number. They returned home late that night.

Three more days passed and there was still no news of the missing RP.

The very next day was May 16th 1961, the day which a military coup d'e tat took place and took over the Korean government. Military junta rounded up hoodlums off the street. Among the arrested were Jung Jae Yi, the mastermind behind the terrorist take-over of the National Assembly, and Hwa Su Lim the east gate division leader.

Military junta executed Hwa Su Lim and his predecessor Jung Jae Yi, while many other notorious gang leaders were given life sentences. RP was still nowhere to be found. Some reports stated that he escaped to Japan in the wake of the military junta round up.

Nearly two weeks following the May 16th military coup d'e tat, Major Thompson stopped by Jean's residence. As Major Thompson entered her house, Jean was beside herself and exclaimed,

"Hello, Major! You are finally my guest today. I missed you so much." She jumped up to him embracing him hard. Major, flattered at the level of affection cracked in smile and asked,

"You haven't forgotten the bidding scheduled for the day after tomorrow, have you?"

"Do you like me, Major?" She asked incoherently.

"Of course I do," he answered.

"Truly?" She asked again.

"Very truly. You know I am madly in love with you." He reassured, then asked, "By the way, are you ready for the bidding?"

"The bidding? I have something more urgent than the bid. I may have to drop it." Her answer was irrelevant.

"Did you say you have to drop it? I thought you wanted it." Major was surprised.

"Yes, I did. But I have a more urgent affair to take care of."

"What is it?" He asked.

"Thompson, do you really love me?" Jean asked him again coquettishly.

"Yes, I do. I do love you madly, Jean." Major was consumed.

"If so, forget the bid and come to my room. I have business to take care of with you." She pulled him in.

Upon entering the room, the two had already started biting off each other madly like two hungry lions devouring their prey. Her bedroom was already dim even in broad daylight; however she turned off the light. She exerted herself with all the technique and coquetry she acquired from her tenure at the Happy Inn, and reduced the spunky Thompson to a pulp for hours. As he was the officer on duty that particular day, he hurried back to his quarters before sunset, leaving Jean asleep like a log.

As the night deepened, someone slid Jean's bedroom door open, and stealthily walked in. It was a bulky man. Jean was sleeping sound when the man swooped upon her in a single motion. Believing it was RP in her dreams, she let it go on for a while. However, she sensed something unusually hectic, and woke up to turn on the light.

It was not RP, the Raw Persimmon. It was PN, the Pig Nose! Stunned at his sight, she screamed,

"What heck are you doing here, Pig Nose?"

"Yes, as you see, I am your Pig Nose," PN answered with unshakable voice.

"Are you crazy? Do you want to get killed?" She shrieked.

"You know I am a man, too. What's the difference between that Yankee and me?

I have been madly in love with you for long long time. You make me crazy. You are responsible for this, woman!"

"You are out of your mind!"

"I am not! I am just madly in love with you. If you don't listen to me, I'll destroy and burn everything up. You got it?" He threatened, gasping hard.

Jean was at a loss for words. She was driven into a corner. There was no way out but to placate him. After PN finished, Jean quickly muttered,

"Okay, Pig Nose, we didn't do anything this night. You were not here and I didn't see you. I forgive you. You got it?"

"Well, we both had a goodtime. However, if you insist, I'll go along with it. We didn't do anything tonight, alright."

"We had a goodtime, fine, but we didn't do anything. You were not here tonight.

Do you understand, Pig Nose?"

"Okay, we didn't do anything tonight. I wasn't here." So saying, PN withdrew.

But that was not the end. PN sneaked into her room whenever he felt, and menaced her, saying,

"I am a fish placed on the cutting board. You can cut me anytime. I am not afraid of anything, not even death. If you reject me, I will shovel out both you and Thompson when you enjoy together. You told me that you had a good time with me. I am only asking for my portion. I think I deserve it. If you take me in and be quiet, I will remain to be your driver and bodyguard." In fact, his molestation had just begun.

PN was suspicious from the very beginning. His cunning intentions were revealed when RP disappeared, and activated when he caught Jean and Thompson in bed. He pledged to sneak into her room right after each time Thompson visited her. Jean resisted and scuffled to wean him off but her efforts were all in vain. His lustful appetite was insurmountable to her to ward off.

At last she pressed charges of rape against PN.

Following a cross examination, the investigator dismissed the case taking the side of PN and his testimony. He spit his words at Jean, saying,

"This woman ridiculed me. She doesn't know what she is talking about."

The chain of events made PN play much in reserve; however PN did not stop his molestations. Jean came to have a heart ailment which caught her with short breath, caused by her pent-up resentment, and her heart was speedily debilitating as the molestation repeated over and over again.

One day, she called out to Thompson,

"Thompson, do you love me?"

"Of course. You know I do. How about you?" He asked.

"I do love you."

"I do love you, too." Thompson embraced her.

"Thompson, if you truly love me, why don't you marry me. I can't stand a day without you," she confessed. However her confession made Thompson flinch and he addressed Jean with a serious look,

"Jean, I wish I could do the same, but next year I'll be gone. Plus my wife will be waiting for me at home."

"You can divorce her, can't you?" Jean suggested.

"I can't divorce her, and I don't want to divorce her. If I were a burden on you, I will stop coming out to your place." He made himself clear.

"Then your love for me is a lie," Jean pouted, cross-tempered.

"It's not a lie. I do love you, but marriage is a different issue. I promised my wife to marry her in my college days and we have a daughter as well. I told you all about it, didn't I? They are waiting for me and they are my family."

"What shall I do, Major? I love you truly. I love you! I love you! I love you with all my heart, with all my strength and with all my life. You are my first love. I can't let you go! Thompson."

Jean confessed her true love, writhing all over. Yet, Thompson was a man of integrity. He was a good man of heart and responsibility. He even supported Jean financially as much as he could. From that day on, he stopped stepping out of the base. Thompson was the first man she truly loved, but this man had to turn around, and yet she had no reason to hate him. She missed him a great deal because her love was truly genuine.

As time passed her shortness of breath got worse and her sleepless nights succeeded on end. Further worse was PN's nightly molestations. He turned a deaf ear to her biting tongue and sneaked in to bulldoze on her ruthlessly. She couldn't stand it anymore. Finally she left everything behind and took flight.

It was with Major Thompson's tremendous help that Jean could find a job at the officers' club on the Yongsan compound. The officers' club provided Jean with quarters. She could shelter herself and had a comfortable relationship with Thompson. Major Thompson had to leave her the following year.

Two years passed since Major Thompson left her, leaving a gaping hole in her heart. Major Thompson was a genial gentleman who sincerely cared for her. He was also an honest man to her, but he was gone! Now, she looked for a replacement for Thompson by the measure that Thompson left in her heart. She exerted herself, spending a lot of time and money in search of the second coming, but she learned that money can't buy a man's heart.

Nevertheless, she never gave up.

Meanwhile, her heart's ailment deteriorated and unexpected diseases came to drain her thin purse. She was slowly paying for what she did.

God is fair and He still anxiously waited for her to come out of the dark mire, as He still does for every living soul. It seemed that calamity overtook her like a storm and disaster swept over her like a whirlwind, while she was wide awake. People thought the judgment comes only after their death, but that is incorrect.

Jean, now went by the name, 'Kathy,' and spent her days and nights by singing and dancing in the uproar of applause through a series of performance tours around subordinate units of the US 8th army. She was one of the more widely known entertainers, but the vacuum in her heart grew larger. The more she struggled to fill it up, madly throwing passion and money all over, the larger the vacuum grew, sucking it back out. Not a single stroke of warm hands touched her heart. Her dreams revisited the same loop played over again and again, which was to be embraced by Thompson just once more. She knew he was gone and his heart couldn't be procured, yet still she kept on searching for it. Alas, can a cracked gourd hold fresh pure water?

On her breaks from the performance tour, she powdered her swollen face and came to the officers' club to sell her song and dance, panting hard from her shortness of breath. Young officers sent roaring applause and in return she would twist a little harder. When she choreographed a funny gesture in her routine, the audience would explode into laughter, grabbing their sides, she could easily win over a crowd.

One day, a young college student arrived and found a job on a temporary base at the officers' club. His goals coming in were to learn English and American culture. At that time learning English was highly aspired among college students.

It was a fantastic opportunity for a young student to find a job among American officers. It was rare luck that may fall on one out of ten thousand students to obtain such a position on a U.S. base. Now he could practice his English on officers during his summer vacation. His name was Yongbum Park.

On the first night that Yongbum worked at the officers' club, which was filled with American officers, he saw an unusually beautiful lady singing and dancing on the stage. He became fascinated by her presence and beauty, which he had never seen before, that he felt like he was walking through a fantasy. It was a confusing spectacle for Yongbum; the lady was not Caucasian yet sang in unknown English words. That day he also observed for the first time that there are Americans that have black hair as well.

As she finished singing, the audience whistled uprising in ovation. Yongbum was just excited in the middle of the up-roaring ovation, and learned that the American audience was outright open and expressive.

On the third day of his stay, Yongbum was walking up the stairs to the club, when he saw a woman on the landing writhing in pain. She seemed suffocating from lack of intake of air. As he approached the woman, he was taken back from surprise, once it registered that it was none other than the lady who sang at the club.

He approached and asked in his unrefined English,

"Hello, Mrs. Aunt (which is a polite gesture of calling a married woman). What's wrong with you?"

"Save me please." To his surprise, the lady responded in Korean.

"Are you Korean? What can I do for you?"

"I can't breathe. I am dying," she pleaded.

"Come on. I'll carry you to the hospital." He squatted and turned his back toward her for her to mount.

Carrying her on his back, he rushed out of the compound and entered a hospital nearby the military base. She was surprisingly light on his back, and he was thrilled.

The doctor at the emergency room received and examined her hurriedly. He stuck the stethoscope into her breast and upturned her eyelids. And then asked,

"Are you a relative to this patient?"

"No, but we work in the same place," he answered.

"She has a severe heart ailment. The valve between cells in her heart is malfunctioning." The doctor was a cardiologist.

"Can it be cured, doctor?" He asked.

"Well, yes and no. This patient needs relaxation in comfort. She shouldn't be disturbed at all."

"What is the cause of her sickness, doctor?"

"Well, it can be inherent. I mean she may have been born with the illness, but judging by her age and symptoms, I believe some time ago in the past she had an enormous shock to her heart either physically or emotionally. Which may have caused the failure of her heart valve to close or open to pump out blood in a timely rhythm," the doctor explained.

"It must be very serious." He was worried.

"Again, the patient needs to be absolutely rested and relaxed. I'll give you medication that is called digitalis's, for you to give to her."

Yongbum carried Jean back to her quarters on his back. There were a double bed and dresser in her room. He laid Jean on the bed,

"Mrs. Aunt, if you please let me contact your relatives, I will let them know that you are seriously ill."

"I am not a Mrs. Aunt, young man." She spit words quite irrelevant.

"I am sorry. Please give me any of your relatives contact information."

"How can I give you what I don't have? I am hopelessly deserted," she continued,

"Young man, I am not Mrs. Aunt," she spoke faintly as her eyes resigned. Yongbum was momentarily confused, asking himself,

'What's the big a deal about being referred to as Mrs. Aunt or Miss Lady? It's completely irrelevant to this emergency situation? Who is this lady? Isn't she the one that sang and danced in the club the other night? That fantastic lady is dying right before my eyes. I have to let someone know about this!' He tried to reach out a lifeline to her once more,

"Then what shall I do, ma'am? Doctor said you need rest and relaxation with this medication. Is there any friend you want me to contact?"

"That's why I told you that I am deserted alone. I have no friends, either. Thank you very much anyways." She gasped to catch up to her breathing and continued,

"You are the one who recently started working in the club, aren't you?"

"Yes, I am. I just started working in the club, and I saw you singing and dancing like an angel the other night. I have never seen such a fabulous scene in my life, ma'am."

"I heard about you. You are very nice young man. Now go back to the club and don't worry about me." She said, wanting to make eye contact but she couldn't keep her eyes open.

Yongbum filled her a cup with fresh water and placed the medication pack next to it, then alerted,

"Mrs. Aunt, here is your medication and water."

"You called me Mrs. Aunt again. I am not Mrs. Aunt. Call me sister." It was painful to see her making out words as she was simultaneously gasping for air.

"Can you raise my back before you go?" She asked.

Yongbum huddled a comforter and put it behind her back to support her. It worked. She breathed with less difficulty. In her sedentary posture, she said, inhaling a deep breath,

"Now I can breathe better." Looking closely at Yongbum, she continued,

"You saved me today, brother. I should have been dead by now without your help. Why don't you go back to your work?" She signaled him to leave.

Yongbum was exited with a weird feeling. He had never been that close to a westernized woman or a lady wearing perfume. His nose was treated to unique female scents for the first time in his life. When he first watched her sing and dance, she looked so alive, exotic and fascinating like a fairy. Ironically the same lady was dying on the landing of the stairs. She also called him brother. All these events aroused a singular sensation in him.

"Thank you very much." He bowed to her and left the room.

The following morning, Yongbum came back to Jean's room.

"I wanted to stop by last night but it was too late after work. How do you feel, Mrs. Aunt?" He asked.

"You called me Mrs. Aunt, again. Call me sister," Jean urged. She looked surprisingly well this morning.

"If you wish, I will call you sister. Then you will have to treat me like your younger brother," he mustered up all his courage to speak out.

"You are right. Since I am your sister, I may use imperative terms to you," and called, "Yongbum!" Suddenly he felt a queer but fantastic sensation.

"Very well, sister" Yongbum answered proudly. In this way, the two became sworn sister and brother.

Since then, Jean struggled up the stairs and stopped at the landing to catch her breath and then, struggled up another flight to enter the officers' club. She kept singing and dancing, panting and gasping, and the patrons applauded her. It was pitiful for Yongbum to watch his sister playing acrobat every night, and he couldn't understand why she should risk her life that way.

One evening, he asked,

"Why don't you stay home and relax? Doctor said you need it, sister."

"Otherwise how can I survive? Who's going to pay for my medication and livelihood?" She retorted.

While she was recovering, confined to her bed, not a single person came to refill her cup with water. How can anyone of such beauty be left so lonely? She needed someone nearby to help her around the clock.

One day, Jean offered,

"Yongbum, how would you like moving in my room and to live together?"

Yongbum's house was one hour ride by bus away in a lodging house. He was a little embarrassed of living together with a lady in the room, but he thought practically and realized it was not a bad idea. He would be able to care for his sworn sister and help her with the lodging fee. He gave her his answer,

"That sounds good because I can be around you and I can help you to pay for your medication with my lodging fee. The problem is that we don't have an extra room."

"What do you need an extra room for? You can pitch a curtain in the middle of this room and put your bed on the other side, can't you?"

Yongbum moved into Jean's place. Since he moved in, Jean's condition improved by the day. Yongbum was gratified with Jean's improving condition and gave all the money he made from the officers' club to aid in Jean's recovery. Now she could stay in bed when she was sick.

After awhile, Jean came across the warm hand she desperately sought and her illness was leaving her. Yongbum unknowingly played the role of Jean's father and mother, and at times even the role of Thompson to her. Her bitter emotional wounds scarred by her forgotten mother's tender love, father's gratifying care, and Thompson's embracing warm heart, became remedied through

Yongbum and his unsparing devotion. In her wretched situation just having another human around her was a big relief. She was really grateful for Yongbum.

"Yongbum, I am grateful to have you. I am very much relieved to have you near me," She complimented.

"Well, it's just a matter of course that younger brothers should take care of his sick sister. I'll do anything to help you become healed, sister," he comforted. Then she would mumble something out of ear shot from Yongbum,

"If I were ten years younger or if you were ten years older..." Lately she openly recited it. Then Yongbum would stop her, saying,

"What are you talking about, sister? I will only be happy if you get well. I will do anything and try my best to get you healed," he promised. His promise was stronger than any of her medications.

"Did you say that you will do anything to heal my sickness?"

"Yes, sister. Whatever is within my capacity."

"You should take charge of what you have just said, okay?"

"Of course, sister. Men should live by their sense of responsibility. That is the motto in my life," he declared.

Yongbum was only nineteen years old. A few days after he declared his promise, he was having a fancy dream in a perfumed room at night, when he felt someone tenderly pressing upon him, and momentarily he was thrown in a spell of hallucinations. The moment he opened his eyes in wonder, his hallucination materialized. Carnal appetite raised its head, numbing any sense of reason. When his senses raced back belatedly, it was no longer a dream. It was a stark reality.

Jean was no longer his sister. She changed to be his lover. Sin has the nature of hiding. When caught, sin would concoct a story to justify and defend itself. Thus Yongbum went astray. Now he had to assume complete responsibility for Jean, and he took it as a matter of justice and love. He claimed that he was a man of heart, a man of conscience, a man of pure love and a man of responsibility. He turned his back on his parents, brothers and friends. He stood stalwart against anyone who criticized his illicit relationship with

Jean. He was rather proud of his being faithful to a dying Jean. He volunteered to be the hero in a story of scarlet literature.

Who warned the young not to gaze at a bottle of wine, when it sparkles in the cup, when it goes down smoothly? In the end it bites like a snake and poisons like a spider. Yongbum, in the prime of life, hid underground like a hibernating serpentine. Chased by despair and agony following behind him, he once attempted suicide. Jean aided Yongbum's demise, as she brutally stomped on his tender stalk for the sake of her own comfort and interest. On the threshold of hell, she received a tender hand and clutched it firmly, without asking whose hand it was and cruelly crushed the tender stalk.

It was stated, 'If anyone causes one of these little ones who believe in me to sin, it would be better for him to have a large millstone hung around his neck and to be drowned in the depths of the sea.' Although Jean heard this some time ago, she had forgotten it along with other aspects of her life.

As fire burns up wood then extinguishes, so does the passion. Illicit passion produces sin and the sinner has to pay for his transgressions. Injustice and immorality cannot last long. God is fair. When the time was up, Yongbum packed up and left Jean, as charcoal turned to ember. Jean begged him to stay, but Yongbum couldn't allow himself to crush his own parents furthermore. When he came to reason, he couldn't give up the true meaning and purpose of his life. Heartbroken, he left Jean.

Jean was left alone again and eked out her sad days in Bupyung as a prostitute. Now she had neither yesterday nor tomorrow. She only had and lived for today. She had nothing to be afraid of or anything to hope for. She deserted herself into prostitution and ensconced herself as a queen in the sex trade, based on her unique techniques and coquetry. She drank and shook in nightly pleasures and was asleep during day.

She prided herself on being a multicultural woman.
She believed she was cultured through her trade and dance tours as she lifted her legs and shook her hips violently, shrieking western songs to receive clapping applause from a drunken audience.

As a cultured woman, she refused tap water and rather drank bubbly soda. She dismissed Korean cultural tradition and jumped on the western bandwagon, pushing aside kimchi and bean paste complaining that, and 'It has too much stench!'

As a typical Korean woman who embraced western culture, she exposed the belly button, died her hair blonde with tight blue jeans or a mini skirt around the hip, shaking from side to side. Homemade shoes were no longer in vogue, and her feet were only adorned in expensive high heels. She was swirled in the manic whirlwind of her daily sensationalizing disillusions of western civilization.

At last her lifestyle broke her body, disaster and distress stormed upon her like burning sulfur: venereal diseases, damage from frequent abortions, insomnia, spinal nerve disease and aggravating heart disease, caught up with her and she finally collapsed. The moment she fell, her world left her like wind. She could no longer sing or dance, but she was still alive.

11.

In His Presence

Parting is never easy especially with someone who just recently arrived back to your life. Even with someone you expect to see in the near future, parting is still painful. Suk's departure was no exception; her parting from the lovely younger children in the house, parting from Pastor and Madam Lady, parting from her always dependable brother Yong, and parting from her kind teacher Sun among her friends and classmates, left her heart very sore on her long flight to America.

Suk was excited when her plane jutted through the cumulus of clouds which relieved her anxiety of flying by herself amongst strangers. She became a little embarrassed when neatly dressed American stewardesses approached her with a big smile speaking in unknown English.

Pastor's farewell blessing was still ringing in her ears,

"May she be always with our good Lord. May her way be wide open and prosperity comes to her in abundance. May she be free from deficiency, discomfort and fear. May she be guided as an apple of His eye?" Pastor repeatedly emphasized that these blessings come as He is always with her.

As Pastor prayed for blessings, God had always been with her in every scene of her life and would remain by her side in the future. Therefore she was always fearless and strong in heart. That was her faith. She lived and grew in that faith.

She had to transfer her flight to Denver at the San Francisco airport. Her first steps in the United States were planted in San Francisco. She accosted a stewardess and asked in broken English,

"I, to Denver. Denver, Colorado, please." Suk found herself speaking with her hands aiding to what she hoped was a successful conversation.

"Are you going to Denver, Colorado?"

"Yes, I go to Denver, Colorado."

The stewardess was generous enough to guide her to the appropriate gate. She waited uneasily for nearly twenty minutes before boarding. She was in America now and a sense of accomplishment overwhelmed her.

When she boarded the plane to Denver, she felt more comfortable with her second flight, though she couldn't talk fluently with anyone but with Jesus Christ, she prayed,

"Lord. No matter how the world changes, wherever I am, whatever these people may think of me, I will always look and rely upon you. Please hold my hand and lead me as you have led me up to the present, for then I will not be afraid of anything. Please do not turn your eyes away from me, Lord." Then she heard Him answer,

"I am with you."

When she landed at the Denver airport, she was overwhelmed with peace and comfort. She followed the passengers blindly to the baggage claim and finally came out of the exit, where Pastor Jonathan welcomed her, waving his hand,

"Suk, Here I am! You look different! You are such a beautiful lady, now!"

"Pastor Jonathan!" She ran into his arms. The pastor embraced her tight and prayed,

"Father, thank you for your holy guidance to have Suk safely arrive here, and we pray for your continued guidance and care of this daughter of yours. I pray this in the name of Jesus Christ."

Is this the American way to serve the Lord? She wondered. This broke away from her traditional prayers at the House of Immanuel, which were conducted humbly on bended knees with a bowed head. Pastor Jonathan prayed hard in a crowd as if he did at the podium, upon embracing her.

She heard a lot in regards to the Colorado sky. Upon her first inspection, she became awestricken at the serenity of the blue sky. The Colorado night sky was painted so marvelously with countless twinkling stars studding the serene indigo canvas. The stars looked whispering within arm's reach. Looking up at its splendor, her fatigue and anxiety were gone instantly.

Pastor Jonathon's wife was a beautiful angel.

"Suk, my name is Lisa. How would you like to take me as a mother while you are in the States? I have two sons but I have no daughter," she asked in a kind motherly tone. Suk was truly honored.

"Thank you. Thank you very much, madam lady," she bowed.

"Don't be like a stranger, Suk. We are a family. Make yourself at home. This is your home as well, Suk." Her persuasive tone was only possible through genuine love touching Suk's heart.

"Thank you. I will try. Thank you, madam lady."

"Madam Lady? Please call me Lisa. How can a daughter call her mother, madam lady?" She embraced Suk tight as if to squeeze out and dispel all the anxiety and misgivings in her, and then followed up with prayer,

"Father, thank you for this wonderful daughter. Keep us both, Suk and I, in your hand and lead us in your way. We pray this in the name of Jesus, Amen."

Suk was shedding tears as she was so thankful to have been so blessed. Mother Lisa released Suk and wiped the tears off Suk's cheek. This time Suk embraced her tight.

"Suk, you are my daughter now. Neither Pastor Jonathon nor I chose you. Our God planned for this a long time ago. If this tear is from the fountain of joy, I should cry too." They wept together.

"That's good enough." Mother Lisa helped Suk up and continued,

"We have lived under two different cultures. It's going to take you awhile to adapt yourself to American culture. I wouldn't be able to prepare you without knowing your history and culture. Therefore I have studied Korean history and culture since I first heard of you, in hopes to help you when you get here." Suk was moved by her commitment and almost burst into tears.

Mother Lisa continued,

"Our foundation is the same Jesus, but our way of living and habits are different. That's the reason why we asked you to come here first."

Mother Lisa meticulously prepared for Suk's arrival down to the smallest of details. While she prayed in the course of preparing for Suk's arrival, Mother Lisa received an answer as to how to ease Suk's transition. The best way to familiarize oneself with another culture is to live within the culture as a family. That's why she suggested to Pastor Jonathan to have Suk spend time with them before her classes started at Stanford.

Suk saw many differences in culture: Americans lived in spacious space, cooked on their feet, ate on tables sitting on chairs, and slept in elevated beds. There were all kinds of utensils and equipments found in the kitchen and each served its unique purpose. In bathrooms were indoor sedentary commodes, a far departure from outhouses she was accustomed to back in Korea. The most striking differences between the cultures were language, way of thought and the way of expression.

Suk landed in the San Jose airport a month later, thankful for the experience with Pastor Jonathon and Mother Lisa, which helped remove the shellshock of living in another country. Truly, God paved His plans for Suk. She could now speak, joke and even wink like an American.

Pastor Jonathon and Mother Lisa helped Suk cross the cultural barrier and introduced her Korean spirit and mind to touch the American heart.

Suk was quickly Americanized. Our good Lord worked a miracle for Suk through the good graces of a blessed couple.

At the San Jose terminal, two students were waiting for Suk's arrival with a signboard, written 'SUK.' Their names were Jane and Susie. When they spotted Suk, they ran and hugged her like an old friend. Suk prayed, holding their hands,

"Father, thank you for these wonderful friends and I thank you for your holy work through them. Help me to be a good friend to them. I pray this in the name of the Immanuel Jesus Christ..."

"Amen!" Jane and Susie responded.

Land was vast in America. The streets were wide and long. There were no oxcarts traveling the streets, instead people traveled by cars, a symbol of extreme luxury back in Korea. The highways were dangerously fast, wide open and straight. Everyday life was different in America. Jane was driving cheerfully while singing a tune.

In the coed dormitory, Jane, Susie and Suk were roommates. Jane and Susie came from wealthy Christian families on the east coast. They were interested in Korean history and culture with due respect. They were well mannered and well educated. Suk once again verified that our good Lord never turns away from His chosen ones.

For the first several months, Suk had a difficult time with English on the college level. Jane and Suk always stood by with, 'Can I help you?' and each of them spent at least an hour a day tutoring Suk in English. As her English improved, her life became that more enjoyable. Suk was gradually becoming better known among her peers and professors.

She began emanating Christian aroma and light. She would stop by to visit the school chapel whenever she had time. She spoke with Christ anywhere on campus but she enjoyed speaking with Christ in His house of worship. She kept Yong and her loved ones in the House of Immanuel informed of every detail of her Christ-led life. Every word of Pastor's farewell prayer was being realized as it materialized in her daily life.

On top of meals at the dormitory cafeteria, the roommates had plenty of healthy snacks and drinks within their pantry and refrigerator. Susie and Jane sometimes showed and read the letters from their mothers, which read,

"The extra allowance is for your friend, Suk."

Financially she was helped along with a job, when her professor suggested,

"Suk, if you'd like, you can work with me at the laboratory for four hours a day, as I need some help."

Suk had her driver's license issued in two months through the help of many other classmates. When Suk went to a Korean church in San Jose to teach young adults, Susie offered,

"Suk, take my car for the weekend."

Suk planned to save enough money to buy her first car, albeit used, by the end of summer break.

Through the generosity of others, she lacked nothing. She lived without a hint of discomfort. She was now widely known among her peers as a beautiful, intelligent and good-hearted Korean medical student. She was bold and strong before God and the world.

In Suk's second year of medical school, Susie's brother, James, came to Stanford Medical School as a resident to the cardiac surgery department. He was a promising cardio surgeon who just finished his internship at Columbia medical school in Manhattan, New York.

He first met Suk through Susie at the dormitory cafeteria, and then quite often in Bible study group. He became quickly attracted to Suk. Susie's father headed the internal medicine department of the Zion hospital in Manhattan. James was an exemplary Christian and a handsome doctor.

The sibling pair were polar opposites in their demeanor, Susie was open and active, while James was prudent and scholastic. James was much taller than Susie whose height was almost that of Suk. James would match his eyes with Suk's before he talked to her slowly and cautiously. When he sat across Suk at a tea house on campus, he would patiently wait until Suk took her first sip before he enjoyed his.

Today he sat across Suk again and said, smiling,

"When I see you, I feel like facing the wonder and mystique of our good Father." Suk didn't understand what he was talking about, confused she inquired,

"I beg your pardon, Doctor James?"

"Look at that. You are so genuine and true. You are truly beautiful and wonderful," he praised. Suk was bewildered for a moment, but eventually she could read his mind,

"Dr. James, you are exaggerating. I am nothing more than a plain female student."

"Look at this. What did I say? On top of your beauty and glamour, your heart and humility are so angelic. You surely are an angel!" This straightened up Suk's posture,

"Dr. James, you are totally wrong. I am an orphan, and I have nothing to be proud of other than Jesus. I am merely a poor foreign student." Her response escalated his admiration.

"How precious you are! How genuine and truthful you are! Didn't He say that the kingdom of heaven is like treasure hidden in a field? When man found it, he hid it again, and then in his joy went and sold all he had and bought that field. I am in that joy," he confessed.

Suk was surprised to hear such compliments and also deeply thankful to him. She just couldn't believe that a promising giant in modern medical science confessed that he was ready to sell all he had for a poor country medical student.

She slowly raised her head and said,

"Dr. James, I am thankful to you. I will deeply cherish what you said to me today, and I will pray for it. Thank you, sir." She stood up and excused herself.

A few days later, Suk faced Susie.

"Susie, I have something to tell you."

"Is it about James? I knew it!" Suk was surprised.

"Don't be surprised, Suk. My brother got lost the moment he saw you. He heard all about you before he came here through my mother. He confessed to me that he couldn't control his burning passion toward you each time he was in your bible study group, and asked for my help. I told him to confess to you directly. He was serious and he is clean, Suk. He said you are the first one he ever fell in love with."

Suk had to close her eyes to hear Susie out and responded,

"Susie, I need your help and you can't say no to me. As I told you before," she paused a minute and cleared her voice,

"Susie, I am honored that your brother has such a genuine heart towards me, and I am deeply grateful to him. It is an exceeding blessing to me before our God and the world, but it is a privilege that I can hardly accept. To be honest with you, I have a hundred and twenty two younger ones and my Pastor father and Madam Lady. I have a sworn brother named Yong, whom I have to return to, upon completing my course here. I have to stick to my promise with them."

"I supposed so. That's why I asked him to tell you directly. We should accept whatever is for and against His plan and purpose. We should make it clear to please our Lord," Susie responded. Suk turned even more serious,

"Thank you, Susie. This decision shouldn't affect our friendship and my respect toward your brother."

"Of course, we aren't teenagers, are we? I am happy to have a good friend like you. A minor problem is that my brother has told everything about you to my mother and she is coming to meet you in person…"

"Susie, stop her from coming here, please!" Suk interrupted.

"Otherwise I'll run away. Please call her right now and tell her not to come."

"Alright, I'll take care of it." Since then, Susie became Suk's best friend, while James went back to New York.

Suk helped the professor in the laboratory and sent a portion of her wage to the House of Immanuel. Madam Lady gathered the young ones at home and lectured,

"Look at sister Suk. She sends us money working herself through school. When she was here, she was the first one to the predawn service, she washed dishes in the kitchen, and then she would set up late to study in her room. Do you remember her?"

"Yes, we remember her. We'll follow her suit!" They answered in concert.

Suk's life became peaceful like a river. She lacked any hint of discomfort and her path was always wide open. What made her so? Was it because she was good natured or smart? Or because she came to know a lot of model citizens such as her adopted parents, Pastor and Madam Lady, Pastor Jonathan and Mother Lisa, Yong, Jane, Susie, and the professor? Did she meet them by accident and by luck?

In Suk's case, there was neither luck nor accident, but justice and inevitability.

In a word, she was always in His presence. He led her and she was carried on His back. That's why she was in her state of comfort and fullness, and enjoyed such prosperity.

Wait a minute! What is His presence? Where is He? Did He lead her? Did He really carry her on His back? Yes, Absolutely Yes! All the answers to the questions are in the Word! Suk comes in His presence and she hears His gentle voice when she reads the words, the words such as,

"Blessed is the man who does not walk in the counsel of the wicked or stand in the way of sinners or sit in the seat of mockers. But his delight is in the law of the Lord, and on his law he meditates day and night. He is like a tree planted by streams of water, which yields its fruit in season and where leaf does not wither. Whatever he does prospers. Not so the wicked! They are like chaff that the wind blows away. Therefore the wicked will not stand in the judgment, no sinners in the assembly of the righteous. For the Lord watches over the way of the righteous, but the way of the wicked will perish. (Psalm 1) The words are the spirit and life that gave her power, wisdom and love.

Now who can dare come out with Four Pillars and Eight Letters, falsely claiming?

"Here are hidden oracles of the Creator written on each pillar and letter." (Four Pillars stand for the year, the month, the date and the time of one's birth, and the Eight Letters are summed up with two letters designated to each letter, derived from the doctrine of the Human Nature and the Rule of Heaven?)

If one can tell the other's predestined fate by the pillar and letter, why one of twins, who were born with the same pillars and letters was so much blessed, while the other was so miserably cursed? Man, how can you, less than a worm dare to peep into the mystery of the Creator? Woe to him who quarrels with his Maker. Can the created say to the Creator, "Why didn't you make me better? Can the clay say to the porter, "Don't crush me. Knead gently."?

You, less than chaff, have you never heard that the Lord works out everything for his own end- even the wicked for a day of disaster? At this very moment someone advises you not to think of yourself more highly than you ought, but rather think of yourself with sober judgment, in accordance with the measure of faith God has given you.

The twin sister's lives could not have been further set apart; at the very moment, Suk was concentrating on her studies in a world famous scholarly institution, while her twin sister, Jean, left everything she owned to escape molestation and found herself back in the streets, ruined as a prostitute.

Four years passed. On August 27th 1964, Pastor and his eldest son, Yong, seated themselves by a window in the middle row of a Northwest Airline airplane headed to America.

"Lean back, Pastor Father," Yong said.

"Thanks, son. You do the same."

"Looks like a smooth ride. All thanks to His mercy," Pastor murmured, closing his eyes.

Placing his hand on Yong's, Pastor continued,

"You did a great job. Now that we have two doctors in our house, I can't ask for more."

For the past four years, Suk studied in America while Yong studied in Korea. Both finished their medical schooling successfully. For the wedding ceremony for the couple, Pastor accompanied Yong, who was to take an internship post with Suk at Stanford Hospital following their wedding. As for Pastor, this was not his first flight to America. He made a couple of trips to meet Pastor Jonathan in Denver on the matter of establishing the Incheon Christian Hospital.

It was Pastor Jonathan who first proposed the idea to build a Christian Hospital in Incheon and Bupyung area. Pastor father found and purchased the site and building. Later Pastor Jonathan came and stayed at the site for a month to supervise the remodeling and interior setup of the hospital. This time around it was Pastor who was to meet with Pastor Jonathan to discuss details for the hospital operation and management, which was to be inaugurated early next year.

"It is wonderful to see that both of you can do the internship together, isn't it?"

"Yes, Pastor. We have prayed for this for years."

"Our God said, 'I will do to you the very things I heard you say.' He surely answered your earnest prayers."

"Thank you. All thanks to your love, Pastor."

"Not in the least, son. We simply worked together in Christ. Look at your own brothers, Yong II and Yong III. How healthy and strong they are! You showed them a good example. All the other children want to follow in your steps."

"Pastor Father, we are not the ones to be praised. It was due to the grace of our good God, and then, thanks to yours and Madam Lady's constant prayers and strenuous efforts for us."

"Again, we worked together in Christ. By the way, your plan is to return together upon completing the internship here, isn't it?" Pastor asked.

"Well, it remains to be seen whether or not we both return at the same time. Suk may be able to practice right away, but I may have to remain behind for further research."

"Then, is it your plan to have Suk return alone beforehand?"

"That seems like the most likely scenario, Pastor. I may need a couple more years. Actually, it was Suk who suggested this and I agreed."

"Well, if that's the case." Pastor was absorbed in thought then continued, "Suk is truly a good girl. She never skipped a month of tithing, working herself through her education. She is in His blessings all the time."

It was true that Suk and Yong were always in His arms. Though they were separated by distance, they were together in their prayers. They lived together. They breathed together in Christ. They never placed their ideals or wills ahead of each other. They prayed and listened to His instruction. They followed His plan and His will. They were always in His presence.

Especially for Suk, Jesus was her companion not by thought but by heart, hand in hand. She talked with Him. She touched His hand. She laughed with Him. She bathed with Him and she slept with Him. She couldn't stand a moment without listening to His voice. The living Jesus never left her alone. She was always in His touch.

As Pastor was praising Jean, Yong answered,

"Again, all thanks to yours and madam lady's prayers, Pastor."

"Truly all thanks to our good Father's love and care. By the way, Pastor Jonathan promised to preside over your wedding. He is coming from Denver." At this, Yong smiled and asked,

"Otherwise, who could lead my bride to me during the service, Pastor Father?"

"You are right. I will hook her up in my right arm and lead her to you, I promise." He laughed happily.

"Thank you, Pastor."

"Madam Lady and sister Sun would miss this wonderful wedding..." Pastor sighed.

"I know. We will try to have another service when we both return home."

"That sounds good. That should be done."

"I will keep it in mind, Pastor."

While they were up in the sky, their conversations were endless, covering each individual in the house to the operation of the Incheon hospital.

Suk arranged for Yong's internship in America. She also discovered and applied for a position for Yong in the research laboratory, so that he can start working right away. Upon his arrival, they were to be married. She found them a small apartment nearby the campus. How many years have they prayed and waited with patience for this reunion?

How many sleepless nights were they thrown into raging waves of irresistible yearning for each other? How many times have they cried out for help to suppress the burning desire to reach and embrace each other? How painful was it to miss each other?

Suk felt those very yearnings. There were times when her heart was burning and her blood was racing. She was pulled in and sometimes shoved into temptation, as she was flesh as well. But she made it! Tomorrow is the day! Finally he is coming, with Pastor! Her heart was throbbing hard like a child on Christmas Eve and she exclaimed,

"Thank you Jesus!"

She became lost in a daydream. Tomorrow is the day our good Lord made. Then, I will face him, touch him, and be embraced in his arms, in his big arms! I will be married! I will no longer refer to him as, Oppa, I will call him, "Honey, My Dear Husband!"

Then her thoughts switched to think of her twin sister, Jean,

'Jean! Where are you? If you were alive, how wonderful it would be.' And then, 'Nay, she is alive! She is alive in good health somewhere! I know it! She is alive.' And then again, 'Oh, I should have made it sure that she clutched at Pastor's sleeve that night! It was my fault...' She fell in another spell of deep remorse. On any occasion, good or bad, Jean always popped into her mind. That night, Suk recorded another sleepless night.

Suk had a two-week long vacation. She stopped by her apartment to make a final round of checks. She set the beds for Pastor and Yong. The bed for Yong was to be their honeymoon bed. She was thrilled at the thought of it. She knew that Pastor would be gone that same day after the wedding.

She went shopping to fill the refrigerator and cupboard. She also made a list of additional items to be purchased later. She checked the living room and the pictures on the wall. Everything looked leveled and aesthetically pleasing. She returned to the dormitory around two o'clock that afternoon. Susie was in the room. She was interning at the pediatric department.

"Susie, did you get off early?"

"No. I was a little tired. I am on my break. How was everything with the apartment?"

"It looks alright. I will fill it up if anything is left missing."

"That's a good idea. You can't fill it up all at once. Suk, we have some friends from the pediatrics coming to your wedding. Let me confirm, the wedding will be held at two o'clock on the 2nd at San Jose Korean church, right?"

"That's right. I didn't mean to disturb them. We are going to make it a real simple ceremony."

"I know, but they all know about your wedding. You expect your Pastor coming from Korea, don't you?"

"That's right, but on the wedding day, the Pastor will leave here for Denver with Pastor Jonathan by six o'clock on a flight. Pastor Jonathan is flying back to Denver after presiding over the ceremony."

"That sounds good. They are pretty much tight-scheduled, I guess. By the way, Jane and I prepared a special song for your wedding."

"Well, that's a surprise. We'll look forward to it." Jane and Susie were truly good friends to Suk.

Sweltering heat smothered the city without an iota of breeze. The estimated time of arrival was six o'clock. When Suk entered the terminal she was treated with a cool and refreshing welcome. As time was fast approaching six, she stood anxiously in the lobby. The plane arrived on time and passengers began filing out. Suk closed her eyes and prayed,

"Father, we thank you for your holy guidance. Please hold me tight as my heart is pounding hard."

Yong appeared from the back of the passage, pushing a luggage cart. His head was wildly swiveling trying to spot Suk, and then there she was. He quickly raised his hands with a broad grin. She wanted to jump in high glee and she wanted to cry out.

Pastor, who was next to Yong waved his hand at Suk. She thanked and cried out in heart,

"Thank you, Lord. He is here! I see him coming!"

She ran to them as they came through the exit. She ran into Pastor's arms. She was embarrassed to raise her head as tears gushed out. Pastor embraced her tight and said,

"Suk, I am proud of you. You are so great!" He patted her shoulder. Suk, raising her head at Pastor, replied,

"You look old, Pastor. How are Madam Lady and Sister Sun?"

"Thank you. Thank you." Pastor repeated his thanks instead of answering her question, for his emotions had drowned Suk's voice, he released her. She then took the longest step of her life as she approached Yong,

"Oppa, I missed you so much!" She went straight into his chest, pushing Yong back a few steps. Yong embraced her with both hands and praised,

"I missed you, too. You look the same!" His eyes were burning at her.

To Suk, Yong looked different. He matured well and became even more attractive. He was short on words but she heard him loud and clear even when he said nothing at all. As they came out to the lobby, Pastor held both their hands and thanked,

"Father, we thank you for keeping this daughter in your arms and letting us to see her in good health. All is in your grace. This young couple faces each other now and they are to be married. They want to glorify you through their marriage. I pray this in the name of Jesus Christ, Amen."

"Amen," both responded. Then Suk instructed,

"Please wait here. It is burning hot outside. I'll go and get the car." She turned around. Yong followed her.

"Pastor, would you hold the cart? I will go with her."

"Go right ahead." Pastor took hold of the cart carrying their luggage.

Coming out of the lobby, hot air flushed their face.

"Wow! It really is burning hot!" Yong exclaimed and held her hand.

"Oppa, I have lived the last four years, drawing your face."

"Thank you, Suk. God knows that I did the same." They tightened their clasp.

"Thank you, Oppa. I have lived in abundance and comfort here in America with many good friends in such wonderful surroundings."

"Well, you did the same in Korea, didn't you?"

"Did I? How have you been, Oppa?"

"I did the same. I was always thankful. I thanked God every time I heard from you. Our good Lord kept us in his arms and our days were filled with thanks."

"So many times, I missed you so much."

"Same here. After all, we both passed the test set forth by God, didn't we?"

"Yes, Oppa, we did pass! How are the boys and girls at home?"

"You'll be surprised. Yong II took my place. He is taller than me now. Sunja grew a lot as well. She is almost as tall as you. She is now twelve."

"Really? I do miss them."

"They do, too. They were disappointed to hear that you extended your tenure in America for two more years."

They walked to the parking lot under the burning heat. As they got in the car, she promptly turned the air conditioning and made a big circle around the parking lot, and pulled off at the entrance of the lobby. Yong and Suk placed the luggage into the trunk and a few other bags into the back seat. As Pastor climbed into the back seat, the cool air circulated in full swing.

"It's nice and cool," Pastor expressed with a smile. Observing Suk pulling out of the airport and driving on the highway, he praised,

"Suk, I am impressed. You are a perfect American!" He was gratified.

"Living in America, everyone does it, Pastor," Suk answered amused, remembering how she was also in awe of driving an automobile, when she first arrived to America.

"We know it was not easy working your way through school. We thanked God and highly appreciated your monthly offerings."

"It is nothing to be appreciated, Pastor Father. It was just a matter of our duty, I thought. I live in abundance thanks to your prayers. How are Madam Lady and Sister Sun? Sister Sun must be ready for a sweet home of her own."

"I know she is, but I haven't heard a word yet. I think she wants to devote her whole life to ministering God's word."

"Well, if that's God's plan, we should follow it. I feel a little guilty about marrying ahead of her, Pastor."

"No, you don't have to feel guilty about that. God has his own time, you know. As a matter of fact, I am going to Denver to discuss with Pastor Jonathan on her case and many others."

"What case about her?" Suk was anxious to know.

"Pastor Jonathan has Sun in mind as the one to run Incheon Christian Hospital." Suk was delighted to hear that and expressed,

"Oh, that's good news! I am positive that she will do a good job."

"But as you know, she has no experience in hospital management and she has no knowledge of it either."

"That's true…" Suk thought there must be a way for her to equip herself with experience and knowledge.

"Lately, Pastor Jonathan proposed…"

"Did he? What did he propose?"

"He proposed to have Sun take a cram course on hospital management in Denver," Suk was lightened up and said,

"That's a wonderful idea. I know she will make it with her zeal and talent. She will gradually pick up experience, running the hospital."

"I hope so, too. I have many other issues regarding the inauguration of the hospital to discuss with Pastor Jonathan. Therefore, I shall leave for Denver on that day with Pastor Jonathan."

"Everything looks perfect for Sister Sun. I think God tested and tried her a lot, and now the time has come for her to be lifted for His purpose. I am so glad, Pastor!" Suk overjoyed at the news

"I think so, too. By the way, is the Korean church far from your place?" Pastor asked.

"It's about a forty-five minute drive. The wedding will be at two o'clock. Pastor Jonathan is to conduct the service, isn't he?" She asked knowingly.

"Yes, how is your pastor of the church. We don't want to be too much of a burden on him."

"Not in the least. I fully explained and he was rather gratified to leave it to Pastor Jonathan."

"That's good. So you are ready for the wedding."

"Yes, Pastor. We are going to make it a simple one, with a mind to make a real one when we get back home."

"Thank you, Suk." Pastor answered.

Yong was just listening to them observing American scenery through the window. They arrived at the apartment and Yong insisted on carrying all the luggage bags. Sitting on a chair, Pastor suggested,

"Let's give thank to our Lord." Yong and Suk kneeled on the floor and Pastor read scriptures.

Suk prepared the dinner table with Pastor's favorite dishes, bean paste tofu soup with grilled fish and seaweed.

"Wait a minute. This is a genuine Korean table!" Taking a liking to the dinner table, he exclaimed.

"Yes, Pastor, we have a Korean grocery store in San Francisco. I haven't forgotten your favorite dish."

"Did you not? Do they serve Korean food at the dorm?"

"Of course, not. We only have American food there."

"Oh, how pleasant it would have been. Suk, can you say grace?"

Suk kneeled down and prayed,

"Dear Heavenly Father. You guided Pastor Father and Yong Oppa on this long trip, and now we sit around the dinner table for the first time in along while. We thank you for this good food and we ask you to keep Pastor in good health and have him live long to glorify you. We also thank you for your love and grace upon our family at home. I pray this in the name of Jesus Christ, Amen."

After dinner, Pastor took a walk around the apartment complex with Suk and Yong.

"Suk, thank you indeed."

"Why do you thank me, Pastor? What have I done?" She asked.

"I do thank you and I am very proud of you. You did a great job. Our youngsters follow your suit. Thank you, my dear Suk." He patted Suk and prayed,

"Father, we thank you for your holy guidance and protection to your daughter. I am grateful to you, Father. This young couple will be married in a few days before You and before the eyes of the world. They will be made one in Christ to glorify you and your name. We thank you for giving them the strength and wisdom to cope with and to step over any hardships that may lie ahead. I pray this in the name of our Savoir Jesus Christ, Amen."

"Amen." The couple responded.

Due to the time difference, Pastor was tired. Suk made his bed for him.

"Have a good night sleep, Pastor. I'll be back early tomorrow morning."

As she came out of the apartment, Yong followed her.

"Oppa, you must be very tired as well. Have a good night sleep."

"I am alright. I will take you to your place."

"You don't need to that. It's only a ten-minute walk."

"That's why I'll take you."

"You are new here."

"I won't get lost. If I am not sure how to get back, then you can take me back." No one could stop him.

"Then, Oppa, remember the name of this avenue and the main street at the end of this avenue."

"I'll remember them. I have never let you go alone, except to America, have I?"

"You are right. You have always protected me."

They came out to a main street, hand in hand. Under the street lights along the walkway, not a single pedestrian was seen. This particular street was quiet with the exception of one or two cars passing by once in awhile.

"That is the front gate of our school straight ahead. We just came out of Parkway Avenue. On your way back, make a left turn at Parkway and then you will come to the apartment."

"Don't worry, Suk. I'll take you to the front gate."

As he came out with Suk, Yong was refreshed with good cheer. In the clear night sky, the crescent moon was lingering about accompanied with twinkling stars. The couple halted under a streetlight.

"Oppa, why don't you go and rest? Aren't you tired?"

"I'm fine. I am in an ecstasy. Things are fabulous to me here." Yong clasped her hand tight and held her in his arms, and was debating to himself,

'Young man! Our God reads your cunning mind. Have you forgotten your oath that you would protect her from your sinful lust until you both stand before God as a married couple?'

He counted the remaining number of days. Five more days to go! He didn't want to stain her purity, her priceless virginity, and he wanted to cherish it deep in his heart.

They resumed walking in silence. Presently Yong asked,

"Suk, what do you want me to do the next few days?"

"Well, everyone knows that you are here today. First of all, you need a good rest, and then I want you to meet our professors and some researchers you would be working with."

"As you can tell, my English is poor."

"The same goes for everyone at first, but that can be your charm. Don't worry about it, Oppa. Oh, and we'll have dinner with Jane and Susie for sure."

"Is that the one whose brother was a cardiologist?"

"Yes, Susie is the one. I am afraid that they may fall in love with you at first glance."

"Don't be silly. Their eyes are not covered with bean crust like yours."

"Why, they saw you in the picture, and they were sold on the spot."

"Don't be kidding, Suk."

"But I am not kidding, Oppa."

Yong paused a minute and switched gears and asked,

"So the next few days, all I will be doing are cleaning the apartment and washing the dishes, I guess." Suk was appalled at his remarks.

"No, why would you be doing that? I told you I have two weeks of vacation. I have never been out sightseeing since I came to America. I heard there are many types of scenery in California."

"That might be a good idea. Once we both start, we may not have spare time to enjoy it together. You are the driver; therefore take me wherever you want." Yong gave in.

"By the way, did you get the driver's license in Korea?" She asked.

"Yes, I did, but I have no experience."

"Then, we should go out practicing for the driving test. The written test is not easy here in California."

They arrived at the front gate. He looked deep into the distance at the main building, thinking to himself 'this is the famous Stanford University!' He waited until she was well into her walk onto the campus, and then, he made a bugle with both hands and shouted,

"Thanks, Suk. Goodnight, my dear."

"Good night, Oppa. I'll be there the first thing in the morning."

The following morning, Suk called Pastor Jonathan.

"Pastor Jonathan, this is Suk. How are you, pastor?"

"Suk! I am fine. I know it's going to be at two o'clock on the second."

"You are right, pastor. We are going to pick you up at the airport. What flight are you coming by?"

"No, you don't have to do that, my dear. You have many other things to take care of. The San Jose Korean Church is on El Camino St?"

"That's right. I am going to make hotel reservation for you, pastor."

"No, you don't have to do that either. I have already made reservations. I'll call you as soon as I check in the hotel. How are your pastor and your fiancé from Korea? Wait a minute. Give me your phone number to your apartment. I only have the number to your dorm."

"They had a good rest last night and they are doing fine. My apartment phone is 408-001-0191. Let me repeat it '408-001-0191'"

"I got it, Suk. I will give you a call when I get there, and then I will stop by your place to see your pastor, okay?"

"Yes, pastor. I'll look forward to hearing from you. By the way, pastor…"

"Yes, Suk, anything else?"

"No, nothing particular. I am just grateful to you."

"You are a cutie. Let's praise the Lord hand in hand."

He was always so gentle and generous. He would fly all the way from Denver to preside the wedding, and he didn't want to bother Suk even by accepting pickup at the airport. After he checks into the hotel, he would stop by her place to see Pastor Father. His love and care of Suk was truly genuine and infinite, and he was a true Christian...

The wedding ceremony took place ceremoniously in Christ. They declared that they were now made one in Christ. No longer was her body hers alone, nor his body was his but hers, as well. They proclaimed that they were a married couple and made a sweet home with Jesus as their master, in which they loved and respected each other. They swore to help and support each other in difficult times to the last day of their lives.

When the presiding Pastor Jonathan introduced the bride and groom, he also testified and thanked how God loved and cared for them through rugged ways in the past, turning the planned simple ceremony into a caldron of wild excitement.

They all shed tears and hailed hearty congratulations.

Pastor Father prayed for the benediction at the end of the ceremony,

"May God bless upon this married couple, fill their hearts with peace and comfort, and lead their way to prosperity to the end of their days. I pray this in the name of Father, the Son and the Holy Spirit, Amen."

"Amen." The bride and groom responded.

Tears welled up in her eyes and Suk said,

"Pastor father. We do thank you."

"You are very welcome, my daughter. I am the one that should thank to you. I am heading for Denver today with Pastor Jonathan." Turning to Yong,

"My son, Yong. Take good care of my daughter." Pastor's eyes were starting to wet.

"Pastor Father, I will do as you wish and I'll send Suk back home in two years. Stay healthy and livelong, please. We will pray for it." Yong was now in tears.

Jane and Susie kissed Suk and hugged Yong. Suk finally burst into tears and wetted her handkerchief.

Before the wedding, Suk discussed their honeymoon with Yong,

"Would you like the sea or the mountain for our honeymoon?"

"Honeymoon?" he wondered.

"Yes, honeymoon. Our honeymoon, which is once in a life time, Oppa."

"Oh, yes! I wanted it, but can we afford it? To me, it is more than a honeymoon that I can face you like this."

"But you would go if we can afford it, right? In fact it wouldn't cost any money."

"Well, if we have a free honeymoon, why not, but even without it I could not ask for more. I am truly grateful that we can work the internship together."

"I am, too, but I want a dreamy honeymoon with you, Oppa. Yes, I wanted and prayed for a quiet place for our honeymoon."

"And then?" He asked in wonder.

"So our good Lord answered my prayer. He gave me two options, one to the sea and the other to the lake in the mountain."

"Are you serious?"

"Yes, I am very serious. In fact, someone asked me about our honeymoon in our department some time ago. I told them that I'd be more than grateful to have it at the apartment, since we can't afford it. Then our chief physician interrupted with a suggestion." Suk recalled her conversation with the chief physician to Yong:

"Dr. Suk, I have a summer house in Lake Tahoe. How would you like having your honeymoon there?" suggested Dr. Smith.

I was overjoyed to hear it and asked,

"Did you say the Lake Tahoe?"

"Yes, it could be a lot better than your apartment."

"I know, but Dr. Smith, I have dreamed of a honeymoon and I have prayed for it!"

"Well, that's nice. Your prayer has been answered. It is not a fancy villa but its quiet there nearby the lake."

Then another resident next to him offered,

"If you don't like the mountain side, I have a villa in Monterey, looking over the Pacific Ocean. It's in on the golf course. If you want, you may use it for your honeymoon."

On that day, I burst into tears. They asked me why I cried, saying that they didn't mean to hurt me at all. Therefore I had to confess to them,

"Doctors, you didn't hurt me at all. I was just so grateful to God, who answered my prayer through you doctors. I am also touched by your unsparing love to me."

"Well, if that's the case, our offers are open. Make a choice and let us know." Dr. Smith said.

Suk concluded her narration of events and asked Yong,

"That's what's happened, now which one would you prefer the ocean or the lake?"

"Well, I prefer the lake in the mountains."

"I thought so, too. I'll pick up the key and will go shopping for our honeymoon."

Thus Yong and Suk had a dreamy honeymoon for three days and two nights at Lake Tahoe.

While Suk was driving up and down hill after hill along the winding highway for more than three hours, Yong fell into a daydream. Just fourteen years ago, he gathered his two younger brothers out of the burning fire, ran away from being certain death as communists, and begged for food door to door.

It was a miracle to come across an angelic girl like Suk, and it was more than a miracle that he could study and became a doctor. Now this former beggar came to America to marry an angelic graceful female doctor. In his ecstasy, he felt like an eagle soaring up to sky as he was heading for Tahoe in a car driven by his beautiful wife! He pinched his flesh. It was not a dream. It was the real.

Glorified by God's presence in his life he began reciting David' psalm aloud,

"The Lord is my shepherd; I shall not be in want. He makes me lie down in green pastures, he leads me beside quiet waters, and he restores my soul. He guides me in the path of righteousness for his name's sake. Even though I walk through the valley of the shadow of death, I will fear no evil, for you are with me; your rod and your staff, they comfort me." Then Suk took the lead and recited loud and clear, as the car was cruising down a hill, continuing where Yong left off,

"You prepare a table before me in the presence of my enemies. You anoint my head with oil; my cup overflows. Surely goodness and love will follow me all the days of my life and I will dwell in the house of the Lord forever (Psalm 23)." Then they chorused in together, "The Lord is my shepherd, I shall not be in want...

The summerhouse was hidden in the forest. It was exactly what Suk had dreamed of, except the lake. It was not a lake she dreamed of. It was a sizable sea surrounded by woods, on which a number of motorboats were racing at full speed. It took nearly a day to circle around it by car.

Entering the summerhouse, they held hands together thanking God. Yong opened the windows for ventilation. Right under the nose below the window, a huge pine tree stood upright way below at the bottom and its branches practically shielded the whole roof with thick foliage. A fat squirrel popped up from nowhere and sat upright on a bare branch, rubbing both hands with popped eyes and then, another hairy one followed suit, racing after the fat one as she scurried up on the trunk. Suk went in the kitchen to set up the cupboard and refrigerator.

As night fell quickly, late autumn rain drizzled, its dripping sound reminding of sweet rain on tender plants. Yong clicked the switch on. The fluorescent lamp on the ceiling blinked a second and then flooded the room with its illumination. Suk cooked in the kitchen, while Yong set up the bed and the bathroom.

After dinner, they had their first family service alone. Yong read the scripture and Suk prayed for the service. They sang aloud, praising the name of the Lord. Yong delivered the message and Suk responded with 'Amen' as they used to do in the House of Immanuel. Most of all, they thanked hand in hand for being made one in Christ as night deepened.

Yong put on pajamas that Suk prepared. Suk turned the light off. Yong embraced Suk on the bed and whispered,

"Are you truly my wife? I thank God for this and I do love you."

Now Suk in his arms, whispered back,

"Are you truly my husband? I do thank God for this, and I do love and respect you."

"Now we are one in Christ. I swear to love you as Christ did the church," Yong declared.

"Since I am in your arms, I will love and obey you as your wife as I do to Christ." She pledged.

"We serve our Lord Jesus as the head of this family and we work together to offer this home as a radiant church, without stain or wrinkle or any other blemish, but holy and blameless, Amen."

"Amen," Suk responded. Thus they declared themselves a blameless beautiful couple before the eyes of our Lord Jesus Christ.

11.

Two Years Later

A giant grandfather clock cuckooed at five-thirty in the morning. Suk headed for the kitchen to brew a batch of coffee. Yong set their bed straight and went into the bathroom. Sitting at the table facing each other, they sang a hymnal. Yong read the scripture for the day. He delivered a brief sermon on the scripture. They meditated on the word for a while and then, closed with the Morning Prayer. It was a twenty-minute service. For them, their Morning Prayers and evening family service were like their regular meals.

Suk went back to the kitchen to prepare breakfast, while Yong went back to bathroom to shave. Suk prepared the table and she went into the bathroom to prepare for her day, while Yong got dressed. Yong then went out to pick up the daily paper to read with his coffee, waiting for Suk to get ready. When Suk came out, both said grace and ate breakfast.

"Did you say that you're conducting surgery today?" Yong asked.

"Yes, I have to open it first. It's a cancer patient," Suk answered.

"You have only a few days before you leave for Korea. You need a good rest."

"I know, but I have to do my best to the last day. Don't you agree?"

"Oh, I agree, but you need rest as well."

"I'll be fine. If things go well, I'll be off around noon."

Suk was preparing to return to Korea in a few days. Yong was to remain behind for two more years to finish up his research project. Upon returning home to Korea, Suk was to head the Obstetrics and Gynecology Department of Incheon Christian Hospital.

In the meantime, Sister Sun completed her cram course in Denver University and now managed Incheon Christian Hospital as director under the supervision of Pastor.

Yong seemed relieved when Suk suggested she may be home around noon.

"That's nice. You need rest. You have a bad habit of enslaving yourself."

"I know what you mean, darling, but I don't want to win anyone's favor when their eye is on me. I want to do the will of God from my heart like slaves of Christ."

"I know you do. But remember God's will as well. You should slow down a little bit and take good care of yourself," Yong suggested.

"Take good care of yourself? That's why I am deeply concerned about you being alone when I am not here. You should slow down and shouldn't skip meals. Otherwise..."

"Don't worry about me. I am concerned about you being alone. You don't skip a meal, madam doctor," He counter suggested.

It was not an easy decision for Yong to stay in America instead of returning home with Suk, but he had to finish his research.

"I'll be okay..." She paused a second and then suddenly changed the subject, "Why don't we have a baby yet?" she asked, looking squarely into his eyes.

"Well, I guess that it is not the right time to have a baby just yet. By the way, what are we having for dinner? I crave bean paste with tofu."

"I expected you to change the subject! I'll go shopping today, the first thing when I get home..." Then looking at Yong's white shirt, she turned serious again,

"Why didn't you change your shirt? I put out the ironed one on the dresser."

"I know, but I noticed that other people wear the same shirt for two days on end. I don't want you to exert yourself too much on my shirts, honey."

"I appreciate your concern, but you are infringing upon the unique privilege of a woman, which was bestowed upon by God."

"Honey, I want you to drop your duties on me and relax at home."

"I appreciate your concern, but I love to take care of you."

Yong smiled and changed his shirt. They both left for work and met on their lunch break.

That night, as they lay in bed,

"It was a big relief that cancer did not spread over other organs of the patient," Yong broached on the issue.

"Yes, it was. Early detection was the key. It wouldn't show up even in regular checkups. By the way, honey, what's the progress on your project?"

"Well, this kind of venture has no projected date of completion. Nevertheless, biomedical engineering is truly infinite. It is exciting probing into the infinite mysteries of our Creator."

"That means you might extend another two years, honey?"

"Not in the least, darling. As a matter of fact, I am tempted to pack my belongings and come with you. Unfortunately, I spoke it out before our God and before you and our Pastor Father, and therefore, I can't take it back. To be honest with you, it is extremely painful not to come back with you," He made a sad face.

"Your mission is your mission."

"You are right, darling. It took four years last time. Although it will be difficult, I think I can make another two years go by. However, if I can't stand it this time, I will fly over to you next summer break."

Suk turned bashful and crawled in his arms,

"Please do so, my dear. I may also have a difficult time with you away. I will start praying as soon as I get home. God always answers my prayers."

"Thank you, Lord." Yong embraced her and continued, "Darling, please make it sure to start praying immediately upon getting back home so that I may crush you next summer break."

Many people made it out to the airport to send Suk off; church members including the pastor from the Korean church, doctors and nurses from Stanford Medical, not to mention Jane and Susie with flowers and farewell gifts, and some ex-patients arrived, to Suk's surprise.

The forty-five mile drive was not easy for them to make. Looking over their precious faces, she had tears welled up in her eyes. They were good-hearted people in Christ. Isn't this true love? It sure was proof that for the last six years, there had been the cross of Jesus in her heart. From that small heart, the light and fragrance of Jesus must have emanated upon those sending Suk farewell. The Holy Spirit moved and touched everyone's heart at the scene.

Suk with tears in her eyes called out to Yong, while boarding the plane,

"Honey, goodbye. May peace and comfort be with you."

Yong raised his hand, responding,

"I trust you. You are my strength. Be joyful in Christ wherever and whatever you do."

"Darling, I am your wife and you are my husband in Christ. We'll meet each other in our prayers."

Then she turned to her crowd of friends and raised her hands,

"May God be with you forever!" She bowed and went through the entrance.

Many of them stayed to watch the plane soar into the sky. Yong stood scanning the plane until it diminished out of sight. In his eyes, tears welled up and shed on his cheek. He whispered,

"Lord, we do thank you."

When she arrived at Kimpo airport, the late autumn dusk was settling. As she came out of the floodlighted exit, a young man came forward,

"Hello, Sister. I am Yong II."

Delighted at the stalwart figure, she looked up at him. There she saw another Yong!

"Brother-in-law. You are now an adult!"

"We are so glad to see you back. You must be tired, Sister. Let me carry your bags. Pastor and other brothers are here waiting for you." He took over the cart.

She heard that Yong II was enrolled in medical school, but she didn't expect him to be that tall and handsome. Pastor Father, Sister Sun and a few other young children were making their way from the lobby. Suk ran into Pastor's arm,

"Pastor Father, you didn't have to come out for me. How have you been doing?" She then embraced Sister Sun.

"I missed you, Sister. How have you been doing?"

"Finally you are home, Suk." Sister Sun embraced her in tears. In fact, this time last year, sister Sun stopped by Suk's place after she finished her courses in Denver on her way back home.

From the airport the party arrived to Incheon Christian Hospital. There were four other college students alongside Yong II. They changed so much that Suk didn't recognize them at first glance. They were all attending schools in Seoul. At the entrance, a volunteer received and guided them into Sister Sun's office.

In the spacious room were paintings under the soft chandelier light. The picture on the wall and the embroidered drooping curtains made an elegant match with the classic furniture nested nicely in the room. Entering the room, Suk thought she sensed Sister Sun's particular taste and propensity.

"Suk, you must be tired. Make yourself at home." Sister Sun offered her a seat.

Pastor took a seat on an armchair and commanded,

"Be seated everyone." Everyone sat on either the sofa or chairs, two young men sat on the floor on a cushion. Suk wished to share her seat with one of them on the floor.

Pastor continued,

"Let's praise the Lord," turning to his hymnal. They all sang with great joy.

Suk took a long look at each student in turn. They were all grown up from six years ago. She talked to herself,

'This must be Myungsik. Yes, he is. He used to live in the House of Faith. The next one is Minchul. That's right. He is Minchul. What about the giant on the floor? He looks like Dukpong who used to live in the House of Barnabas. That last one, he must be Daekeun.' She could recognize them, scrutinizing each one's figure and contour from the past.

Sister Sun prayed to start the service. Pastor then conducted his sermon, tailoring his sermon to the theme of welcoming and thanksgiving. As the service ended, Pastor went to Suk,

"You need a good rest today. We can talk tomorrow."

"Pastor, I am alright. I want to reach out to the young brothers." Suk walked toward the first one,

"You are Myungsik, who lived in the House of Faith, aren't you?

"Yes, sister. You have not changed much. How is brother Yong?" Myungsik asked.

"Oh, he is bent on his research project. He is doing fine. Which school do you go to?"

"The same school as Yong the Second, Sister."

"So, you go to the medical school."

"Yes, sister."

"I am glad and grateful to our Lord!" She turned her attention to the next student,

"Minchul. Aren't you?"

"Yes, Sister. You recognize me, thank you."

"You are grown up. You were a third grader when I saw you last."

"You are right, Sister. When you left, I cried a lot, I remember," Minchul replied.

"Did you? Minchul, which school do you go to?"

"I go to the same school as Myungsik goes, Sister."

"Then, you too go to the medical school."

"Yes, sister." Now Suk facing to Pastor,

"Pastor Father, we have three doctors in this room."

"You are right, Suk, All thanks to you." Pastor could not have been more proud.

"Why, Pastor? All thanks to your prayers." She then turned to another boy.

"You are Dukbong, aren't you?"

"Yes, that's me, Sister."

"Which school do you attend?"

"I just entered law school, Seoul National University."

"Congratulations, Dukbong!" Finalled she faced Daekeun. This time, Daekeun answered before being asked,

"I am Daekeun, Sister."

"I know you are. You were cute like a puppy. Now you are grown up. Which school do you go?"

"I was admitted to the same school as Dukbong, Sister."

"So you are enrolled in Seoul National University?"

"Yes, Sister."

Suk, thoroughly impressed looked to Pastor and Sister Sun, asking,

"Therefore, all these five students are KS marks, isn't it?"(KS stands for Korea Seoul National University)

"Of course, Pastor Father wouldn't send anyone from Busan to Seoul unless they are KS marks," Sister Sun answered.

Suk closed her eyes and prayed thanking the Lord. When she opened her eyes, she cleared her voice and said,

"Brothers, I am glad and I am so grateful in the direction you all are heading for. People in the world may be proud of you or even envy you as you are racing straight along the track of success. Success, defined by the world is important, but it shouldn't be the purpose of our lives. We should be able to see the true purpose of our lives, which is beyond worldly success. There is a greater and higher purpose, which we were called for and assigned, even before the beginning of the world; this is our true original purpose we were born with.

Someone must have put us on this righteous track. Who could be this someone? Have you thought about it? Our race has just begun. We press on to take hold of that for which Jesus Christ took hold of us. I do not consider myself yet to have taken hold of it, but one thing I have done is to forget what is behind and strain toward what is ahead as I press on." She addressed and encouraged them.

Who picked up those wretched ones on the street and transformed them into stately men of duty? Was it due to the efforts of man's good heart, money or power? Not a chance! Who else but the spirit of Christ who will not break a bruised reed and will not snuff out a smoldering wick? Who can work that miracle other than the spirit of Jesus Christ?

Did Pastor and Madam Lady play an instrumental part in their success? Yes, they worked hard to provide, yet they worked as His tools. The truth is that Christ Jesus worked miracles through them. Christ declared,

"I shall lose none of all that He has given me, and no one takes any from me." He works day and night in us, for us, with us, and through us. Suk encouraged the young brothers to allow to Christ work through us as He planned. She stressed that was the purpose of our lives.

Time flies like a darting arrow, as two years has passed since Suk was assigned to Incheon Christian Hospital. Tomorrow was the day she had waited for so long, Yong was finally coming home.

On the flower-bed at the entrance of the clinic, a bunch of cosmos, bathed in the early morning dew, seemed wiping their pretty faces in the breeze with the ray of rising sun in the eastern sky.

As Suk, wearing rimless glasses, pushed in the door to the medical facility, the intern and nurses on duty greeted,

"Good morning, doctor."

"Good morning, Dr. Kim and Miss Lee."

Her agile walk led her to the doctor's locker room. She changed her shoes and put on her white uniform in front of the mirror. She placed her stethoscope around her neck and smiled at herself in the mirror. She then closed her eyes with both hands clasped together.

"Thank you for your being my shepherd. Make me the fragrance of Sharon in your holy guidance on this day." She then headed for the clinic.

Suk, now a thirty-year old obstetrician of Incheon Christian Hospital was starting her day. She worked at the clinic until noon and in the afternoon she worked the operation room in the main wing. She also volunteered for dispensary work in Bupyung recreation district.

Though she worked strenuously from morning till night, her gown was always clean and white, and her benign smile never left her lovely face. She was not alone. She was always with Jesus Christ. Since the living Jesus was with her, she was always happy, thankful, and vigorous.

Still, she had a sad story, the story of Jean, her twin sister. Recalling back sixteen years ago to the night of the air raid, she regretted, soliloquizing,

'That was a serious mistake. I should have made sure that she clutched at Pastor's pants or sleeve. I always took care of her until that night. Then I totally forgot her! What was I thinking? It surely was my fault that she is still missing.' But, strangely enough, her remorse was always followed and overwhelmed by singular conviction that 'Jean is still alive. She is not dead.'

Around sunset on Saturday, Suk returned home from Bupyung dispensary. Entering her room, she threw herself on the bed. Accumulated fatigue swooped upon her and she was resigned to snoring softly. Her housemaid heard Suk coming in and hurried to the kitchen to prepare the dinner table for her, whining,

"How hungry you must be! Please come out and wash your hands. I'll ready everything for you in the bathroom, and I'll bring in the dinner table right away."

Presently sliding the door open with the dinner table, she heaved a deep sigh at the sight, pleading,

"You should eat first and then go to bed!"

Smacking her tongue, she shook Suk up. It was no use as Suk was affixed to the bed. In cases like this, the maid would withdraw the dinner table, for this was not the first time Suk came home only to crash minutes later.

As dusk fell, sea gulls in a neat formation flew over in the twilight sky.

Tooting whistles from ships in the harbor touched the maid's despondent heart, resounding in the unsettled breeze of the night.

This lady came to Suk's house as a housemaid two years ago through the introduction from the pastor of her church. She could number the days with her fingers that she had dinner with Suk since she had arrived. The maid would be left alone all day and night and talked to herself,

'What a good and pretty doctor she is! She is God's daughter, alright. Not a thing of hers is of waste. How could she keep herself so busy solely for the sake of others? Well, tomorrow is the day. Her husband is said coming home. Hopefully she will be settled by then.'

The clock on the wall struck 7:30 in the evening, and simultaneously the phone rang. The maid came out quickly and answered the phone,

"Hello,"

"Hello, this is the hospital. Is the doctor in?" It was an urgent voice on the other end.

"Did you say Hospital? Wait a second. Doctor is at rest. I will wake her up. Please wait."

At the sound of, hospital, Suk woke up and came out of her room to receive the phone,

"Hello, this is Dr. Suk."

"Doctor, we need your help!" It was an intern on duty at the emergency room. He continued,

"We have an urgent crisis, a patient with hemorrhage. She was brought in while undergoing surgery. When I opened and looked inside the vagina, thick blood poured out and I couldn't locate the hemorrhage points, doctor."

"How many months into pregnancy, and the patient's age?"

"It looks well over three months. The patient is in her thirties. She has had repeated abortions in the past, doctor."

"Have the anesthetist ready for the operation," Suk ordered.

"The anesthetist is on his way. We conducted blood and urine tests, X-rays and EKG, and we are set for blood transfusion. I have already dispatched the emergency car for you, doctor," the intern reported.

Presently an ambulance with Suk in the passenger seat was dashing towards the hospital, deafening the night with its screams to make way.

As Jean collapsed, her world left her: money, jewels, clothes, pleasure, love, and finally her health packed up and was about to depart, leaving her on the threshold of death.

On that day, she counted the days away on her sick bed. It was well over three months. She hired a neighboring prostitute to take her to the quack doctor nearby the military base.

She was placed on the surgery table and she opened her legs. The quack doctor, examining between her legs, grumbled,

"Repeated abortion is dangerous."

Nevertheless, he picked up a pair of rubber gloves off the wall and inserted his equipment into her vagina. He started digging in, tearing pieces to pull it out little by little, and then all of sudden his hands were trembling and then shook violently.

Blood gushed out and flooded the surgery table, dripping on the floor. Frazzled in fear, the quack doctor picked up a bundle of swabs and jammed them into Jean's vagina in an attempt to stop blood flow. As Jean felt warmth under her bottom, she thought death was approaching, as she was losing consciousness.

With the help of the prostitute that Jean hired for the day, the quack doctor kicked open the emergency room and the intern on duty ran to the patient.

"Blood started gushing out while she was undergoing surgery," the quack quacked. The other woman was holding Jean's hand.

The intern on duty performed emergency procedures and then quickly moved the patient to the operation room. He unplugged the swab out of her bottom to examine and then immediately he plugged it back with a new bundle of swabs. He rushed his pre-operation procedures with his assistant and nurse, and then he grabbed the phone to call up the chief obstetrician.

As Suk entered the operation room and signaled to the anesthetist, Jean was immediately put to sleep under the mask of her respirator. The anesthetist at her head was monitoring her blood pressure and breath counts.

Suk was at the foot of the patient, bowing her head with eyes closed and prayed.

The intern and nurses followed her. It was a brief prayer as immediate medical attention was at the utmost urgency.

She quickly applied iodine on the patient's belly and made a long slit across. Blood smeared out and yellow fat revealed to the surface. She simplified the blood clotting procedure. The womb presented itself. She stanched the flow of blood into the uterus and readied her scalpel.

She started cautiously opening the uterus. She then cleaned out the uterus. Inside the walls resembled rugged furrows. Blood vessels were cut and torn out here and there. In this case, the easiest way to help the patient was to remove the womb, but she came to think of the patient's interests, a lady who was only in her thirties. Suk couldn't rob the patient of life. She knew what she had to do in this case no matter how intricate and cumbersome the process was. She started carefully repairing broken vessels one by one. She had the okay signal from the anesthetist.

Strangely enough, Suk had an unusual sensation from the beginning, inexplicable pain and odd pressure upon her heart. She took it as a warning sting and she performed a slow but thorough operation which lasted nearly an hour just to repair the broken vessels.

She kept praying,

"My Lord, have mercy on this lady. Forgive her for whatever wrongs she did. Keep her from the path of the wicked. Make her humble before you. Have her surrender to you. I'll suture and wrap up her wounds, but you are the one to heal them, Lord. Guide and lead her to your light. Have mercy upon her."

The inside of womb was stitched like a wrinkled cabbage-leaf. She closed up the wound and sutured the cut together in line. She gave post-operational instructions to the intern and left for home. For the first time that day, she felt her stomach empty. The patient was carried to the recovery room.

Suk came home exhausted and hungry. That night she was tossing about on her bed and she couldn't find sleep. She couldn't figure it out why. Was it because of Yong who was coming home by 7:30 flight tomorrow evening? That couldn't have been the cause, because she would have slept really sound. What else, then?

There were two ministers in the Incheon Christian Hospital, both were female. One minister was Sister Sun, who was also the director of the hospital. The other was Minister Min who was the resident minister to the hospital.

Minister Min came to the recovery room for the third time since last night. The doctor on duty signaled and the nurse next to him approached her,

"Minister Min. Doctor wants to see you"

"Does he?" Minister Min who was walking toward Jean's bed turned to the doctor on duty.

"Minister Min," the doctor called with a serious look,

"That patient has been sobbing harder since you left at dawn. Was it your second visit?"

"Yes, I left her around midnight and came back at five this morning. Now I have come to bring her some seaweed soup."

"The patient needs rest, as you know," the doctor warned.

"I know, doctor, but God's word heals the patient, as you know, doctor."

She walked to Jean's bed. Last night, Minister Min waited until Jean woke up from the anesthesia. As usual she placed her hand on the patient's forehead and whispered prayer into her ears,

"Living God, you are the Mercy. You loved this daughter so much that you gave yourself up on the cross. Please open her ears and have her listen to your voice of love. You are the love. I pray this in the name of Jesus Christ, Amen." Then Minister Min spoke softly to Jean as she was opening her eyes,

"The living God is here with you. Doctor performed a successful operation. Let's praise and thank God, sister."

As Jean was coming back to her senses, she faintly remembered the warmth of blood under her bottom. At that time she believed she was dying, but presently she became cognizant of her surroundings, and realized that she had survived another day. She looked up at the fluorescent lighting affixed to the ceiling and suddenly fell into nostalgia for the sweet old days.

Someone whispered something into her ears but she couldn't make out what she heard. Instead the softness of the tone had invoked sweet memories in her. Am I sleepwalking? She asked herself. Whatever state of consciousness her mind was in, Jean did not want it to end. She wanted to cling to her past memories, for they helped her escape her reality. Then she sensed someone watching over her, ending her state of peace.

"Where am I?" Jean asked.

"You are in the recovery room," Minister Min answered.

"What is the time?"

"It is two minutes past midnight."

"Who are you that come this late to see me?"

"I am Minister Min, sent by our good Lord who loves you so much."

"I am hopeless! I am done!" Jean protested.

"I beg your pardon. You will be fine. You are not done, sister." Minister continued,

"To our Lord, you are more precious than the world itself. However, it's no time for talking. It's time for you to calm down and relax. If you could, please meditate on his words, recalling all your days." Minister comforted and left the patient.

When minister Min came back at five o'clock, Jean was sobbing hard once again. Minister Min consoled her,

"Sister, you shouldn't be agitated. You should be relaxed. Let me pray for you." She placed her hand on Jean's forehead, which instantly activated a burning heart in Jean. As her heart was racing hard, she vividly saw herself running into the church hand in hand with Suk. Over her pale cheeks were tears flowing in a stream.

Minister Min prayed,

"Dear Lord, you loved this sister. You loved her so much that you were nailed and thrust onto the cross. What is your plan for this sister? Why have you waited so long and met her now in this difficult situation? Please help her surrender to you this very minute because she wants to be in your good favor. We thank you for receiving her, her tears and her prayer. We thank you, our Lord. I pray this in your name, Lord." Minister Min then whispered in Jean's ear,

"I'll go and get some seaweed soup for you."

"Seaweed soup?" Jean opened her eyes excited and exclaimed,

"I love and I crave for it!" She wanted it very much and her swollen face in the dim light stroke out the contour of her juvenile jovial face.

"I'll be right back, thank you." Minister Min, saying unfitting thanks to Jean, stood up and whispered in her hears again as if to an old friend,

"Our Lord is a forgiving God. You know that, don't you? Even murderers can be forgiven the moment they turned to Him. I know our good God would give you the precious moment of recollecting your old days to get yourself cleansed. Then He will guide you to the bright world. Trust him." And she left.

Now Minister Min was coming back with the soup. She walked up to Jean and pulled a chair to face her. Jean was in a sedentary position with her back propped against the headboard of the bed.

Minister Min placed both her hands on Jean's right hand and prayed. She asked the nurse to take off Jean's respiratory mask and to place the food on the food panel attached to the bed.

Jean was eager like a simple naïve girl, looking down on the soup bowl. Her face, though swollen, was lighting up as steam from the soup dewed upon her face. She still looked very much like she did in her youth.

"Help yourself, sister," Minister Min offered.

"Thank you, minister." Jean scooped the soup in excitement with her spoon, her fingers shaking, and then suddenly she halted on the way and dropped the spoon back into the bowl, sobbing in tears,

"Minister, are you sure that a sinner like me can be forgiven?"

"You said it. You don't know how pleased our God is at your confession. You don't know how dear the tears that you are shedding are. Our good Lord has waited for this wonderful moment with patience for all these years. Now let's try the soup while it is still warm," she offered earnestly.

"Thank you, madam. I thank you very much, minister." Jean scooped the soup, trying to slow her tears, and carried it to her mouth. Then she dropped the spoon again, whimpering,

"Minister, I am a cursed lewd girl and..." Minister Min instantly stood up and came close to stop Jean, placing her hand on her shoulder, saying,

"God knows. He is omniscient. Have you ever seen anyone not lewd in the world? We humans are all lewd in nature. You know the precious blood of Jesus Christ, don't you?"

"Yes, I know. I heard a lot when I was a girl, but I have completely forgotten about it." Leaning back upright, Jean was having shortness in breath.

Minister continued,

"Then, you know the truth that you will be cleansed by His blood and all your sins are to be forgiven once you come before him, don't you?"

"Yes, I do. I'm starting to remember." Jean continued, protesting,

"I am afraid that I am not entitled to that grace. I am too terrible. I am a prostitute," Jean, spitting words, burst into tears.

Minister Min patted Jean's shoulder,

"You are truly forgiven by His grace. Not a single soul is entitled to his forgiving love, but we are all forgiven when we confess that we are not entitled to it. By grace of God, your sins are all cleansed white like snow. Do you believe that, sister?"

Silence fell for minutes, finally Jean lifted her face and spoke, "Yes, I believe it. I do want to believe it, madam."

"Very well, He just said on the cross, 'It is finished.' Now help yourself to the soup. While you eat, I have good news to deliver to you. You know I am a minister, sister." Jean picked the rice bowl and dumped it into the soup. She sipped a spoonful of soup. It was surprisingly delicious like the soup she begged and shared among street boys at the Seoul Station sometime ago.

"How old are you?" Minister asked.

"I am thirty years old. I am an old woman."

"No, you are not. You were just born again. Is your name Kathy?"

"Yes, Kathy is my nick name. My real name is Jean," Jean answered while enjoying her soup. The soup was even more enjoyable as it soaked her dry throat.

"Then, I will call you Sister Jean. Our God has his unique plan and purpose for each one of us."

"Then, does God have a unique plan and purpose for me, too?" Jean asked.

"Yes, he does. He is perfect and accurate. He has a distinctive plan and purpose for each individual fairly and equally. You were born with your own plan and purpose in life, which is unique."

"I don't quite understand."

"You see, your name, your fine figure, your pretty face, your life, your voice, your bright eyes, your glamour, your good heart, your love, your passions even your hatreds, jealousy, thought, wisdom, intellect, memory, creativeness, imagination, patience, all kinds of strength, will, power, attachment, possessive desire, feeling, all on this list is given to you, it is going to be endless."

"Well, I do speak English better than others. Is this a talent given to me by God?"

"It goes without saying that everything was given to you. In a way, they were not given but loaned out to us, because when the time comes, we will have to return all to Him."

"I still can't understand clear," Jean expressed. Minister continued,

"I can't blame you. As I told you before we are not meaningless beings. We were born with specific meaning and purpose. Where can we find our purpose?"

"Yes, where can I find my purpose?" Jean asked eagerly.

"Well, suppose you buy an expensive machine. When you open the box you will come across its manual. The manual explains the machines functions and gives instructions how to use and maintain it. Now if you want to run the machine, what would you do first?"

"I'll read the manual." Jean answered.

"Otherwise you may end up breaking the machine. The same is with humans. We should read our manual."

"But, we are not machines," Jean protested.

"Of course, not. We are the created by the Creator. We are a lot more important than machines. Our Creator is responsible and dependable. He wrote a good manual for us."

"Where is this manual?" Again Jean asked in earnest.

"This is the manual." Minister pulled out her Holy Bible, continuing,

"The Bible reveals the path to our mind, our body, and our spirit. It gives important instructions to us on how to live, what to do, how to love, among many other important aspects of life. The Bible guides us to execute and fulfill the plan and the purpose that we were born with.

It is our mission. While our soul is in our body, we should carry on our mission to prepare for the day when we would stand before our Creator. We should be holy and perfect to be admitted to the eternal Kingdom of God, but we cannot carry out our mission without Jesus."

"It is too difficult for me to understand," Jean confessed.

"Have you heard of the parable of wheat and weed? Wheat will be stored in heaven and weeds will be thrown into the fire. For example, if your soul does a good deed according to the instructions of the bible, as long as your body breathes on the earth, you will be a good grain. However, if your body is tempted and your soul follows the devil's way, you will be a weed to be cast into the fire."

"If that's the case, I am already a rotten weed!"

"Jean, you may be right, but I have never seen anyone that is not a weed. Besides, our journey has just begun. As I told you, no matter how serious the sins we have committed, if we turn to our Lord and confess them, our good Lord will cleanse us with His precious blood, and make us into a new creation."

"But still I am a filthy obscene person!" Jean cried out.

To this, Minister closed her eyes and praised,

"Hallelujah! Father God." Minister continued,

"If you are a wicked obscene person as you said, all you have to do is to turn around and stand before our Lord. Confess from the bottom of your heart. Then our good Lord would not only cleanse you, but He will also instill in you a state of peace that only can be obtained through Him. He will lead you to another brilliant tower of victory on your past. Nothing is too late as long as you are breathing."

"Do you really mean I still have a chance?" Jean asked.

"Of course, you do. You will be dearly used for his purpose. I know you have a great mission ahead. Solely for that mission, you might have been through so many sad days and nights, which may be the reason why we are here face to face." Still it was not enough to clear Jean's face and she pouted,

"But you never knew me. You can hardly imagine that I used to be a hopeless prostitute. How could you, an angelic minister imagine of such a sinister world that I have lived through? How nice would it be if all sins were cleansed upon confession? I am too rotten and incurably ill to be forgiven," Jean whimpered.

Minister stood upright, approached Jean against the raised bed, and stared at her holding her head with both her hands.

"Jean, you must have been a bright smart girl up until some-time ago. Then one stormy night you were thrown into a pit with no reason and you lost your grip with our Lord Jesus. Satan and his devils are rampant in the pit and you were further enmeshed in the mire, as you lost the sense of direction. Even now, God warns us not to be surprised when confronted with painful trials, as the world we live in is the pit.

You, like many others were ear plugged to his warnings. As you know well, there are innumerable victims at this very moment wallowing in pain and torment within the dark pit. We need someone to go down to the pit and rescue them back into the light of Christ. Our Lord Jesus Christ is searching for this someone, as his mercy is ever pouring all over the world. Yes, you could be this someone."

To this, Jean upturned her eyes, questioning,

"Are you saying that wretched ones like me could be used for His work?" Jean bit her lower lip, grimacing with pain from her abdomen.

"You are very right. Now you know how precious you are and how anxiously He has been awaiting you."

"Oh, my! If I could be spent for something beneficial to the world!" Her eyes glimmered.

"Yes, you want to dedicate yourself to something beneficial to the world, don't you? That's what you are! Our Lord wants you to be what you are! Let us put an end to your past and stand on top of it to acclaim, 'Hallelujah! Thank you, Lord!' Oh, how anxiously our Lord has been waiting for this minute! No turning back now, sister."

"Has he? If so, I am grateful!" Jean exclaimed.

Minister Min was delighted and continued,

"Congratulations, you are in His arms, Sister Jean! The old Jean has just been crucified, and the new Jean has just been born. You are new! You are a new creation in Christ! All you have to do is to look upon Him and follow Him." Jean broke into tears as she was deeply moved. Minister Min continued,

"Now we are sisters in Christ. Frankly I am a little jealous of you, because you have so many things that I don't have. God values every bit of your experience, good or bad. Please don't throw it away. You'll need it when you come out to the world. Now, we together can help others to be born again, into new brothers and sisters, new husbands and wives, new mothers and fathers, new grandfathers and grandmothers to expand the kingdom of God."

"But what can I do?" Jean asked.

"Our good God has everything in store for you. We were very blessed this morning, Sister Jean. I have to go now. In the morning, our director may come to see you, since she is a minister, as well."

"Is the director of this hospital a minister, too?" Jean wondered.

"Yes, she is. She is a wonderful minister. She will definitely come to see you today. Let us pray together now." Minister concluded. This time they prayed hand in hand.

In the prayer, Jean turned pale as she was confessing in tears,

"My Lord, I am a dirty prostitute! Could I be really forgiven?"

Her heart burnt, her face flushed, and then, she heard a voice at heart, a clear voice soft and tender,

"My Daughter, Where are your accusers? I will not condemn you either. Go and sin no more."

As the hospital director entered the room at ten o'clock in the morning, the doctor and nurses on duty stood up and greeted in concert,

"Good morning, director"

"Good morning. How is the patient who had surgery last night?" Director asked.

"This is the patient, madam. Her name is Kathy." The doctor on duty guided Director Sun to the patient, explaining,

"Dr. Suk performed the operation. The patient is doing well. However, the patient has been sobbing all these hours since Minister Min left this morning."

"Has she?"

Director Sun walked toward the patient and picked up the chart at the end of the bed. She screened the chart, the patient covered her face with right her hand and was sobbing hard.

Director Sun called out,

"Hello, sister."

The moment Jean dropped her hand away from her face, Director Sun's eyes fixed on the swollen face of Jean. At the sight, Sun's eyes quivered in a second and her body was temporarily frozen. She narrowed her eyes in misgiving and then came closer to stare at Jean again, upon confirmation she exclaimed,

"Isn't this Jean? Jean! You are alive! Hallelujah! You are alive!" She exploded into acclamation. To this, Jean upturned her eyes in surprise and glared at Sister Sun, crying out at the top of her lungs,

"Sister? Sister Sun? You are Sister Sun, aren't you?" She recognized Sister Sun instantly and attempted to sit up in excitement, but she lost control and collapsed, falling over forward.

Startled at the sight, Director Sun dashed to Jeans aid, screaming,

"Jean, Jean, you are alive! Wake up, Jean! Hallelujah! Wake up Jean!"

Holding up Jean's drooping head, she shook her frantically to prevent Jean from falling deeper into her faint. Director Sun kept on screaming and roaring in frenzy that it shook the entire hospital,

"Wake up, Jean! Jean! Wake up! You are still alive! Wake up, Jean!" In an instance, the floor emergency crew scurried to the scene.

At this very moment, Dr. Suk was entering the recovery room to check up on the patient, and stood dumbfounded in astonishment to hear the words she recited in her dreams, "You are still alive! Jean!" Suk dashed to the scene, shrilling,

"What? What did you say, Sister Sun? Is Jean alive?" She shoved off Director Sun and reached Jean, and then shouted aghast,

"Jean, you are alive! My Lord, she is alive!" Panic stricken at the sight of Jean falling down in a swoon, Suk shrieked,

"What's the matter? What's wrong with you, Jean?"

She took Director Sun's place and shook Jean and shouted for her emergency staff, sticking her stethoscope onto her sister's heart. Her heartbeat was faintly audible but not much irregular. Jean was breathing hard; her respiratory mask was falling off her mouth. Suk caught the mask and fixed it back to Jean's nose and she ordered in panic,

"Cardiac Stimulant!"

A nurse hurriedly injected a syringe of stimulant into Jean's bloodstream through intravenous solutions. Now Suk, gently leaned her twin sister back into the bed. She was silenced to feel the pulse and narrowed her eyes to scan through the graphic readings on the monitor screen. Jean's heartbeat was returning back to normal. Tense moments were lifted.

With a sign of relief, Suk made sure that Jean was asleep. Watching over Jean's swollen face, Dr. Suk suddenly swooped down upon her, embracing her as their cheeks met, sobbing violently,

"Jean, you are alive! My dear Jean! You were alive! Thank you! You have been alive this whole time! Yes, you surely are alive!"

Then Suk raised her head to look upon Him with both hands up, tears flowing over her closed eyelids, and thanked,

"Thank you, my Lord. Praise and Glory is to you, O Lord. You heard my cry and You answered me! You are merciful and I adore you forever and ever, Amen."

Printed in the United States
217040BV00002B/1/P